Reinhold Visuals

Study Guide

Reinhold Visuals

Study Guide

John Lidstone and Stanley Lewis

with Sheldon Brody as Photographic Editor
for Volumes 1 through 8

VNR **Van Nostrand Reinhold Company**
New York Cincinnati Toronto London Melbourne

Published by Van Nostrand Reinhold Company
A division of Litton Educational Publishing, Inc.
135 West 50th Street, New York, NY 10020, U.S.A.

Van Nostrand Reinhold Limited
1410 Birchmount Road
Scarborough, Ontario M1P 2E7, Canada

Van Nostrand Reinhold Australia Pty. Ltd.
17 Queen Street
Mitcham, Victoria 3132, Australia

Van Nostrand Reinhold Company Limited
Molly Millars Lane
Wokingham, Berkshire, England

16 15 14 13 12 11 10 9 8 7 6 5 4 3 2 1

CONTENTS

What the Visuals are

Today we live in an environment richer in visual imagery than that of any earlier period. Television, motion pictures, pictorial books and magazines, advertising media—all barrage us daily with ideas expressed through images. We have, as a result, developed an unprecedented awareness of visual forms.

The Reinhold Visuals comprise a range of examples as wide as that found in the environment: they represent the art of many ages and places, different media, and diverse modes of expression. They provide a working collection of image material that matches the excitement and sophistication of our visual surroundings in a way impossible within the traditional, limiting format of illustrated books or standard art reproductions.

Each Portfolio in the series takes as a starting point one of the elements or aspects of art—Line, Mass, Organization, Surface, Color, Movement, Perception, Space, Light, and Fantasy and Illusion. Each group has been researched and edited to provide a coherent and meaningful sequence of image ideas. But the organization of the Visuals upon this basic framework is open-ended. It relies on the concept that in any sequence of images each of us will find significant underlying relationships that unite some by similarities, comparisons, and affinities and oppose others by differences, contrasts and polarities. The works selected are calculated to produce lively discussion and to suggest constantly unfolding levels of insight, new vistas that help to reinforce our understanding of the universal application of each art element and each work of art. The images are intentionally evocative and provocative—and sometimes even controversial—in order to stimulate the viewer to take a new look at art and the environment. Because the organization of the Visuals is flexible, the viewer can make his own creative interpretations and rearrange the order to reveal new relationships. Versatile in themselves, the Visuals encourage versatility in seeing.

Because the Visuals range through such a wide variety of imagery, the significance of an art element becomes very apparent to the viewer who may experience it in the design of a fabric, the decoration of a primitive mask, the facade of a building.

When one element, line, for example, is observed again as the predominant force unifying an urban landscape, defining the surface of a shell, and enhancing the chance juxtaposition of utilitarian objects, we become acutely aware that all art is enlivened and energized by a common set of elements that exist in and out of "art" and persist in all forms of expression. In providing a diversified but coherently organized selection of visual material, the Visuals help the viewer to move beyond knowledge and appreciation, to a fundamental understanding of art and its dynamics.

How the Visuals Can Be Used

One of the most dynamic ways of learning about art is through the visual and physical manipulation of images, and the Visuals offer unlimited opportunities for such exploration. The moment one begins to thumb through the posters, ideas on how to use them spring to mind. Each Portfolio is planned to facilitate a wide range of teaching approaches and learning experiences, not only in art but in other fields as well. An activity-oriented program, a curriculum favoring the humanities, special areas of study such as social studies, cultural history, creative writing, and interdisciplinary courses, all can benefit from the scope of the Visuals. They can be used effectively in any number of ways, and the suggestions made here are intended only as a point of departure for individual imagination.

The text supplied with each Portfolio includes, for each work, full identification data as well as a brief commentary, which appear on the back of the poster described. This ensures that the basic information will never be accidentally separated from the work and provides convenient reference when a particular poster is being studied. In addition, the same text, together with identifying reproductions and color indications, is compiled in this book. The entire contents of all ten Portfolios are thus available for reference and comparison.

The commentary on each work is meant as an introduction—it indicates the general nature of the work, its main features, and its relationship to the theme of the Portfolio and other posters (cross-referenced in boldface type). Like the Visuals themselves, however, the commentary should be considered open-ended, a stimulus to further exploration and discovery.

Because the Visuals require no darkened room or special equipment and are large enough to be seen from a distance, they are extraordinarily adaptable to a wide variety of teaching-learning situations, including the classroom, studio, seminar, television, and individual study. A few basic ways to use them are:
—as a school or college exhibition (duplicate the text for captions or make your own);
—as a classroom exhibit (tack them to a display board or wall);
—as general reference material (to catalog them for library collections, simply transfer the identification data for each poster to catalog cards, using the Portfolio and poster numbers as the call number, for example, **1:1**, and adding the appropriate subject headings);
—as the basis of an art collection for study and display (expand each Portfolio by adding other examples; mount them on 18 x 24″ cover stock and number them from 25 on);
—as presentation material for discussion and debate (prop them on a chalk rail or easel or hand them around the class, singly or in selected groups, according to the context);
—as a source of ideas for student projects of all kinds (original art work and photography, creative and critical writings, illustrations for oral reports).

It cannot be too strongly emphasized that these suggestions are only a beginning: individual needs should be the guide to effective use, and the range of exciting possibilities the Visuals present is as wide as imagination makes it.

The Visuals are grouped in ten subject areas, but there are innumerable subgroupings that cut across these categories, each reflecting a different emphasis or point of view. A work of art can be appreciated in many ways according to the particular interests and attitudes of the viewer. Therefore, plates selected from various portfolios in the series may be clustered so as to provide a visual core to support projects in any number of curriculum areas. Eight sample groupings with different objectives follow.

A studio-type project about lettering might make good use of the following plates:

Portfolio 1 (Line)
   plate 16 (Oriental brush lettering)
   plate 17 (contemporary street graffiti)
Portfolio 3 (Organization)
   plate 3 (lettering as part of a painting)
   plate 4 (poster lettering)
   plate 8 (billboard lettering as part of a photographic composition)
Portfolio 4 (Surface)
   plate 24 (lettering as part of an assemblage painting)
Portfolio 5 (Color)
   plate 13 (a Hebrew letter as the principal motif in a fabric design)
   plate 23 (lettering on a book jacket)
   plate 24 (a circus poster)
Portfolio 7 (Perception)
   plate 15 (comic-strip lettering)
Portfolio 8 (Space)
   plate 8 (advertising lettering)
Portfolio 10 (Fantasy and Illusion)
   plate 4 (19th-century wooden printing type).

A discussion theme concerned with the relationship between form and function could be built on:

Portfolio 1 (Line)
   plate 5 (old-fashioned wire ice-cream-parlor chair)
Portfolio 2 (Mass)
   plate 15 (stacked boxes used by Japanese street vendors)
Portfolio 3 (Organization)
   plate 6 (a chambered nautilus seashell as a classic example of natural organization)
Portfolio 8 (Space)
   plate 2 (space in the architecture of an airline terminal)
Portfolio 9 (Light)
   plate 12 (neon-lit building entrance as walk-through sculpture).

A unit on motifs in art might use the following Visuals to explore the persistence of the circle as a design:

Portfolio 3 (Organization)
   plate 2 (decoration of an Apache devil dance headdress)
   plate 7 (traditional Japanese family crests)
Portfolio 9 (Light)
   plate 14 (a halo as the dominant compositional force in a 19th-century religious engraving)
Portfolio 5 (Color)
   plate 17 (lumagram slide for a multi-media theater production)
Portfolio 6 (Movement)
   plate 14 (spiral design within a circle—contemporary kinetic painting)

A photography project could explore different views of urban subject matter in:

Portfolio 7 (Perception)
   plate 1 (a building-size mural giving dramatic identity to a run-down commercial neighborhood)
Portfolio 8 (Space)
   plate 4 (alternating glass and granite producing a pattern of light and shadow)
   plate 7 (a city building incorporating a twelve-story garden core of greenery
Portfolio 9 (Light)
   plate 23 (brilliant reflections from city windows, waterfront machinery, piled-up cargo and rooftops)
Portfolio 10 (Fantasy and Illusion)
   plate 15 (a stunning painted landscape)

A related-arts class studying rhythm in the arts could compare musical rhythms to visual patterns in the following:

Portfolio 1 (Line)
  plate 3 (a computer print-out enploying typewriter characters abstractly to create a rhythmic pattern)

Portfolio 2 (Mass)
  plate 16 (identical cubes of color in a lively op-art counterpoint)

Portfolio 3 (Organization)
  plate 1 (a syncopated pattern of stars and curving organic shapes in Matisse's design for a stained-glass window)

Portfolio 4 (Surface)
  plate 6 (the opposition of varied patterns in an African bronze head)

Portfolio 7 (Perception)
  plate 24 (fishes becoming birds; a pattern in which positive and negative shapes are exchanged)

Students studying comparative religion in a humanities program could discover both information and new points of view in:

Portfolio 2 (Mass)
  plate 1 (Nepalese sculpture embodying the perfect tranquility and peace Buddhists strive for)

Portfolio 5 (Color)
  plate 14 (early 15th-century painting of "Saint Ursula and her Maidens" illustrating sumptuous and reverential treatment of Christian saints)

Portfolio 10 (Fantasy and Illusion)
  plate 6 (a Surrealistic painting with an unusual representation of the Crucifixion)
  plate 14 (an 18th-century Hindu painting of holy figures)
  plate 21 (an African religious relic to which healing powers were attributed)

The following Visuals provide provocative starting points for a class discussion on the relationship between art and science:

Portfolio 5 (Color)
  plate 3 (an extraordinary reflecting cube composed with the aid of space-age light technology)

Portfolio 6 (Movement)
  plate 6 (movement recorded by strobe photography)
  plate 20 (transmutation of a shape into two different shapes by computer programing)

Portfolio 7 (Perception)
  plate 16 (a single videotape run to multiple television sets forming an "electromedium" for a kinetic light environment)

Portfolio 8 (Space)
  plate 1 (photomicrograph of a crystalline structure)

Major developments in the history of painting since the Renaissance can be observed in the following:

Portfolio 5 (Color)
  plate 3 ("The Poplars," 19th-century impressionist painting by Monet)
  plate 4 ("Door to the River," 20th-century abstract expressionist painting by De Kooning)

Portfolio 6 (Movement)
  plate 18 ("The Harvesters," Renaissance work by Pieter Bruegel the Elder)

Portfolio 9 (Light)
  plate 2 ("Young Woman with Water Jug," 17th-century baroque painting by Vermeer)
  plate 20 ("Invitation to the Side Show," 19th-century post-impressionist painting by Seurat)

Portfolio 1, Line

Line in Art

String and wire are forms of line that have physical reality—we can place our hands around them; they have mass and cast shadows (lines). A line that is drawn, painted, or incised is also tangible—it can bend or twist; we can measure its breadth. But we also perceive line where no real two- or three-dimensional line exists: in the contour line that serves as the boundary or edges of a shape, the dividing line between two buildings or two colors, the connecting line between a series of points. These lines are implied and conceptual; that is, we perceive them through the use of imagination.

The artist works with both real and imaginary line to create form and space—the delicate network of a wire construction, the sinuous curves of a figure carved in stone or suggested by the partial contours of a charcoal sketch, the architectural plan translated into steel lines that support a building, the illusory depth of perspective. Line is important as a means of giving thrust and movement, direction and speed, rhythm and unity to works of art. While the emotional impact of surface and color may be more immediate, that of line is just as significant. We often associate line with clarity, precision, reason, and order, but the range of feelings it can evoke is reflected in the familiar phrases we use to describe its effects: we speak of the "clean" lines of one form and the "soft" lines of another.

Line

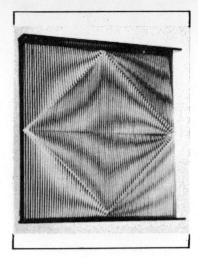

Peruvian **embroidered** mantle, detail showing three figures, pre-Inca period, ca. 600 A.D., from the Coastal Region, early Nazca Culture. Wool embroidered with colored wools. 103 x 55" (overall). The Metropolitan Museum of Art, gift of George D. Pratt, 1932

Line in art can serve many functions. It can define and describe; it can provide rhythm and movement; it can suggest mood and evoke feeling; it can imply dimension and indicate direction. In this embroidered mantle, woven in Peru over a thousand years ago, line is used imaginatively to delineate ritual figures and to create rhythmic patterns. A natural fusion of art and craft, the mantle illustrates how line can serve both as a means of communication (in its religious subject) and as decoration.

The ancient craftsman who made the mantle was alert to the full possibilities of the technique, even while he worked within the limits of a cultural tradition. In the angular quality of subject matter and design, for example, he exploited the straight-line patterns inherent in the hand looms of his time.

As we look at this detail spread flat, we must remember that it is part of a garment meant to be worn draped in soft folds. The flatness of the design is an advantage, for the pattern will take on depth when the fabric hangs on the body. Had the weaver created a design with a feeling of depth in itself, it would have become visually confusing when rearranged into folds. The lively line is reinforced by strong, vibrant colors and keeps the eye moving continuously over the entire surface. This eliminates any possible center of interest and makes an overall pattern appropriate to fabric design.

"Acceleration **Number 19, Series B,**" 1962, by Yvaral (Jean Pierre Vasarely) (U.S., b. 1934). Plastic and wood. 23⅞x24⅜x3⅛". Collection The Museum of Modern Art, New York; gift of Philip C. Johnson. © 1968 The Museum of Modern Art, New York. Photo by O. E. Nelson.

As its title suggests, this construction uses linear patterns to imply physical motion. The sculptor takes three-dimensional line (plastic "string") and overlays one series of straight lines with another. This forms the basis for a sequence of changing moiré patterns that are brought to life when the observer shifts his angle of view.

Unlike traditional sculpture, which generally makes a complete statement and involves us with its subject matter, "Acceleration" has no subject matter and demands the active participation of the viewer himself to set the work in motion. The viewer, thus, completes the statement. The sculpture is, in essence, a motivation for optical involvement, and as such it is an example of contemporary Op art.

Although the structure of "Acceleration" is rigidly geometric—a square within a square—once optical movement begins to operate, an infinite succession of line relationships and complex three-dimensional images suddenly are manifest upon an originally inert surface. While such optical experiments may not gratify us emotionally in the same way that works with representational subject matter do, we enjoy visual delight, intellectual fun, and physical release when we look at them.

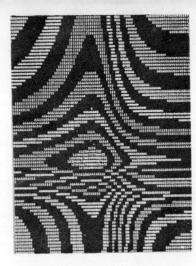

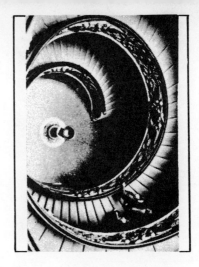

Line

Computer print-out **(the intensity of a magnetic field** distributed over a thin sheet of super-conducting material), produced at the IBM Thomas J. Watson Research Center, Yorktown Heights, New York. Courtesy The IBM Corporation.

A print-out is the visual result produced by a programmed computer. This enlarged print-out of the intensity of a magnetic field is similar to the designs created when iron filings are scattered on a magnetized surface: in both cases the particular design structure is determined by physical laws. To explain the print-out in another way, if one were to analyze a musical composition by computer, the print-out would be a graphic equivalent of the music's underlying mathematical structure.

In the past the artist found concepts of ideal beauty and form in nature. Today science affords us the means to explore the universe in unprecedented ways, revealing natural phenomena never before experienced by man. The artist as well as the scientist of tomorrow will work in a world of tremendously expanded horizons. It is because of its implications for art that this print-out is exciting to us. In its rhythmic pattern we see line made up of texture; the line contributes movement and structure to the composition, and the texture gives it variety and dimension.

In the Peruvian textile **(Line 1)** the subject matter is expressed in linear form dictated by the mechanics of the loom; here the linear form is organized by natural laws. The pattern produced on the primitive machine and the one made by the most sophisticated machine man has yet conceived are very different. But they share a machine-like quality that discloses their method of production, the weave of the fabric resembling in its grid structure the typographical spacing of the print-out.

"Vatican Stairway," 1964, photograph by Sheldon Brody. The Reinhold Visuals Collection.

In the Peruvian textile **(Line 1)** and the computer print-out **(Line 3),** line moves across a surface, indicating two-dimensional direction and organizing two-dimensional space. We are dealing with a very different idea of line, used in a very different way, in this photograph of an architectural detail, the Vatican Museum stairway. Here line is not a tangible element; it is perceived in the edge of three-dimensional mass. Yet we can speak of line and analyze the architectural use of it. It spirals freely through three dimensions, creating depth and defining spatial relationships; its man-made structure is strikingly similar to the natural structure of the chambered nautilus shell **(Organization 6).**

The linear organization of the Vatican stairway as shown in the photograph is like that of the tire painted by Lichtenstein **(Mass 19).** Both are formed of off-center rings and have a strong pivotal point; in both, too, the circular linear movement is accentuated by radiating lines that compel us to fix our attention on the axis of rotation. The painter has unconsciously mirrored three-dimensional structure on his flat canvas in order to create the illusion of depth.

The bird's-eye view of people on the Vatican stairway, like the oblique angle of the painted tire, increases the feeling of depth by making the viewer look down. But the presence of the figures makes it clear that the stairway is more than geometric pattern. The viewer feels the surrounding space here, and enjoys a heightened appreciation of air volume carved by architecture.

Line

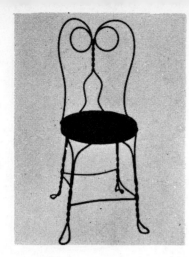

"Ice-Cream Parlor **Chair**," 1967, photograph by Sheldon Brody. The Reinhold Visuals Collection.

Line forms the basic structure of this whimsical chair. Line is three-dimensional here, like the string in Yvaral's "Acceleration Number 19, Series B" **(Line 2)** and the cable in Brody's "Brooklyn Bridge" **(Line 7).** It is tangible and solid rather than conceptual line, as in "Vatican Stairway" **(Line 4).** The fact that the wire of the chair has been bent and shaped and can obviously support the full weight of a person reinforces our acceptance of line as physical material.

The chair's wire curves and twists stand out in sharp silhouette. The clean lines are not only functional, although function is the primary consideration of the design; the economical use of line to fit the purpose is in itself satisfying. In addition, the decorative, almost frivolous handling of the wire makes this an object to look at as well as to sit on. The chair seems to have a personality of its own, and a sense of humor, in its curled-up feet and fanciful back, where we may or may not discern a face. These qualities emerge because the photographer has pictured the chair without background detail, even without shadows, thereby giving it importance as a linear design that is not merely functional, but an object to enjoy visually.

"Bicycle," 1967, photograph by Sheldon Brody. The Reinhold Visuals Collection.

The versatility of line is astonishing. Besides the infinitely varied ways it is used for purely aesthetic ends, it is an exquisitely practical form of matter, as we can see in the design of objects such as the ice-cream parlor chair **(Line 5)** and the Brooklyn Bridge **(Line 7).** And, as this photograph illustrates, the design of the bicycle is a perfect example of line used functionally and expressively to create motion.

The straight spokes and the circular rims of the wheels, the soft curves of the brake cables, and the bold tubing of the bicycle's frame, all contribute to its effectiveness as a working machine. Its design is not accidental, as is that in "Sidewalk Cracks" **(Line 23),** but carefully thought out to provide the lightness and balance that best serve the purpose of the vehicle. When the thin, action-packed line of the bicycle is viewed abstractly, however, the machine emerges as a kinetic sculpture. The automobile fascinates some artists and typifies for them the depersonalization of a too-complex industrial age—this is the case in Rosenquist's "Ultraviolet Cars" **(Mass 18).** The bicycle, in contrast, has meaning for others such as Brody, and Shaw, in his "Bicycle I" **(Mass 6),** who see in its purity and simplicity of line a symbol of speed and youthful vigor.

Line

"Brooklyn Bridge," 1967, **photograph by Sheldon Brody**. The Reinhold Visuals Collection.

The structural wires and cables that support the span of New York City's Brooklyn Bridge form the visual elements of this linear composition. Brody creates an abstraction by showing us a portion of the bridge rather than a literal, overall view. By silhouetting the delicate web of lines and overlaying the identical line patterns, he minimizes the three-dimensionality of the subject and reveals an aesthetic organization that is satisfying in non-objective terms.

The photograph stresses the beauty of the bridge's structure rather than its function. We see the cables as diagonals radiating from the mass of three stone towers and the wires as verticals in counterpoint. The lines, held taut by solid areas of stone and steel, weave a pattern of pleasing regularity against the sky. While this poetic treatment of wire and cable makes us acutely aware of the bridge's design in aesthetic terms, in the end it also heightens our appreciation of its functional physical structure.

"Sky Thrust," **1967, photograph by Sheldon Brody. The** Reinhold Visuals Collection.

We live in two physical worlds—the world of nature and the world we have made ourselves. The world of man-made things was once derived wholly from the materials of nature, and its outlines were softened by these roots. We are moving farther and farther away from nature, and we have created a new landscape in the process. Twentieth-century architecture proclaims its origins in monolithic structures of aluminum, steel, and glass that reflect man's ingenuity and technological progress rather than the emotions of the individuals who build them.

The soaring lines of "Sky Thrust" scribe out a picture of contemporary architecture in all its monumentality. Hard edges outline the towering mass of city buildings against the sky, and the photographer stresses the upward sweep of the buildings by taking the picture from the point of view of the passer-by on the sidewalk below. But this architecture is not oppressive. Although unrelieved by natural surroundings of trees and grass, the monotonous regularity of verticals rising from base to top is broken up by contrasts of light, dark, and reflecting surfaces, by varied, predominantly horizontal fenestration, by changing widths of lines and line relationships. The architect has, without diminishing the functional purpose of architectural line, used it to transform what might have been overwhelming mass into a pattern of dynamic space sequences.

Line

COLOR

"Untitled III," by Piero Dorazio (Italian, b. 1927). Lithograph. 26 x 18¼". Courtesy Marlborough Graphics Gallery, New York. Photo by O. E. Nelson.

This composition has no "meaning" in the traditional sense of telling a story or making a statement that can be expressed in words. It is an artistic experiment with line, color, and transparency. The interweaving of bands of color produces subtle color changes and changing depth relationships as the bands pass under and over one another. While each band contributes to the central complex, it maintains its own individuality, that is, we can follow it from end to end. But Dorazio gives us more than a simple interweaving of color bands. Sets of bands spell out a variety of constructs, for example, the shape formed by the green lines alone, or by the blue lines, or by the lines made of negative space. There are squares and rectangles, crosses and bars, and a variety of colors formed by the crossing of the bands.

The artist plays change (overlay) against non-change. All the bands are of approximately the same width and length, but they terminate in a number of ways, so while the top and sides of the structure present ragged outlines, the bottom edge is squared off. All the bands intermesh at right angles except one—and that one, the only yellow band in the work, cuts across the entire design surface. This controlled counterpoint of similarity and difference, and the multiplicity of possibilities presented by the simple arrangement of a few elements, both animate and unify the composition.

"Zigzag Dress," 1967, photograph by Sheldon Brody. The Reinhold Visuals Collection.

Optical art is the result of the contemporary artist's exploration of optical phenomena and human perception. Some examples of the Op artist's interest are seen in Noland's "Bend Sinister" **(Line 11)** and Anuszkiewicz' "Primary Hue" **(Line 20).** This candid photograph illustrates the spontaneous interaction of art and life, for the zigzag line of the girl's dress and the graph-paper line of her stockings are motifs that have been adopted intact from Op art and enthusiastically incorporated in popular design.

The Op artist uses line to explore the nature of perception, setting up a unique situation under controlled conditions. In contrast, the fabric designer who utilizes Op motifs makes use of the artist's experiments to produce a repeated pattern, the end use of which he cannot determine. He is not concerned with whether the fabric is draped on the figure, spread flat against a wall, or fitted to the contours of a chair—his object is to create a pleasing overall pattern.

COLOR

COLOR

"Bend Sinister," 1964, by Kenneth Noland (U. S., b. 1924). Plastic paint. 94 x 76". Collection Joseph H. Hirshhorn. Photo courtesy The Jewish Museum, New York.

We live in a complex world to which artists react in many different ways. Antonakos, for example, wholeheartedly accepts contemporary technology in his sculpture, "Marie's First Neon" **(Line 18),** for he uses neon tubing, a modern industrial product, as his medium of expression. In "Bend Sinister" Noland chooses one of the most ancient of design motifs—the chevron—as the subject for his huge canvas. It is his purpose that is contemporary—he is concerned with optical phenomena. He works only with the basic elements of line and color. Noland uses line not to delineate subject matter, create texture, or express emotion, and not as an element of a complex organization, but in and for itself.

The color stripes of "Bend Sinister" are not inert: vibrancy started by the red and adjacent blue chevrons is carried over to the others, and the asymmetrical relationship of the chevrons to the background keeps the whole in dynamic tension. The direction of the lines, like an arrow, creates a downward momentum, while the diagonal axis moves our eyes back upward. Active visual ambiguity is created by the fact that we can read the lines as flat bands or as a series of triangles superimposed on one another in shallow space. In contrast to the dizzying movement of Yvaral's "Acceleration Number 19, Series B" **(Line 2)** or the dazzling sensation of Anuszkiewicz' "Primary Hue" **(Line 20),** Noland's canvas is a subtle challenge to our visual perception.

Paintings by Ellsworth Kelly (U. S., b. 1923). Exhibition at The Sidney Janis Gallery, April, 1965. Courtesy The Sidney Janis Gallery, New York.

This photograph of an exhibition of Kelly's work is shown in place of a single painting in order to bring out the startling vitality of his line, best seen when his huge canvases are juxtaposed. Paintings such as these are called "hard-edge" because the edge of each high-key color area slams up hard against the edge of the next. (The light line that appears between colors in some parts of the paintings is a photographic effect and does not exist on the canvases.) The artist carries one flat color up to the very limit of the shape defined, butting it against the flat color of the neighboring color-shape.

The large, simple shapes of Kelly's paintings firmly maintain two-dimensionality—even when actually extended into space at right angles, as in the red, blue, and yellow composition seen through the doorway. This is in marked contrast to the effect of the soft, floating shapes in Rothko's "Number 10" **(Mass 14).** Yet, situated in intense color-space, the hard-edge shapes also play tricks with our eyes. We are never sure what is background and what foreground: we are visually tempted to merge one form with the next and, at the same time, forced to establish lines of demarcation between them, a situation of perceptual conflict that makes the edges seem to vibrate. Although no line exists between the color areas, the effect of line that is optically generated exists as emphatically as a painted line.

Line

"Studies for Stone Sculpture," 1938, by Henry Moore (British, b. 1898). Pencil. 11¼ x 7¾". Collection The Museum of Modern Art, New York; gift of Mr. and Mrs. Simon Askin. © 1968 The Museum of Modern Art, New York. Photo by Soichi Sunami.

The hand of the sculptor is immediately evident in these beautiful line drawings by Henry Moore. His studies show us how the artist can use line to explore and analyze form and space. With free-curving sweeps and short, stabbing strokes, he feels out and distils into its essence the volume of the human figure, rediscovering in each study the beauty of its topography.

Line here conjures up the movement of muscles and the unseen framework of the skeleton, as well as the softness of flesh and drapery. It describes inner and outer anatomy but it is always an inseparable part of the whole, never a perimeter or a symbol. While drawn on the flat surface of paper, Moore's simple line clearly communicates the plastic solidity of his subject as though it were carved in stone.

"Theater Director Miyako-Dennai III," by Toshusai Sharaku (Japanese, late 18th century). Colored wood-block print. 14⅜ x 10" The Metropolitan Museum of Art, Whittelsey Fund, 1949.

This wood-block print shows the masterly use of line to define mass, pick out detail, create surface, and express character. The skillful Japanese artist depends wholly on the line he carves into the wood to give life to his subject, so it is through varying the line that he achieves variety of effect.

Although he does not attempt to render volume directly, Sharaku gives body to the figure with the heavy broad lines that indicate folds in the garment covering it. Volume is so clearly implied by these strong curves that it is not destroyed but given richness and beauty by the areas of linear, geometric pattern applied to the surface in flat, wallpaper fashion, regardless of the body underneath or the natural drape of fabric. While the volume of the body is represented with broad lines, character is rendered by the artist's economical use of highly expressive fine lines that bring to life the furrowed forehead, pouched eyes, and intent mouth. Thin, closely packed lines indicate the texture of the hair; a single, sweeping line ending in a spiral creates the contour of the scroll.

Sharaku's rather formal, schematic line is, and looks, very different from Moore's exploratory, suggestive, sculptural line in his "Studies for Stone Sculpture" **(Line 13).** But both are tremendously sure and evocative, and the substance of the figures in both cases comes through in a physical way. As Moore's feeling for line is evident in his pencil drawings, the Japanese artist's love of line and his sensitive understanding of its possibilities are revealed in the grand rhythms of this woodcut.

Line

COLOR

COLOR

"A Clown," by Honoré **Daumier** (French, b. **1808**, d. 1879). Watercolor and charcoal. 14⅜ x 10". The Metropolitan Museum of Art, Rogers Fund, 1927.

Scene from "The **Burning of the Sanjo Palace**," copy of Heiji scroll, Japanese, middle Kamakura Period (ca. 1249-ca. 1287). 16½" high (approx.). The Tokyo National Museum, Japan (original in The Museum of Fine Arts, Boston). Photo by Sheldon Brody.

The sketched line of Daumier's "Clown" is kinetic. Unlike Picasso, whose line is firm and decisive in "Grande Tête de Femme au Chapeau Orné" **(Line 22)** or Anuszkiewicz, whose line is immaculately precise in "Primary Hue" **(Line 20),** Daumier has used several strokes of his charcoal where one would suffice. Yet none of the lines are superfluous—in unison they give the work an almost cinematic movement. We feel that we have caught the figures in action, an effect easily pinpointed in the multiple lines of the drummer's stick and especially strong in the rendering of the clown's wild gestures. The watercolor energy and quickly drawn line of this sketchbook page give the impression, too, that we have interrupted the artist—that we are seeing a sketch in progress.

Calligraphic line plays a double role. Not only does it provide the vehicle for written language; it is also used, with no reference to language at all, as a means of artistic expression. The beauty of the calligraphy here lies in the elegant brushstrokes, where curving line is played against straight, thick line against thin, complex line against simple, yet the overall impression is one of complete unity. The animated Japanese characters, standing out against the neutral background, create a texture balanced by the finely delineated forms of bowman and rider who sweep dramatically toward them. The brush line of the characters serves as the inspiration for the treatment of the figures. The calligraphic style appears particularly appropriate in the detail—the horse's tail, the bow and swords, the musculature of the bowman's legs. Like the writing, the figures benefit from the unembellished background that allows the nuances of the brush to stand out in crisp clarity.

In the frantic lines of the clown and the hunched posture of the drummer, Daumier does far more than record the outward appearance of the street entertainers; he emotionally communicates his feeling for the human tragedy they represent. Far from detracting from the sketch, the loosely drawn detail, scribbled accent lines, and transparent washes (rather than thick, carefully laid in color) give Daumier's work its immediacy, its emotional depth, and its power.

While the execution of the line is free and fluid, the basic form of the writing is, of necessity, fixed by the demands of a written language. Yet the artist has been able to employ its traditional style to meet the creative challenge of figure drawing. He imbues his line with energy and expression to which the calligraphy becomes a living complement, making the transition between language symbol and art symbol seem easy.

Line

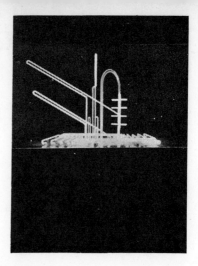

"Peanut Ricky," 1967, photograph by Sheldon Brody. The Reinhold Visuals Collection.

There is much more mischief and joie de vivre than craftsmanship in this egotistical message, but there is also an undeniably close union of idea and technique, casual as they may be. The same message carefully carved in italic script or printed in a line of formal type would look inappropriate and uneasy and would lose its spirit. As it is, the impudence and bravado behind the words give it style and flash.

Whoever wrote "Peanut Ricky as Thunder Bolt" would laugh if someone called him an artist. But in the moment that he boldly scrawled his manifesto for all the world to see, on the rough wall of a building, he acted as an artist and made an artistic statement in an artistic way. His spontaneous expression is a lively component of the environment, not only as a source of amusement to the passer-by and of annoyance to the owner of the building, but also as a reminder of the impact and appeal made by a free and honest statement of feeling.

COLOR

"Marie's First Neon," 1965, by Stephan Antonakos (U. S., b. 1926). Neon tubing and enamel-coated aluminum. 44 x 48 x 48". Collection The Whitney Museum of American Art, New York; gift of The Howard and Jean Lipman Foundation, Inc.

We are at home with the neon glow of hundreds of flashing signs and glaring displays that assault our eyes every day, and we accept them as a medium of communication. In much the same way that we read a neon message, we involuntarily "read" Antonakos' sculpture of colored light by scanning its lines over and over.

Sculpture in conventional materials often tempts us to run our hands over its lines, to test and savor its surfaces. The bare glass lines of this maze of tubing, endlessly bending back on themselves, offer no stimulus to the fingertips, but they capture our eyes. Antonakos' sculpture is pure line shot full of vivid, electric color. As the color pulsates within the glowing tubes, it expands and dynamizes the work. A new optical dimension is created, challenging traditional concepts of what line is.

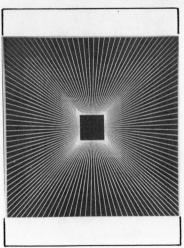

Line

COLOR

Favrile glass **vase, by Louis C. Tiffany** (U. S., b. 1848, d. 1933). 13½″ high. The Metropolitan Museum of Art, gift of H. O. Havemeyer, 1896.

Function has often served as motivation for the artist, but never has it been fulfilled more elegantly than by Tiffany in the production of his distinctive glass. In this slender vase we see refinement carried to an extreme; function has become a very secondary consideration. Elegance here is seen in the attenuated line, elongated silhouette, and ethereal colors that underline the fragility and decorative exaggeration of the piece. Graceful almost to the point of being frivolous, delicate almost to the point of being impractical, the vase is nevertheless a tour de force of style and craftsmanship.

By exposing hot glass to metallic fumes and oxides, Tiffany was able to produce a sparkling iridescence that, although widely imitated, has never been equalled in quality. The free-flowing lines of Tiffany glass became world popular at the turn of the century with the rise of Art Nouveau. This movement stressed the imaginative stylizing of curving, organic forms and placed a premium on hand-produced objects, in rebellion against the new machine age.

Much of the glass produced by the Favrile process was heavily ostentatious, but in this vase we can see the superlative restraint and appreciation of form that give some pieces an almost spiritual beauty. As Antonakos today is fascinated by the luminosity of neon, so was Tiffany excited by the luminosity of translucent glass. But while the slim lines of "Marie's First Neon" **(Line 18)** are lit by electricity, the slender shafts and shells of Tiffany's best work themselves gather in and hold the light that illuminates their shimmering, gemlike lines.

COLOR

"Primary Hue," 1964, by Richard Anuszkiewicz (U. S., b. 1930). Liquitex on canvas. 66 x 66″. Collection Mr. Richard Brown Baker, New York. Photo by Eric Pollitzer, courtesy The Sidney Janis Gallery, New York.

The Op artist forsakes not only subject matter but also the traditional dramatics of art, such as perspective, modeling, and foreshortening, and chooses instead to work in that narrow but exciting no-man's-land which exists between physical fact and psychic effect.

Everything has been drained from "Primary Hue" except surface sensation and surface illusion, and the nerve-tingling surface is created entirely by the artist's manipulation of precisely painted lines of color. Colored line and line on color create an illusion of depth and movement. Although the canvas is flat, we are compelled to see into it deeply. While there is no real motion, we sense a pulsation originating in the central square, and behind the striated surface, squares of color flicker as we look. The painting is kinetic, that is, it implies movement although it does not actually move. The movement we perceive is the result of the combination of color vibrations (predominantly red against green) and the interruption of the lines. The artist does not allow us to reach a final resolution of what the forms in the painting really are. The optical sensation is constantly changing and in itself is the object of the painting.

Line

African mask *(kifwebe)*, Republic of the Congo (Kinshasa). Wood and paint. 17½" high. The Museum of Primitive Art, New York. Photo by Charles Uht.

COLOR

"Grande Tête de Femme au Chapeau Orné," 1962, by Pablo Picasso (French, b. 1881). Linoleum cut. 25¼ x 21". Courtesy Marlborough Graphics Gallery, New York. Photo by O. E. Nelson.

We know very little in the way of fact about this mask: who the artist was, what tools he used, what motivated his work, and what tribal conventions may have dictated its form. But the powerful result is itself evidence that the carver possessed a sure command of his technique and a vigorous style of expression.

The artist employs a rigid system of parallel lines to develop form—form conceived abstractly, but with full awareness of the structure of human anatomy. He intuitively makes use of the visual phenomenon whereby parallel lines that change direction create a feeling of depth. Thus areas of line are manipulated so that the planes of the face are expressed and the mass of the head implied. The herringbone pattern of the forehead gives the mask three-dimensionality, which is accentuated by the contrasting smooth swath extending down from the crown of the head. Similarly, by the juxtaposition of line areas the artist conveys the gaunt concavities under the eyes and the blunt protrusions of the jaw.

The smooth areas of the eyes, nose, and mouth stand out markedly not only as physical features but as major design elements. The necessary apertures of eyes and mouth give the mask its strong emotional presence, for through the elongated eye slits and completely abstract design of the mouth are projected the menace and mystery of the face. The lines are repetitive but never monotonous. By their change of direction and contrast with smooth areas, the carver achieves the drama and unity of his work.

Line in this linoleum cut has the vigor of the tool cutting through the resistant material. Here is neither the softness of a brush nor the nuance of pen and ink, but the scalpel-like clarity of swift, free, incised line. Yet the line carved by Picasso is very different from that seen in the African mask **(Line 21)**. Although both the African artist and the contemporary master treat the head in an abstract way, Picasso's line is employed to make a highly sophisticated interpretation and analysis of mass presented on a two-dimensional surface.

Picasso discards the traditional, straightforward treatment by which the head is represented from one viewpoint (the front, for instance, or the side) and presents simultaneously multiple views. He depicts what he knows as well as what he sees. This is why there are two heads that, clearly or ambiguously, share an eye, an ear, a chin, and other features—he is showing us the same head from the front and the side at once.

Picasso's virtuosity in handling line is amazing. A black line on a light ground becomes light line on black ground; here a line is edge, there shape; elsewhere it defines a detail, in yet another place it establishes major mass. Swooping lines that begin as decoration turn into dynamic, principal lines. Lines are sharp-edged, single, slender, rough, double, broad. Through the reconciliation of seeming opposites—front and side, line and shape, flat and solid, positive and negative—Picasso creates a composition of distinct unity.

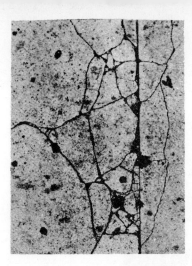

"Sidewalk Cracks," 1967, photograph by Sheldon Brody.
The Reinhold Visuals Collection

What art is and what is art are questions to which there is no one
answer. Certainly a pattern of cracks in a sidewalk, the chance
result of time and weathering, is an environmental feature that
we ordinarily pass without a glance, occasionally regard in a
negative manner (as a pedestrian hazard), and rarely consider in
aesthetic terms. But the juxtaposition of fracture lines in a section
of pavement is recognized in this photograph as a lively example
of linear design.

An alertness to the positive values of chance effect is characteristic
of many contemporary artists, who take advantage of it in their
work and draw inspiration from the natural art that exists in the
environment if only one looks for it. In "Sidewalk Cracks" the
photographer singles out a particular area of pavement for us to
look at, so that our attention is drawn to it as if to a painting.
There is nothing symbolic, informative, or romantic here, only a
spontaneous structure of lines and areas formed by them, visually
relieved by texture and subtle changes in tone. Seen in this way,
it is an accidental "abstraction" that has an easy flow of line and
relaxed composition which we often admire in studio art.

COLOR

"Thorn Heads," 1946, by Graham Sutherland (British, b. 1903).
Oil on canvas. 48 x 36". Collection The Museum of Modern Art,
New York; acquired through the Lillie P. Bliss Bequest.
© 1968 The Museum of Modern Art, New York.

Line is a principal element in Sutherland's painting, for with it he
creates the sharp-pointed, spiky shapes that are the abstract
subject of the work. He uses line to strengthen mass, emphasize
area, increase volume, accent focal points, pick up the quality of
detail. Crisp black lines are sliced into the painted surfaces with
vigor, and passages of color are more than often outlined by
the same bold lines. Thick slashes seem to carve out of color the
forms the painter seeks. Color areas, too, serve as line, sometimes
accentuating and complementing the black, often independent
elements adding power to the composition.

Sutherland's painterly line has the freedom of Daumier's in
"A Clown" (Line 15), but none of its looseness, the sculptural
quality of Moore's in "Studies for Stone Sculpture" (Line 13), but
none of its experimental suggestiveness. Sutherland's line is
free but firm—even hard-bitten—searching but just right when set
down, knife-sharp but imbued with nuance and variety. Line in
"Thorn Heads" smells of oil paint, suggests the thick and thin and
drag of the brush, and sits well on the canvas because it is,
above all, a painter's line.

Portfolio 2, Mass

Mass in Art

The word "mass" suggests things that have volume and weight, things that take up space. We all recognize mass in a metal or stone sculpture: the sculptor works with materials that are tangible and occupy space; he works directly with mass. On the other hand, a straight line drawn on a flat surface does not seem to have mass. But if it curves so that it encloses space, a shape emerges—for example, a circle—and, in a sense, we can speak of its mass. If the circle is filled in with black, it takes on added weight; if it is modeled with shading or textured with dots, it appears as a sphere, an object having volume as well as weight. We know, of course, that such forms are two-dimensional, but we nevertheless perceive them as mass, and they can have all the effect of three-dimensional mass.

Mass never exists by itself. It is defined by line, surface, color; it has a definite relationship to the space around it. Its character and impact depend entirely upon what the artist does with it. The significance of a particular form as mass is not always the same in art as it is in life, or even the same in two works of art. The artist can assign mass whatever importance or qualities he wishes, making a rock seem light, a feather heavy, a cube flat, and a plane deep. Mass can be floating or stable, delicate or overwhelming, hollow or solid; it can be ominous or lighthearted, amusing or sad.

Mass

Nepalese figure of Avalokiteshvara (disciple of Buddha), ca. 14th century. Copper gilt. 36" high. Collection The Golden Monastery, Patan, Nepal. Photo by O. E. Nelson, courtesy The Asia Society, New York.

Mass is tangible form—solid, having volume and weight, occupying space, three-dimensional. Mass is all around us; we handle it, we move it, we shape it. The artist manipulates mass in innumerable ways, for a variety of aesthetic ends, with results as diverse as the monumental pyramids of Egypt and the shifting weights of a Calder mobile.

This Buddhist sculpture is a magnificent example of expressive mass in traditional art. The graceful symmetry and lyrical modeling of the body, growing naturally from and supported by the weight of the folded legs, give the figure stability and evoke a feeling of perfect repose and tranquility; its quiet majesty is reflected in the smooth, simple definition of mass in the face. However, in the rounded contours of the figure, in the broad shoulders flowing gracefully from the slender waist, and in the intricate detail that sets off the overall smoothness of the sculpture, there is vitality and latent power. Through his sensitive handling of mass, the artist has created a figure that is serene yet imbued with inner energy, sensuous yet inspiring reverence and devotion. His work has a spiritual significance that, as the offering of flower petals by Buddhist monks shows, still endures today.

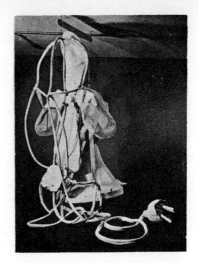

"Giant Soft Fan (Ghost Version)," 1967, by Claes Oldenburg (U. S., b. 1929). Canvas, wood, and foam rubber. 120 x 124 x 76". Collection The University of St. Thomas, Texas; gift of Mr. and Mrs. John de Menil. Photo courtesy The Sidney Janis Gallery, New York.

Because of our overfamiliarity with everyday household objects, we tend to overlook their expressive qualities. Here the artist takes a commonplace appliance—an electric fan—and draws our attention to its aesthetic possibilities by greatly exaggerating its scale (the sculpture is ten feet high). The soft and limpid treatment of what we know is a rigid object isolates and heightens its artistic effectiveness. The removal of the fan from its usual context provides sensational and provocative impact; the inflation of the mass is at once whimsical and sardonic. Oldenburg makes us see mass in a new way. Through this caricature of stereotyped assembly-line production, he opens our eyes to personal excitement in impersonal things.

"Tubas," 1964, photograph by Sheldon Brody. The Reinhold Visuals Collection.

When Oldenburg exaggerates the scale and contradicts the rigidness of a commonplace object in his "Giant Soft Fan (Ghost Version)" **(Mass 2)**, he makes us acutely aware of aspects of its form that before passed unnoticed. In "Tubas" the photographer gives us fresh insight about mass not by physically changing its structure, but by composing his picture so that it is brought to our attention in a new way. Through repetition, he makes us aware of both the differences and the fundamental similarities of the mass ' of each instrument.

Mass in the tubas is functional, because they are designed to make certain musical sounds, and bulging mass is required to produce their deep tones. But this functional volume is visually emphasized in Brody's photograph by the curving highlights of the polished metal, and the contrast of narrow, involuted tubing with the broad smooth expanse of bell-shaped horns. Most of all, perhaps, the mass of the tubas is given prominence by the amusing disparity in size between the instruments and the musicians, who must reach around awkwardly to grasp them. Mass is so ponderous here that the real actors on this little stage are the tubas themselves, which are so imbued with presence that the human figures become hardly more than foils or background.

 COLOR

"Untitled," 1966, by Tom Doyle (U. S., b. 1928). Fiberglassed wood. 5½ x 12 x 12'. Courtesy The Dwan Gallery, New York.

Mass exists in many forms. In McCracken's sculpture, "Manchu" **(Mass 17)**, mass is heavy, solid, and compact, with hard edges; in Chamberlain's "Heng" **(Mass 21)**, it is soft, porous, and springy, with soft edges. Here, in Tom Doyle's freestanding sculpture, mass takes on a completely different character. The sculpture stretches out, its cantilevered construction extending it so it virtually creates its own environment. It is skinny, spidery mass, which reminds us of insect movement, suggesting a giant grasshopper or a praying mantis.

Shadows emphasizing the solidity of the base, eye-catching highlights on the edge of the red area, and changes from thickness to thinness within the structure, all serve to focus attention on effective sculptural mass. Notice how the heaviness of the horizontal base contrasts with the pinpoint support of the sweeping red shape to evoke a feeling of heaviness and lightness at the same time.

Because works of this type are uncomplicated in construction and utilize basic, simple shapes and colors, they are often referred to as "primary structures." Though large in scale, sculpture like this is characteristically devoid of detail, and is therefore also called "minimal art," or even "A B C art." Although this sculpture is non-objective, it suggests, too, the form of practical things—the release bar on a typewriter, the automated arm of a record player, airport architecture, twentieth-century furniture.

Mass

"Kendo," 1955, photograph by Sheldon Brody. The Reinhold Visuals Collection.

Kendo is the traditional Japanese sport of jousting. In this photograph, as in Tom Doyle's sculpture **(Mass 4),** mass is extended into space, but here the subject is in the realm of human physical activity. Although the photograph is two-dimensional, mass is seen as energy and momentum—the athlete engaging in a dramatic and dynamic contest.

The manipulation of positive-negative areas is an effective way of shaping mass, as this action study shows. Mass is created by the contrast of dark tones against a white field; Shaw, in "Bicycle I" **(Mass 6),** reverses the technique, making the figure white. By silhouetting the thrust of the fighter here, the photographer eliminates eye-slowing detail, and the figure is blurred to heighten the feeling of motion. The photographer takes advantage of the fact that mass need not necessarily be a static, weighty element occupying a fixed space, as in McCracken's "Manchu" **(Mass 17),** but can express vigorous motion in free space.

"Bicycle I," 1965, by Kendall Shaw (U. S., b. 1924). Liquitex on canvas. 52 x 29". Courtesy The Tibor de Nagy Gallery, New York.

"Bicycle I" is a fine example of how the illusion of mass can be successfully created on a two-dimensional surface by the manipulation of flat positive and negative areas. Both in Brody's photograph, "Kendo" **(Mass 5),** and in Shaw's painting, major emphasis is placed on silhouetted movement, but in "Kendo" the action moves in an unrestrained manner across and out of the picture, while in "Bicycle I" the action is frozen and locked into place by black negative areas.

Mass is presented here as balanced weight. Bicyclist and bicycle merge to form an aesthetic whole, the result of a perfect equilibrium of man and machine. Yet the painting projects a sense of the nervous energy associated with the shifting weight of the rider. Compare the way the artist uses mass here and in the Nepalese sculpture of Avalokiteshvara **(Mass 1)** to achieve opposite effects. If we look at mass in each case as a triangle, in the painting we find the base of the triangle at the top, precariously poised over the angle formed by the convergence of the other two sides. In the Nepalese work the triangle is reversed—the broad base supports the weight and gives us the feeling of stability.

"Bicycle I" is compelling because of the artist's crisp black-and-white treatment of mass, yet implied detail (seen in the machinery of the bicycle) adds liveliness to its simplicity, and the smooth flow of line forces our eye to constantly explore the canvas.

Mayan whistle in the form of a seated figure, from Mexico, Campeche, Island of Taina. Clay. 7⅛″ high. Courtesy The Museum of Primitive Art, New York. Photo by Charles Uht.

In ancient cultures beauty often grew in an organic manner out of artistic solutions to practical problems. Sculptured whistles, for example, are common in pre-Columbian art (the art of the Americas before 1492). Realizing that the pitch of a whistle is determined by the size and shape of the tone chamber, Mayan craftsmen fashioned whistles in great variety to achieve tonal range. The shapes that were evolved began, in time, to suggest subject matter, and the sculptured whistle became a perfect blending of form and function.

The ancient whistle shown indicates how effective such a union can be. With great simplicity and naturalness, mass is used for practical purposes, while the fluid lines and smooth surfaces of the figure show an understanding of the physical possibilities of clay as a sculptural medium. Broad and bland areas dominate the work, producing a quiet, lyrical effect accentuated by the contrast of details—bracelets, beads, and headgear.

Although small in scale, the sculpture conveys a feeling of restrained dignity and majesty. The treatment of the subject matter, with its fusion of naturalism and design elements, shows a sophisticated approach to the figure by the unknown Mayan craftsman whose art still has universal validity.

COLOR

Chinese ritual vessel, late Shang Dynasty (1766-1122 B.C.) Bronze. 9¼″ high. From The Sackler Collections. Photo by O. E. Nelson.

This Chinese ritual vessel demonstrates how form and function can merge into a satisfying aesthetic unity, but in a way totally different from that of the Mayan whistle sculpture **(Mass 7).** Every detail of this ancient bronze contributes to both its utility and its beauty. The work demonstrates, too, how mass can be changed to serve varied ends: the full roundness of the central mass to be a receptacle, the attentuated mass of the legs to be graceful and economic supports.

Commonplace vessels are often visually unexciting (think, for example, of the average teacup), but the craftsman devised this ritual object so that all its parts have inner vitality and combine to form not only a sturdy vessel but a work of art as well. The expressive boldness of its form reflects, too, the vigorous agrarian life of the Shang period, and its fascination with the powerful forces of nature.

The antiquity of the bronze might suggest that it is the product of a primitive technology, but in fact quite the opposite is true. It is representative of the finest works made by the lost-wax process— a complex and painstaking casting technique brought to perfection during the Shang Dynasty.

Mass

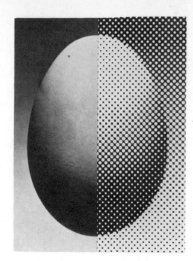

Egg seen in terms of continuous and discontinuous gradation, from the IBM exhibition, "Mathematica: A World of Numbers . . . and Beyond," designed by Charles and Ray Eames. Courtesy The IBM Corporation. Photo by Charles Eames.

Designers consider the egg to be a classic example of functional mass as a package because the interior of the egg offers the most effective possible accommodation for its contents, and the exterior is a fine piece of pure sculpture. The egg shown here (used by IBM to graphically explain mathematical principles on which different types of computers are based) demonstrates two ways of creating mass.

The left side of the egg shows mass as our eyes, and the camera lens, ordinarily see it—in terms of realistic three-dimensional solid form. The right side of the egg has been overlaid with a halftone screen, which produces the kind of dot pattern familiar to us from newspaper photographs. As a result of this pattern, we see mass at first as a flat, two-dimensional texture. As we look, however, a feeling of volume builds up through optical illusion. This phenomenon is caused by our "reading" of a mechanical symbolic language—the dots—which we unconsciously translate into the three-dimensional form we know mass to be in reality.

The artist constantly makes use of both our instantaneous recognition of "real" mass and our tendency to interpret symbols meaningfully. He can manipulate our perception according to his purpose. Like Brody in his "Sports Car Tire" **(Mass 20),** he can present a straightforward representation of mass; or, like Lichtenstein in his "Tire" **(Mass 19),** he can force us to question, to consider multiple truths, to seek meanings behind the surface.

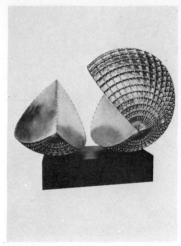

"Untitled," 1964, by Robert Bart (Canadian, b. 1923). Cast aluminum. 40" high. Collection Mrs. Vera List. Photo by John A. Ferrari, courtesy The Leo Castelli Gallery, New York.

Sharp-edged steel, cold concrete, modular detail endlessly repeated, massiveness unrelieved—these are the features that make up the dehumanized geometric mosaic of our industrialized society. Mass, as we see it in our surroundings today, is often hard, unyielding, and brutal. Skyscrapers, factories, shopping centers, drive-ins, and billboards crowd our cities and towns, spilling out along every multilane superhighway and engulfing the once tranquil and untouched landscape. This is the reality from which the disquieting forms of Bart's sculpture emerge.

The bolts and seams of this work, its giant forms, its ironic non-functioning, its forbidding insularity make it an accurate but chilling symbol of twentieth-century life. The dual machine shapes are severe, riveted, and impersonal—just the opposite of Chamberlain's "Heng" **(Mass 21),** with its soft, pliable, spongy forms and sensuous lines. While "Heng" invites a caress, Bart's sculpture says, "Hands off!" This is characteristic of modern "brutalist art."

At the same time, Bart's overwhelming conception is an example of precise craftsmanship and sharp aesthetic awareness. It is executed in a way that reminds us of machine production. Real rivets and bolts are placed with the precision required by a functioning machine. Mass is boldly accentuated by emphatic latitudinal and longitudinal lines and by a strident contrast of plain and broken areas. By slicing a section out of the sphere, the artist gives an intense solidity and weight to the parts. Mass is logical and self-evident; nothing is left to the imagination, and every detail reinforces the relationship of Bart's sculpture to the technological age that it personifies.

Mass

COLOR

"The Castle of the Pyrenees," 1959, by René Magritte (Belgian, b. 1898, d. 1967). Oil on canvas. 78⅝ x 55⅛". Collection Harry Torczyner, New York.

The bizarre use of mass in "The Castle of the Pyrenees" challenges the logic of perception. We know that the situation presented by the painter is impossible, but at the same time he renders it so skillfully and with such inner logic that we are tempted to defy reason and accept the impossible.

The expanse of the sea stretching into infinity and the limitless sky with its light, fleecy clouds make us feel that the central rock, in contrast, is real three-dimensional mass—solid, heavy, impenetrable. The strong, depth-modeling shadows reinforce this impression, and the miniature castle growing out of the rock's overwhelming bulk makes it appear still more gigantic. By surrounding this mass with free space, suspending it against the sky, the artist convinces us that a huge rock crowned with a fantastic castle is actually floating in the air.

Although each element of the subject matter—sea, sky, rock, and castle—is depicted realistically (for instance, the waves and spray), the scene does not add up to a real world. Everything is viewed with the strange clarity that we experience in dreams, where things seem to be more than what they actually are. The exploration of this irrational world of super-realism was the purpose of Surrealism, a movement (founded in 1924) of which Magritte was a leading member.

"Rocks and **Children**," 1967, photograph by Sheldon Brody. The Reinhold Visuals Collection.

Our reaction to mass in a work of art is highly subjective and can be tempered by many factors. One way the artist can control the effect of mass is by his use of scale. Magritte, for example, uses distorted scale to baffle our sense of reality by endowing mass with impossible properties in "The Castle of the Pyrenees" **(Mass 11).** In this photograph, the tiny figures of the children set against the massiveness of the rocks make the rocks more solid, more huge, more challenging than they would appear without the contrast.

To heighten the effect, the photographer excludes by cropping any detail, such as a tree, that might give us a clue to the real dimensions of the rocks. He eliminates the ground line and silhouettes the rocks against a sky completely empty of detail. Because the rocks appear formidable to the viewer, the efforts of the children climbing them, in turn, take on a more heroic stature. We might even feel, when we look more closely, that this picture of Sunday-afternoon fun in the park begins to have deeper significance, perhaps symbolizing man's struggle with Nature.

By intentionally narrowing his field, the photographer creates this mood. If the camera pulled back to reveal the mild relationship of the rocks with their actual environment—Central Park surrounded by the towering skyscrapers of Manhattan, a different feeling of scale would be established, and the illusion of heroic mass would be destroyed.

Mass

IBM Laboratory, Uithoorn, The Netherlands, 1963, designed by Samenwerkende Architectenbureaux. Courtesy The IBM Corporation. Photo by Jan Versnel.

Architecture is always concerned with function, because buildings must be designed with particular purposes in mind. A well-designed building reflects its purpose. The architect organizes space so that function is best served, and as space is created, architectural mass comes into being. Its effect is heightened by the play of light and shade, by variations in surface, and by the optical impact of perspective lines and the patterns they create. The architect has a special problem, therefore: he must be aware of all the elements that will come into play the moment his two-dimensional design, the blueprint, becomes the three-dimensional structure of steel, concrete, and glass.

The IBM buildings shown illustrate how form can echo function to form visually stimulating architecture. Basically, the buildings are composed of simple rectangular shapes, each in itself of little interest. But the architect has organized the total mass within a completely controlled environment so that it generates a geometric excitement which reflects the research function of the laboratory and alerts the attention of the viewer.

Research in automation and the computer, for which the IBM complex is designed, marks a new peak in man's intellectual endeavor, extending his control of the machine for rational purposes to an unprecedented extent. While the buildings lack the intimacy and warmth of traditional architecture, they provide a handsome and suitable atmosphere for intellectual research, for everything in this abstract and timeless environment—even the mathematically concise treatment of the paving—is the product of human rational activity.

COLOR

"Number 10," 1950, by Mark Rothko (U. S., b. 1903). Oil on canvas. 90⅜ x 57⅛". Collection The Museum of Modern Art, New York; gift of Philip C. Johnson. © 1968 The Museum of Modern Art, New York.

"Number 10," which is almost eight feet high, is a deceptively simple painting. Rothko is noted for his use of large blocks of color on canvases seemingly built up wholly in terms of surface. While the two-dimensionality of "Number 10" cannot be dismissed, the areas of color possess a luminosity and inner energy that expand them beyond the limits of their two dimensions and force us to perceive them as tangible mass as well as painted surface.

The artist creates the glowing and almost floating quality of the color blocks by dissolving their edges so they seem to hover within the boundaries of the blue ground, like independent units held in loose check by some mysterious magnetic field. The effect is heightened by subtle variations in the intensity and texture of the color.

In this painting we see what are basically uncomplicated rectangular forms in a composition similar to that of "Stacked Boxes" **(Mass 15).** But while the boxes are rigidly defined and positioned in space, in "Number 10" nothing is fixed, and we are drawn into the painting to ponder relationships of mass that are constantly changing.

Mass

"Stacked Boxes," 1958, photograph by Sheldon Brody. The Reinhold Visuals Collection.

The artist works with three-dimensional mass in many ways—carving, welding, modeling, casting. Intuitively, passionately, with calculation, and even taking advantage of accident, he plays with mass to achieve aesthetic ends. But mass can have an effective aesthetic impact outside the studio as easily as in it. The arrangement of these boxes, stacked with no aesthetic intent on a street in Japan, has a strength and serenity that underline the close relationship between art and life.

"Fine art" is labeled; we know it was made to be looked at. The environment, on the other hand, often contains chance compositions more than often disregarded by the passer-by, but perceived by the sensitive eye. The photographer, in this case, recognized the aesthetic value in an everyday street scene—the rhythmic alternation of simple box shapes complemented by a circular accent—and shares its beauty with us. The visual stimulus, as in the IBM buildings **(Mass 13)**, is the asymmetric arrangement of geometric shapes. Here, however, happenstance repetition of the pleasing rectangular volume of each box generates the vivacity that transforms these ordinary utilitarian objects, when combined, into an artistic structure.

COLOR

"Positon," 1966, by Victor Vasarely (Hungarian, b. 1908). Oil on board. 33 x 33". Courtesy The Sidney Janis Gallery, New York. Photo by A. M. Desailly.

The two simplest and most basic forms in which we can imagine mass are the sphere and the cube. In "Positon" Vasarely selected the cube as the basis for a highly complicated, intellectual painting. A first glance suggests that the artist here manipulated mass in obvious variations on a simple theme, much as one might manipulate building blocks. But as we look, our perception clicks into an expanded vision. We suddenly experience shifting depth relationships and realize that the painting is a super-exploitation of the cube, presenting an endless vista of both color and space interpretations. This effect is related to the mathematical calculation of infinite permutations.

As opposed to the loose arrangement of rectangular shapes in "Stacked Boxes" **(Mass 15)** and the architecturally functional IBM buildings **(Mass 13),** "Positon" represents an analytical exploration of the possibilities of the cube as an artistic element. The artist communicates his fascination with his subject to the viewer, with the result that he is involved not as a passive observer but as an explorer himself.

Mass

COLOR

"Manchu," 1965, by John McCracken (U. S., b. 1934) Wood, fiberglass, and lacquer. 44¾ x 62 x 14½". Robert Elkon Gallery, New York. Photo courtesy The Jewish Museum, New York.

COLOR

"Ultraviolet Cars," 1966, by James Rosenquist (U. S., b. 1933). Oil on canvas with plexiglass, motorized. 88 x 74". Courtesy The Leo Castelli Gallery, New York.

Contemporary sculpture owes much of its vitality to the fact that many artists today are well informed about the nature of perceptioı and use their knowledge to good effect. They know, for example, that they can control our perception of mass with color if they use it in certain ways. It can make gross, heavy forms appear light and puny or, on the other hand, give solidity and weight to what otherwise might be insignificant mass.

McCracken expands the optical volume of "Manchu" and emphasizes its three-dimensionality by his choice of high-keyed, shiny primary colors and by the strong, vibrating effect of the incised chevron. The stark contrast of these complementary colors reinforces the effect of expansion; if pale related colors were used instead, the mass would appear to diminish. Although the physical chunkiness of "Manchu" is in itself mass, color calls attention to its volume and, in addition, charges the sculptural surface with vitality.

In "Ultraviolet Cars" Rosenquist exaggerates mass by implication. As we look at the painting (to which a hidden motor is attached), we see the ends of two overblown, overstyled automobiles actually approach each other slowly, as if to collide. We mentally ready ourselves for the sound of the impending crash. The cars barely touch, and then ponderously move apart to begin the pantomime again.

The sculpture is a study of mass impinging on mass. Mass is suggested first by highlights that punctuate the opulent curves of highly polished chrome and lacquered metal. But it is even more strongly emphasized by the suspense that we subconsciously feel can be broken only by the shock of two heavy automobiles slowly crunching into each other, massive fenders crumpling, as if in a slow-motion film.

Unlike Bart, who in his untitled sculpture **(Mass 10)** surveys the whole contemporary scene with the eye of a removed beholder, Rosenquist chooses one aspect of it and comments with all the unflinching immediacy of a candid camera. His painting does more than zero in on a disturbing scene—its real, motor-driven action forces us to become eyewitnesses to a drama presented in time and constantly repeated. We share his frustration with the inadequacies—which opulence cannot soften—of our high-speed urban world, yet we share, too, a fascination with the chrome and glisten of a brash new age.

"Tire," 1962, by **Roy Lichtenstein (U. S., b. 1923).** Oil on canvas.
68 x 56". Collection M. Grosso. Courtesy The Leo Castelli Gallery,
New York. Photo by Rudolph Burckhardt.

"... but is it Art?" How many times do we hear this question? In
the case of Lichtenstein's "Tire," the question is a natural one
because there seems to be very little distinction drawn between
subject matter and real-life object; the painting looks more like
an advertisement than what we are accustomed to see in museums.

Closer scrutiny indicates, however, that the power and punch of
this work are achieved through strictly artistic means, which
elevate it above the level of comic-strip illustration to that of
a work of art in its own right. The mass of the tire is made
overpowering by linear repetition and by its isolation in space.
The feeling of mass is built up through the use of off-center circles
created by three-quarter view, by the radiating lines, by the immense
scale of the painting, and by the stark contrast of blacks and whites.

Roy Lichtenstein is considered a pioneer of Pop art, and "Tire" is
an outstanding example of this movement, which developed in
the early 1960's. Like other Pop artists, he is intrigued by mass
media, by popular images and everyday objects: movie stars, light
bulbs, soup cans, all are Pop themes. Lichtenstein's fascination,
too, with the expertise of modern advertising art is revealed by
his slick technique, reminiscent of the commercial art of the
billboard, magazine, or supermarket, that makes no concessions
to subtlety and nuance. By this means he reduces all of the attributes
of the tire to blunt symbols; for instance, the shine of the chrome hub
cap is rendered as a series of terse, schematic lines. But paradoxically, while draining the subject of flesh-and-blood realism, he
produces a super-tire—that is, in a sense, a tire to end all tires.

"Sports Car Tire," 1967, photograph by Sheldon Brody. The
Reinhold Visuals Collection.

This photograph has the same general subject matter as
Lichtenstein's painting, "Tire" **(Mass 19),** but the photographer
approaches it in a very different manner. The painter depersonalizes
mass, rendering it in the technique of Pop art, and the image is
reduced to a symbol. In the photograph, on the other hand, mass is
located in a recognizable setting and presented in a matter-of-fact
and straightforward manner. It is personalized, specific, familiar.
Instead of the sharp contrast of blacks and whites and the
three-quarter view of Lichtenstein's work, which result in a dramatic
illusion of three-dimensionality, here depth is minimized by soft
gradations of light and shade, and the flat side view emphasizes
the disklike character of the tire rather than its volume. The
concentric circles of hub, rim, and treads, echoed in the surrounding
shape of the fender, give us a feeling of stability and balance—
the antithesis of the jarring, rolling sensation evoked by the painting.

The photographer makes the viewer conscious of the existence
of outer reality: dirt and grime, road debris, the changing time of
day in terms of reflections and shadows. He is unconcerned
with symbolism; he sees the tire as functional mass, bearing the
weight of the car. By careful framing of the composition, however,
he draws our attention to visual elements—the symmetrical star
pattern of radiating spokes, the contrast of varied surfaces, the
lively play of line against mass—and he reveals to us the aesthetic
qualities of a practical design.

Mass

"Heng," 1967, by John Chamberlain (U. S., b. 1927). Urethane. 54 x 54 x 36". Courtesy The Leo Castelli Gallery, New York. Photo by Rudolph Burckhardt.

COLOR

Chinese tomb figure of a court lady, T'ang Dynasty (618-907). Ceramic. 18¾" high. From The Sackler Collection. Photo by O. E. Nelson.

"Heng" is not only a challenging sculptural form achieved in a non-traditional material (urethane), but also an art object in which the traditional concept of a work of art as expression decisively frozen in time and space is discarded. Chamberlain has created sculpture seemingly in process. Compared to the serene inertia of the Mayan figure **(Mass 7)** or the immobile solidity of McCracken's "Manchu" **(Mass 17),** this is pliant, ready to spring into new shapes, bursting with internal energy. It is mass that undulates and pulsates; it turns in upon itself and writhes as if alive, straining to snap back to its original shape.

Presenting no established front, back, or side views, "Heng" intrigues the viewer to move around it, to search for relationships between its soft, spongy parts. Gentle modulations and shadows played against strange pitted slashes give the sculpture a mysterious and exotic quality. The artist's choice of material and his treatment of its surface affect our perception of mass as well. Thus, for example, in "Mustang Sally McBright" **(Surface 1)** Chamberlain employs a similar compositional theme—elements that bend and fold in upon themselves—but there the unyielding automobile metal, with its hollow volumes and jagged outlines, crackles with electric energy. The brittle, synthetic, reflecting surfaces make a neon-sharp statement and mischievously cause any attempt at interior inquiry to ricochet, keeping our fancy engaged instead with the gleaming exterior. The porous, cellular consistency of "Heng" makes an entirely different kind of mass; it suggests a dynamic inner core and tempts the imagination to probe its hidden secrets.

This figure of a court lady, although created in a far-distant place and long-distant era, has a timeless charm and grace. The T'ang Dynasty was a golden age of art, music, and poetry marked by the fusion of Indian Buddhist values with traditional Chinese art forms. While this sculpture is disarmingly frank in conception, simple in construction, and emotionally low-keyed, its beauty is nevertheless the culmination of generations of religious and worldly thought.

The stylish and genteel court lady, with her self-assured air and wry humor, is the aristocratic embodiment of a sophisticated culture. Her fashionable coiffure, elegant attire, and graceful stance give us the impression that here is nothing more than a lady of fashion, her head filled with the frivolous concerns of a Chinese noblewoman. But the more we look, the more we sense a quiet and subtle dignity, an inner calm reminiscent of the calm that characterizes the Buddhist religious figures such as the Nepalese sculpture **(Mass 1).** Its presence in this sculpture reflects the pervasive influence of Buddhism on the culture of the T'ang Dynasty.

The sculptor conveys the duality of a life-style that extolls the contemplative ideal yet expresses it in profane subjects. He handles mass in a restrained and economical manner, organizing it so that one ovoid shape grows softly out of the next. This treatment of mass, which has much in common with Rothko's handling of abstract blocks of color in his "Number 10" **(Mass 14),** is conducive to the expression of the contemplative state. The absence of naturalistic detail frees the mind to grasp fundamental truths about spirit as reflected in the beauty of pure form.

Mass

COLOR

"The Diner," **1964, by** George Segal (U. S., b. 1924). Plaster and mixed media. 8½ x 9 x 7'. Collection The Walker Art Center, Minneapolis. Photo courtesy The Sidney Janis Gallery, New York.

We find ourselves asking, "Is it art?" when we look at Lichtenstein's Pop painting, "Tire" **(Mass 19).** "The Diner," Segal's Pop "environment," provokes our curiosity even more deeply, and we wonder, "What is real and what is not real?"

"The Diner" is an assemblage, that is to say, an aesthetic arrangement of diverse elements, some of which are from the real world (the lunch counter and stools, coffee urn, mirror, and fixtures) and others (the plaster figures) created by the artist specifically for the work. Segal's sculptured people interact in a real-life situation that we all have witnessed many times, made more convincing because they are set in an environment of startling reality. In ordinary experience such a scene would be so commonplace as not to elicit a second glance, but in its gallery context, "The Diner" grips our eyes and imagination. Although both the figures and the props are life-size and set in true space, the unearthly pallidness of the figures and the fact that they are virtually featureless give the scene a macabre air. Thus, while Segal confronts us with a real setting and goes so far as to make his figures from plaster casts of living models, his intention is to create people whose individuality has been obliterated, who wear the modern mask of anonymity. The ambiguous swing from reality to unreality and back again draws the viewer into the world of "The Diner" and prompts him to ponder his own life, his own anonymity and isolation in a world of plastic and chrome. Although "The Diner" represents a complete break with sculptural tradition, the profundity of its intention and its ability to move us indicate that it is a serious work of art that rises far above the limitations of its subject matter.

COLOR

French armor, 1555. (**Armor of Aнne de Montmorency**, Constable of France, 1493-1567.) The Metropolitan Museum of Art, Harris Brisbane Dick Fund, 1932.

The natural armor of creatures such as the turtle and armadillo defines the living mass that it encloses and protects. Such armor is invariably beautiful in its functional articulation and its perfect and logical relationship to the body underneath. This French suit of armor is an example of man's attempt to provide a similar protective covering for himself. Unlike its counterpart in nature, it is an accoutrement that must be carefully planned so that the wearer can support its weight and move with some degree of freedom.

In the endeavor to keep armor as light as possible without sacrificing strength, armorers over the centuries fashioned each individual suit to precisely fit the dimensions of its owner. As they searched for solutions to practical problems of strength, weight, and mobility, the basic components were arranged, rearranged, and refined, and handsome as well as utilitarian designs emerged. The manipulation of the mass involved became as much an aesthetic concern as a practical one, leading to such decorative results as that shown here.

Leaving aside the purpose this suit of armor was created to serve, it is a work of art in its own right, a powerful expression of man's physical vitality and spirit. It is, as well, a fine example of mass sensitively organized and controlled, its major volumes enhanced by nuances of delicate tracery, and its hard strength set off by the contrast of soft suede. In common with the padded solidness of the modern football player or the pressurized bulk of the astronaut, the sturdy, steel-clad form of the knight in armor stands as an extraordinarily energized expression of mass ready for action.

Portfolio 3, Organization

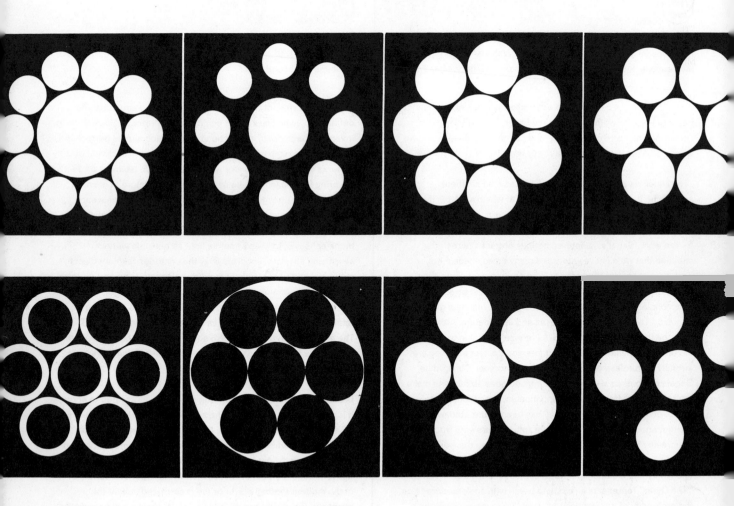

Organization in Art

The individual elements of art, such as line or mass, do not in themselves form a work of art. Anyone can take color from a paint tube
and put it on a canvas, but it remains for the artist to put it down in
such a way that we experience an underlying order. The ordering of
elements into a meaningful unity is visual organization.

It may help us to understand why organization is necessary in art if
we realize its importance in nature. To give only one example, the
skeleton, blood, and organs that make up the human body cannot
work on their own. A coherent interrelationship—organization—is
essential to life. Similarly, organization is essential in the man-made
world. Unless its parts are ordered, a building will not stand nor a
machine function.

Some artists consciously structure their work; others arrive at it
intuitively. There are no absolute rules by which aesthetic organization can automatically be created. Although we can name such
factors as symmetry and balance, it is impossible to list all the means
artists use to give their work unity. But even if we cannot at first
glance comprehend the organization of a work of art, we are immediately affected by it; it shapes our perceptions and our feelings. As we
know, by our unease, when organization is lacking, so we recognize
its presence by our sense of harmony and completeness.

Organization

COLOR

"Nuit de Noël," 1952, by Henri Matisse (**French**, b. 1869, d. 1954). Stained-glass window (in four sections). Approx. 11′ 1″ high (overall). Collection **The Museum of Modern Art, New York**; gift of Time Inc. © 1968 The Museum of Modern Art, New York.

The artist works with many elements—subject matter, purpose, the physical properties of his medium, and the formal elements of design such as line, mass, surface, and color. All of these components must "hang together" in order to form a work of art; that is, they must be organized. In "Nuit de Noël" the arrangement of stained-glass pieces forms an ordered composition that makes a direct appeal to our senses. The relationship of the parts seems uncomplicated, but sophistication is at the heart of the window's unity. The design was carefully planned in a collage made by the cut-and-pasted-paper technique, where Matisse coaxed his brilliant color-shapes into ideal relationship to one another and to their frame. Only when perfect harmony was achieved with paper was the design transferred to glass and the window assembled.

Every piece of glass here has equal importance; every one is distinct and vibrant. But there is a definite organization, for every one is strictly positioned in relation to a main axis—the ascending central blue column. The pattern of stars and curving, organic shapes rises within the axis and symmetrically on either side of it, culminating in the bright star at the top. Matisse's sophistication—and his genius—are expressed in his use of imperfect symmetry to animate the composition. While every shape is locked into place by the heavy horizontal bars and more delicate lines of leading as tightly as the pieces of a jigsaw puzzle, the individuality of each infuses it with life and gives the whole an air of ease and spontaneity.

Apache devil-dance **headdress**, United States (Arizona). Cloth, wood, paint, metal glass (mirror), and cord. 35″ high. Courtesy The Museum of Primitive Art, New York. Photo by Charles Uht.

The triangle and the circle are the chief design motifs in this Apache headdress. In contrast to the Nigerian sculpture of a guardian spirit **(Organization 16)**, in which the basic triangle is given mass (that is, it becomes a wedge), here the triangle is treated as a flat form. Although this is a three-dimensional construction, the shapes are more closely related to those of Matisse in "Nuit de Noël" **(Organization 1)**. Matisse plays the jagged star against curving shapes; the Apache craftsman opposes the serrated sunburst to circular and semicircular shapes. A central vertical axis is the basis for a symmetrical disposition of the motifs, producing a balance that is especially important here because of the headdress's practical function. The Apache, like Matisse, is interested in two-dimensional pattern, and his forms become even more abstract as they are manipulated. But although the organization of the Indian work is comparable in these ways, there are essential differences between it and "Nuit de Noël."

The pattern created by the Apache craftsman is regular—the symmetry varied only by the freehand repetition of shapes (the sunbursts on the left originally had inner circles like those on the right). The basic motifs do not lose their identity. While Matisse makes his carefully planned design seem spontaneous and loose, here we are conscious of a strict and formal geometry. Appropriate to its ritual purpose, this is a work that will evoke awe as the dancer, his face obscured by the cloth head covering, moves under its impressive height and bold design.

Organization

COLOR

"Semé," 1953, by Stuart Davis (U. S., b. 1894, d. 1964). Oil on canvas. 52 x 40″. The Metropolitan Museum of Art, George A. Hearn Fund, 1953.

Both "Semé" and Matisse's "Nuit de Noël" **(Organization 1)** are built up of cut-out shapes and strong, bright colors, but the two works seem to represent opposite poles of visual organization. The structure of "Nuit de Noël" is deliberate and immediately clear. In "Semé" there are many basic elements—the rectangle, the circle, straight and curving lines—and many recognizable figures—the arrow, the "X," words. No two are alike, and all are intermingled with an equal variety of irregular shapes in a wholly unpredictable pattern. The work is well described by its title, a French word meaning "strewn." But the organization of "Semé" is not at all haphazard.

Davis' composition is perfectly balanced, not through the fixed structure of symmetry, but by a free-flowing organization of shapes and colors. It has a restless quality that is created by the variety of its parts and by their relationship to one another and the whole. The floating shapes of the periphery contrast with the overlapping shapes of the main complex. Shapes are interrupted, and we are never quite certain of their spatial relationship. Another kind of dynamic uncertainty is created by the combination of recognizable and ambiguous or abstract shapes: the ease with which we identify the former makes our involvement with the others searching and active. The feeling of movement in "Semé" contributes to its balance rather than disturbing it. Through the constant movement and interplay comes the resolution of its changing shapes and colors, and thus, paradoxically, its unity.

Poster for an exhibition of works by Takis (Vassilakis) and Raphaël-Jésus Soto at the Rudolf Zwirner Gallery, Essen, Germany, 1961. Designed by Schmitt. Courtesy Rudolf Zwirner, Cologne.

The purpose of this poster was to announce an exhibition of two artists noted for their kinetic work. Taking a readably sturdy, rigid style of type, the designer creates an exciting composition by making it move. He noticed that each name occupied almost the same amount of space when set in type and observed relationships that appeared when one was placed above the other: the roundness of the a echoed in the o, the verticality of the k continued in the t, the curves of the s repeated in the o. Then he began to imagine that the word *Takis* was actually changing into the word *Soto* by a gradual transformation. This is the fanciful idea on which the poster's organization is based.

By nature we are organizing beings. When we look at things that have begun to change, we are not content until we see the change completed and are even compelled to go and help. This is what makes the poster work—the typographic transformation is not at all mechanical and arbitrary. The designer does not merely give us half of each word in the intermediate stage. The t is the only letter cut in half horizontally; the a, k, and i are sliced at different angles, all pointing downward and creating momentum toward the bottom line. This motion is accelerated by our tendency to complete by closing and merging things that are not really closed and merged—we continue the line of the i in the half-i beneath it and the vertical of the k in the half-k. We also continue the contours indicated by the black lines, so that the white areas, or negative spaces, become dynamic elements of the transformation, and we extricate ourselves from this action to seek the final, stable resolution of the bottom line.

Organization

 COLOR

"The Grande Chartreuse," detail of manuscript page, from *The Belles Heures of Jean, Duke of Berry,* by the Limbourg Brothers. French, produced about 1410-13. The Metropolitan Museum of Art, The Cloisters Collection, purchase, 1954.

This manuscript illumination (shown enlarged) is a striking example of how physical and intellectual discrepancies in a work of art can be visually reconciled by effective organization. The artist has two themes: the monumentality of an important monastery and the humble life of the monks who live there. The naive combination of various perspectives gives us an impossible view (we see the church from below, but look down on the courtyard behind it) and impossible proportions (the figures are too large in relation to their distance from the buildings). The fantastically decorated sky defies all logic. Nevertheless, all these elements are brought together in a balanced, charming, and finally plausible whole.

In contrast to the perfect perspective space that unifies Botticelli's "The Three Miracles of St. Zenobius" **(Organization 15),** here contradictory space is held within a painted frame, which merely encloses the various elements and cannot organize them. But there is a strong cohesive principle within the composition. Interlocking bands of color and shape cross the picture surface from side to side in an orderly way. Each major area of the work—grass, water, buildings, hills, and sky—forms an integral part of this system, building up an underlying stability. Against these horizontal bands, relating and energizing them, rise verticals—the uprights of the dam, the piers, windows, and spire of the church, the peaks of the hills, the tree trunks that reach into the gold-foliated sky. This close-knit organization unobtrusively makes the work hang together, setting us at ease with and allowing us to enjoy the serenity of this microcosmic world.

"Chambered Nautilus," 1967, photograph by Sheldon Brody. The Reinhold Visuals Collection.

Organization in nature is always successful because it is a prerequisite for survival. In technology, too, it must be successful because it is fundamental to function, that is, the parts of a machine must be perfectly articulated if it is to work. Similarly, organization is essential to a work of art; we feel that an arrangement of colors, shapes, lines, and volumes has no "life" and does not "work" if we do not sense underlying order in it.

Nature has always provided the artist with ideal proportions, and the spiral, characteristic of many natural forms, has from earliest times been a popular design motif. The chambered nautilus shell is a classic example of natural organization. It is admired by the scientist for its economical and effective pattern of growth, by the mathematician for its precise expression of the equiangular spiral, and by the artist for the beauty of its symmetry and the clarity of its structure. In this photograph the paper-thin shell is shown in section, revealing the perfect relationship between interior and exterior as well as the harmonious development of the chambers. In the delicate, sinuous lines, unfolding volumes, and polished surfaces of the chambered nautilus are absolute logic and beauty.

Organization

Japanese family insignia, from *Hyojun Mon-cho (Directory of Standard Family Crests)*, published by Someori Kanko Kai (Society of Weavers and Dyers), Japan, 1956.

The Japanese family crests shown here are selected from a collection of thousands. The book from which these two pages are reproduced is used by craftsmen who decorate kimonos with the wearer's crest. The insignia are superb examples of effective organization achieved despite design limitations of the most stringent kind. To serve their purpose—identification—each crest must be both unique and immediately legible. All, by tradition, are confined in a circle (whether used or, as in some here, implied). All are two-color or, more accurately, use only positive and negative space. All, finally, are composed of a minimum of design elements or motifs—in these examples, only one: the circle in one group, a comma-shape in the other. Yet it seems clear that the possibilities are inexhaustible.

The organization of each crest is based on the imaginative manipulation of simple variables. Thus, in the lower group, the number of circles ranges from three to eleven. Although four crests are composed of three circles, in one the circles have a different relationship (they overlap). The remaining three crests are distinguished by a changing figure-field relationship: in one the shapes are defined by contour; in another they are solid, or positive; in the last, negative. Other variables are size and direction. In the upper group these factors are varied with striking results. Different effects of movement are created—the crest in the upper right corner spirals "more quickly" than that on its left. The power and elegance of the designs grow from the simplicity and economy of their organization. The crest in the left-hand column, fourth from the top, is perhaps the most remarkable—in its completely self-possessed design, most of the circle is completely empty!

"Street Posters," 1967, photograph by Sheldon Brody. The Reinhold Visuals Collection.

On a long-neglected wall layer upon layer of posters are pasted; they are peeling off, tattered, and scrawled on. The photographer has found, in this chance product of time and weather, an assortment of design elements: lettering of various kinds, a single recognizable shape, many irregular shapes and outlines. He carefully selects and frames a portion of what he sees and creates an ordered composition.

The accidental nature of this arrangement is in direct contrast to the controlled organization of such works as Matisse's "Nuit de Noël" **(Organization 1).** Here the placement of forms is arbitrary, yet the photographer's choice imposes a certain order. While there is no considered motif or plan, there is an equilibrium of light and dark, positive and negative. There is a pleasing flow of torn edges and rough, evocative shapes complemented by the sharp, decisive lines of the dancing leg, the fragments of words. We are reminded of an imaginary map, quickly changing storm clouds. This reaction is quite the opposite of our reaction to Brody's "Store Front **(Organization 18),** where the strict, rectilinear pattern keeps our ideas specific. The very vagueness of these free-form shapes, the unpredictable quality of the design, and the movement and life of the organization opens the doors of our imagination.

Organization

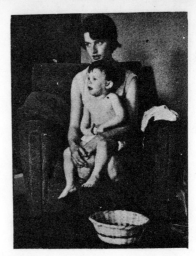

"Rome—Tourist with Ice-cream Cone," 1964, photograph by Sheldon Brody. The Reinhold Visuals Collection.

Amusing and serious at the same time, this photograph is a masterly study in incongruity. Its subject in one sense is the woman with an ice-cream cone. She is the center of a little drama revealed if we look at the details: the camera slung over her arm identifies her as a tourist; the handkerchief, which serves as an improvised hat, evidently protects her from a hot midday sun, while the ice cream refreshes her. But equally demanding of our attention here is the cheap reproduction of a Renaissance painting, Raphael's "The Madonna of the Chair," which is hung on a peeling wall that takes up more than half of the photograph. In itself it is incongruous— a copy in a frame ornately decorated with a silk-tasseled rope, a masterpiece tacked up on a dilapidated wall.

The photograph is organized in quite a simple way through visual as well as intellectual contrasts. The two subjects are isolated from the environment and each other by the different textures of their rectangular backgrounds, but balance is achieved by the similar positions of the figures on either side of the composition. The unequal size of the rectangular shapes and the extension of one in the upper right corner keep the composition from breaking into two separate, unrelated scenes and give it visual unity.

This photograph represents a visual relationship that existed for just one brief moment—our daily lives are filled with such phenomena that pass unnoticed. It is artistic perception and creation that isolate and transform them into organized structure, and we sense a new opening up of experience in this sharing of the accidents of life.

"Mother and Child," 1955, photograph by Sheldon Brody. The Reinhold Visuals Collection.

In this contemporary version of a universal theme, the photographer records the warmth and dignity of a simple, unposed scene. The genre quality is created by the unselfconscious figures in their casual surroundings—the rumpled bib, plain basket, and ordinary furniture of an ordinary home. But we cannot mistake this for a family snapshot. The photographer captures a moment of natural visual order, and the scene becomes timeless.

The emotional as well as the visual center of the photograph is the single form of mother and child. The two figures are fused by the close-knit relationship of mother enfolding child and by the interlocking arrangement of arms, hands, legs, and feet. The unity of the smooth, softly rounded mass of the figures, modeled by light and shadow as though by a sculptor, is set off by the broad, rougher curves of the armchair and the flat wall. The subdued, grainy quality of the photograph suffuses the entire scene with softness, but every form is clearly stated and immediately understood. It is through the lack of artifice that the inner serenity of mother and child is expressed.

Organization

COLOR

"The Crucifixion with Saints and Scenes from the Life of the Madonna," detail of triptych, from the workshop of Duccio di Buoninsegna (Italian, ca. 1255-1319). Tempera on wood. 22 x 15¾". The Metropolitan Museum of Art, bequest of George Blumenthal, 1941.

A forthright exposition of theme presents us with a fine opportunity to observe the formal organization that underlies the grandeur and dignity of this medieval religious painting. Everything is calculated to lead our eyes to the figure of Christ. It occupies the center of the composition, and the other figures are either reduced in size or relegated to the lower half of the painting. While there is far more weight in the lower part, the focal point of the work is the head of Christ. Here is the crossing of the Crucifix, the center of the semicircle of angels, and the apex of triangles formed by base points in the upward gaze of two figures, in the head and shoulders of the outermost two, and in the ends of the ground line at the bottom of the painting.

The upward motion is repeated in the rocks and in the upright of the Cross. But at the same time, the artist keeps our eyes from moving out of the painting by the strong horizontal of the Cross and downward-pointing triangles such as that formed by the arms of Christ. The flat gold background (only traces of its rich decoration still show) eliminates any suggestion of pictorial space, pushing the figures to the foreground plane. While the formal structure of the painting gives the scene its monumental quality, the emotional content of the subject is also fully expressed. In the attenuated arms and downcast head of Christ and the elongated, contained figures of the mourning saints the artist has concentrated all the moving drama of the Passion.

COLOR

"Hatos," 1966, by Victor Vasarely (Hungarian, b. 1908). Tempera on board. 33 x 33" (approx.). Courtesy The Sidney Janis Gallery, New York. Photo by A. M. Desailly.

The structure of this Op painting is of a completely different order from that of Duccio's "Crucifixion" **(Organization 11),** but the work is no less carefully structured. While Duccio's object is to fix our attention on one point, and the entire painting is organized in relation to it, Vasarely is interested in the pure sensation of visual perception. There is no center in "Hatos"—every part of the painting is equal to the rest in emphasis. The artist does not tell us where to look: he simply provides a stimulus for optical involvement. For this reason it is essential that we become active viewers. Unless we explore the sensations provoked by the painting, it will remain a simple composition of geometric forms.

If we concentrate on what we see, however, we will begin to experience the variety of visual perception. The painting suddenly becomes alive: it is kinetic. The circles pulsate; the cubes resolve in ascending, steplike arrangements within a complex spatial structure. If we concentrate long enough, we will see the ambiguity of this illusory space, in which the top of one cube can be read as the bottom of another. Our original perceptions are turned topsy-turvy, our sensations change constantly, and we feel the excitement of optical illusion.

Organization

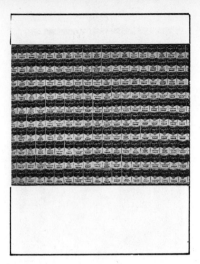

COLOR

"Tropics" (date not established), by Henri Rousseau (French, b. 1844, d. 1910). Oil on canvas. 45 x 64". The Metropolitan Museum of Art, bequest of Miss Adelaide Milton de Groot (1876-1967), 1967.

The circle is a major motif in "Tropics" as it is in Vasarely's "Hatos" **(Organization 12)** and Warhol's "200 Soup Cans" **(Organization 14),** but Rousseau was not concerned with either the objective study of visual perception or the detailed treatment of individual objects. Whereas Vasarely uses the circle as an abstract geometric concept, Rousseau's brilliant oranges are living symbols of a mysterious, imagined jungle. He painted directly on his canvas his impressions of a romantic, personal world and grasped intuitively the means of organizing the fantastic, dreamlike scene.

At first this painting may appear naive, but a strong compositional structure supports the decorative surface. Every element is part of a spatially coherent stagelike setting for the two storybook monkeys in the center. They sit between the dark verticals of the tree trunks, under the arch woven by diagonal branches; the sky dips down to them, and the two other creatures become part of the background. The overall pattern of luxuriant foliage is a backdrop and a snug frame, its shadowy subdued greens complementing the warm reddish-brown of the main characters. Against it, too, the almost glowing oranges stand out and give rhythm to the whole, culminating in the single orange that draws us to the focal point of the composition. The organization of color, shape, and line evokes the hush of a steamy afternoon, and, for a moment, we feel we have intruded on the lives of the fictional monkeys who stare out at us.

COLOR

"200 Soup Cans," by Andy Warhol (U. S., date of birth not known). Casein on canvas. 72 x 100". Collection Mr. John Powers. Photo by Eric Pollitzer, courtesy The Leo Castelli Gallery, New York.

Few artists would consider the repetition of a basic unit two hundred times as an appropriate organization for a painting. There are no points of emphasis in "200 Soup Cans," no balance of pictorial forces, no suggestion of movement, no nuance of color or modeling, and no indication of depth or solidity beyond the most schematic representation of the cylinder. We see only two hundred soup cans stacked in regimental order as they might be in a supermarket. Yet in turning his back on all the "rules" of organization, Warhol achieves a novel structure—a non-organization that works effectively and has a kind of unity.

In the manner of the Pop artist, Warhol emphasizes the unique identity of a banal object. He does this not by painting a monumental soup can isolated in space, as Lichtenstein treats the automobile tire in "Tire" **(Mass 19),** but by insistent repetition—by filling every inch of his huge canvas with the image on which he wants us to concentrate. This is an organization that hems us in; we cannot visually escape. Once we begin to explore the painting we become aware that the artist has not duplicated the image with the exactness of a rubber stamp: there are intentional irregularities in the lettering, and, perhaps with a touch of humor, many varieties of soup are scattered throughout the rows, reminding us that we are not, after all, in the ordered world of the supermarket.

Organization

COLOR

''The Three Miracles of St. Zenobius'' (date not established), by Sandro Botticelli (Italian, b. 1444-5, d. 1510). Tempera on wood. 26½ x 59¼''. The Metropolitan Museum of Art, Kennedy Fund, 1911.

Like a modern comic strip, ''The Three Miracles of St. Zenobius'' is organized so as to express a sequence of events in time. The cartoonist represents time by a convention we recognize and understand —the action is repeatedly stopped in successive boxes. Although the subject matter of this Renaissance painting is unfamiliar, the narrative sequence becomes clear as soon as we understand the conventions used.

Botticelli presents simultaneously three episodes in the life of St. Zenobius and tells us how to ''read'' them by the careful arrangement of every element in the composition. A single, exact perspective unifies the painting as though the actions were taking place on one stage. Then, like a director, Botticelli leads our eyes from one tableau to the next. Thus, the scene at the left is pushed to the very front of the stage by the mass of the building behind it— and that is where we begin. We see the Saint (identified throughout by his robe, miter, and posture of blessing) raising a dead youth to life. Then, as our eyes travel naturally along the diagonal perspective lines into the central space of the painting, we come to the second miracle: the Saint reviving a messenger who was killed bringing him relics (the skeletons). Again our eyes are drawn along diagonals (the sides of the coffin), through open space, to the scene at upper right, where the Saint hands St. Eugenius a cup of holy water. Finally, following the line of the steps and the direction of St. Eugenius, we see the miraculous revival of his relative. Despite the subdivision of the painting, the overall unity of the work is never lost, for color, line, and mass are perfectly balanced in the grand plan of the composition.

Nigerian guardian **spirit (*ejiri*), Western Ijo or Urhobo**. Paint on wood. 25½'' high. Courtesy The Museum of Primitive Art, New York. Photo by Charles Uht.

The organization of this wood sculpture derives its strength from a vigorous abstraction of natural shapes. The organizing principle of the work is that of theme and variation, the theme being the geometric wedge shape. Reading the sculpture from the top, we immediately see the dominant shape inverted to form the nose of the seated figure. (Less clear in this photograph, but still evident, are the wedge shapes that compose the top and back of the man's head.) The pattern of teeth, a major variation of the theme, is repeated schematically in the chevrons that form the eyes, the scarification of the cheeks, and the design of the fingers. The wedge is powerfully restated in the tusklike spikes protruding from the sides of the animal and in its massive legs. Unifying these elements is the overall shape of the sculpture— a wedge that stands securely with its weight at the base.

The emotional tone of the sculpture, in keeping with its purpose as guardian spirit, is ferociousness. This quality is created by the recurring pattern of teeth—in the face of the man, the gaping mouth of the animal, and the sepulchral heads that decorate its legs—and emphasized by the feeling of powerful mass. The architectonic structure of the work grows naturally from the artist's handling of his material: he retains the solid, blocklike character of the wood. Thus he makes no distinction between the figure of the man and the body of the animal, while opening up the mass so that space becomes an active element, and each part relates logically and dynamically to the next.

Organization

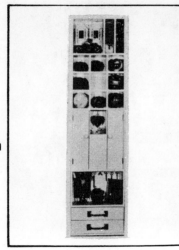

''Repository,'' 1961, **by George Brecht (U. S., b. 1926)**. Wall cabinet containing miscellaneous materials. 40⅜ x 10½ x 3⅛". Collection The Museum of Modern Art, New York; Larry Aldrich Foundation Fund. © 1968 The Museum of Modern Art, New York. Photo by Soichi Sunami.

The apparently miscellaneous objects we see arranged in this assemblage are only some of the things provided by the artist. Among the items not shown are a pocket watch, bottle caps, playing cards, pencils, a postcard, a miniature Statue of Liberty, a page from a thesaurus, and a preserved worm. The viewer is invited to rearrange the elements —the organization is thus unfinished; it is open-ended.

Two themes dominate this thought-provoking work. Many of the objects included are directly associated with childhood: here we see wooden blocks, a toy motorcycle, a skate key, and a variety of balls— a star-decorated rubber ball, an autographed baseball, a wooden puzzle ball, and a ''ball'' of string. Other objects, not specifically associated with youth, nonetheless are memorabilia of the sort that fill anyone's junk drawer: a heart inscribed with a long-past date, an old photograph, used toothbrushes, a plastic persimmon. This is the useless collection we each keep because it is not anonymous—it is privately meaningful. The artist's intention that we consider it our own is made clear by the inclusion of a mirror, which reflects our presence in the work. The second theme is that of mystery. Here are objects we cannot quite identify, closed doors, a barrier of wire mesh, an empty space (what belongs there?)—and an assortment of keys that will not unlock the mystery. No matter what we do, the result will be ''organized'' by the fixed pattern of compartments and the character of the objects the artist has given us. No matter what we do, these elements will add up to feelings about a half-remembered past and the unanswered, unanswerable questions about ourselves we all carry locked in our memories.

''Store Front,'' 1967, photograph by Sheldon Brody. The Reinhold Visuals Collection.

Unlike the artist, the photographer does not create the subject matter of his work—he finds and organizes by selection and editing the images that move him. This is a creative process, as Brody's ''Store Front'' shows us, for the photographer has revealed the aesthetic content of an inconsequential scene. In a deserted, dilapidated section of building and pavement he sees, and makes us see, a composition of rectangular shapes, strong contrasts of light and dark, and varied surfaces.

The emphatic pattern of rectangles gives the organization its underlying strength. The large, boarded-up area, covered with a rich texture of lines, dominates the composition. It is echoed in the major shapes of the windows above, the metal doors below, and a variety of minor rectangles within the larger ones, in the recesses between the buildings, and in the store front at left. The diagonal perspective lines in the sidewalk show a kinship with the uprights of the buildings, and the grid motif of the metal doors is recalled in the wire screen. The cylindrical shape of the rubbish can, with its rectilinear ridges, is subtly varied in the column rising beside it. The surfaces are diverse, and there is a balanced range of value from light to deep shadow. Whether we become absorbed in the abstraction of the scene or consider its content, our appreciation and feelings are heightened by the photographer's art.

Organization

 COLOR

Paintings by Jim Dine (U.S., b. 1935). Exhibition at The Sidney Janis Gallery, October, 1964. Courtesy The Sidney Janis Gallery, New York.

In the three paintings shown here we see five different versions of a single subject—a bathrobe—and, consequently, five different kinds of organization. In the diptych at left, Dine treats the panels as parts of one organization, tying them together with a common field color and elements that extend from one to the other—the black area, the footstool, and the painted horizontals. The artist's unwillingness to be confined to a two-dimensional surface is evident in his use of solid objects such as the towel rack and shelf attached to the right-hand panel, but he carefully maintains the unity of the pictorial space, for both of these elements merge with the painted horizontals. While the two panels are also related by the similar placement of the bathrobe on them, closer study shows that the technique of representation is varied—for example, there is no realistic modeling of drapery in one.

The painting in the background shows still another technique of representation and another kind of organization. The bathrobe is painted decoratively in flat colors applied with sharp definition. In this work, too, the artist confounds us with the interchangeability of two- and three-dimensionality, for the upper edge of the frame is a solid rod and over it hangs a real bathrobe cord.

A still greater transformation of subject matter and composition is seen in the diptych at right. On one panel a careful pencil drawing of a bathrobe is divided into twenty-eight squares by a grid. On the other panel only the squares remain, here brightly colored. In this ultimate version, Dine gives us an abstract organization that captures the essence rather than the outward form of his subject.

"Greek Mother and Child," 1964, photograph by Sheldon Brody. The Reinhold Visuals Collection.

The feelings evoked by this photograph of a mother and child are specific and intensely emotional, in deep contrast to those prompted by the same photographer's "Mother and Child" **(Organization 10).** The figures here arouse questions with social implications: Who are they? Where do they live? What misfortunes have overtaken them? Their faces are grim and troubled—they appear to be the principals in some tragic occurrence.

It is not only the expressions on their faces and the obvious poverty of their surroundings that distinguish this mother and child from the other. Despite the general similarity of the pose, the differences are significant. Though related by proximity as well as emotion, this pair does not function as a unity. The boy leans against the woman rather than being securely held; they gaze in different directions. There is a pronounced discontinuity between their bodies, the checkered shirt and white knees of the boy standing out against the somber black of the woman's clothes. The background occupies a greater area than the figures here, and although the figures are primary, the pathos of the scene is inextricably bound up with the setting. The flat shapes behind are impersonal and unyielding; the closed doors and boarded-up windows are inhospitable, seeming to refuse shelter to the forlorn pair. There are no curves and no softening of surface in the background—the strong rectangles of wood and blank wall serve only to press the figures down on the hard, empty ground.

Organization

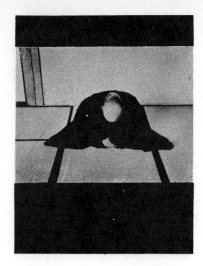

 COLOR

"Marilyn," 1962, by James F. Gill (U.S., b. 1934). Detail of triptych. Oil on composition board. 48 x 35" (each panel). Collection The Museum of Modern Art, New York; gift of Dominique and John de Menil. © 1968 The Museum of Modern Art, New York.

The subject of this Pop painting is one of the most popular images of our day—the movie star Marilyn Monroe. Every detail of Gill's powerful work expresses his concern with the problem of identity and the tragic destruction of personality by the glamor of a public image.

The organization of the painting is sequential, as is Botticelli's "The Three Miracles of St. Zenobius" **(Organization 15).** Here, however, time is compressed drastically, and the effect is cinematic. Gill presents a double series of stop-action photographs that catch the exaggerated poses and stereotyped facial expressions of publicity pictures. The repetition provides visual continuity, but more important is the carrying over of the photographic treatment to the main portraits. In the left panel, the head seems lifted from the frame behind; on the right it is pointedly "underexposed," so the flesh-and-blood personality becomes the celluloid image.

The figure is the focal point of each panel—the bright red dress stands out against a touch of complementary green, the muted colors and abstract shapes of the background fix it in place, and the lines of thrust formed lead directly to it. But Gill makes it clear that, as there is no depth in the painting, the image is surface too. In the poignant flatness of the glamorous image, he captures all the pathos of the dazzling but anonymous Hollywood star.

"Zen Monk," 1957, photograph by Sheldon Brody. The Reinhold Visuals Collection.

In this photograph, as in Brody's "Greek Mother and Child" **(Organization 20)** and Gill's "Marilyn" **(Organization 21),** a number of rectangles are played against a central form. In each case, however, the artist's purpose is quite different, and so is the resulting organization. While this work is dominated most strongly by the central form, it is a basically abstract composition of light and dark. It expresses a state of mind in which we become participants rather than observers. There is no suggestion of arbitrary manipulation; although the photographer has carefully selected a particular view, we are as unaware of his presence in the room as is the Buddhist monk.

The framework of the organization is the spare geometry of black lines made by the binding of the *tatami* mats. Each of the lines leads to the focal area, which is emphasized by perspective, and the rectangles outlined lock the central form into place. The figure of the monk is abstract and suggestive rather than specific, and this is the reason for its impact. There is no explicit body—all detail has been suppressed and, instead of a familiar silhouette, we see a flat, black, symmetrical shape. The impersonality of the figure is heightened because the monk's face is hidden. Thus our eyes travel from the white crescent of his collar to the sphere of his head, and come to rest on the clasped hands at the very base of the shape. The bare lines, lack of detail, and perfect balance of the composition make it a precise visual statement of the reserve, dignity, and absolute quiet concentrated in the person of the praying monk.

Organization

COLOR

"Entrance of the Thugs," from *The Miraculous Mandarin; Homage to Béla Bartók* (a series of six prints), 1966, by Colin Lanceley (Australian, b. 1938). Screen print. 30½ x 22⅛". Courtesy Marlborough Graphics Gallery, New York. Photo by O. E. Nelson.

The mechanical images of this silk-screen print are the artist's interpretation of complex and evocative characters in a ballet with music by Béla Bartók. Lanceley's images, too, are suggestive and puzzling. Though we seem to recognize in them the technical illustrations of a textbook, we cannot make them make sense. The artist provides just enough information to convince us the machinery will work: schematic views of engines, directional arrows, apparently mechanical relationships. But when we attempt to relate the parts, they do not fit together. The wheels and cogs have no more logical place than does the outsize, yellow jigsaw-puzzle piece.

The puzzle piece is a clue to the unorthodox, intellectual organization of the work. Lanceley is actually presenting us with the plan of an almost-real system—a puzzle that cannot be solved. He confounds our senses by playing with the traditional elements of art and traditional methods of organization. Shapes are repeated in an apparently meaningful way; mass and space are balanced; color and texture give emphasis. But all the element play ambiguous roles. The mottled surface of the black and white mechanism on the left gives it three-dimensionality, but it is juxtaposed in an impossible way with the completely flat puzzle piece. The striped shape at lower left is very slightly distorted so we cannot easily tell what position in space it occupies. It is in the shuttling back and forth of our imagination from reality to unreality that the work achieves its energy, and in the illusory continuity of its parts that we perceive its organization.

COLOR

Scene from "The Going of the Emperor to Rokuhara," Heiji scroll, Japanese, middle Kamakura Period (ca. 1249—ca. 1287). 16½" high (approx.). The Tokyo National Museum, Japan. Photo by Sheldon Brody.

This detail from a Japanese scroll is like a scene from a film in that it depicts one episode in a continuing drama. The remarkable skill of the artist is illustrated by his ability to organize the elements of the picture so that we see a completely self-contained action—a visual entity—that has all the verve and momentum of a grand procession.

Every element that lends stability to the picture is balanced by one that implies motion. For example, the continuity of action indicated by the corner of drapery that is disappearing at the extreme left is countered by the braking stance of the figure in green who pulls at the first horse's head and by the backward glance of the horse's rider. The flow created by various horizontal forces, such as the direction of the feet, the streaming tails of the horses, and billowing drapery, is offset by the placement of most of the figures to the rear (right of center), the upward thrust of the bows, and the eye-catching patch of empty space in the very center of the procession. The repetition of tall black hats provides a lateral rhythm, yet simultaneously holds the action in place by defining its upper limits.

The flat colors, stylized draperies, and delicate calligraphic lines making a band across the neutral background create the impression of a decorative frieze, while the obvious movement gives life to the painted figures. In this sensitive and elegant way, the artist captures and communicates the form and tempo of his highly sophisticated age.

Portfolio 4, Surface

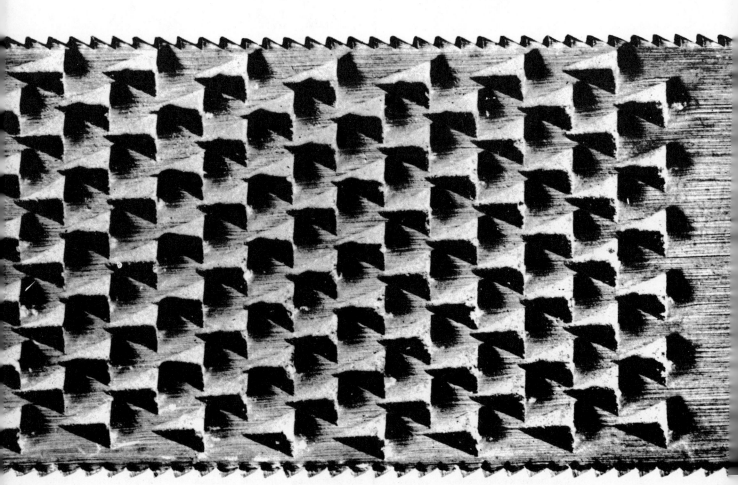

Surface in Art

No element in art makes such an immediate appeal to our senses as surface. Surface is not something abstract—it is a direct, sensuous link with environment. We react to it physically when we touch things, feeling their roughness, smoothness, and many other tactile qualities. We also react emotionally: some surfaces are pleasant, others repellent. Touch is so much a part of our sensory knowledge of things that we are hardly aware how much we rely upon it. But we expect surfaces to feel a certain way (skin is smooth, bark rough), and we are shocked when a surface seems inappropriate. Surface is thus of great importance to the artist, for it will clearly influence our response to his work.

We do not actually have to touch a surface to feel it, because we constantly translate what we see into tactile sensation. The artist therefore does not have to depend on our touching his work—or even on actual texture. The texture we perceive evokes reactions as strong as texture we experience physically, and the artist can make our reactions even more intense, if he wishes. He can also modify or reduce sensations, or make them changing or ambiguous. His treatment of surface can invite us to run our fingers over a work of art or keep us at a distance, draw our eyes into its depths or over its planes, put us at ease or disturb us. Surface in art is not just a skin of polish or paint—it is a powerful, moving factor, and its quality shapes our experience of line, mass, color, and space.

Surface

COLOR

"Mustang Sally McBright," 1964, by John Chamberlain (U.S., b. 1927). Welded and painted metal. 60 x 50 x 70". Courtesy The Leo Castelli Gallery, New York.

Although we do not usually think about it, our sense of touch helps us relate to our environment. Our attitude toward objects is highly influenced by our tactile response to their surfaces: soft fabric, polished wood, rough stone have textures we "see" through our fingertips and "feel" through our eyes.

For Chamberlain the automobile is material for a brilliant, abstract sculpture of sensuously gleaming surfaces. In his characteristic, crushed-car works, the automobile is removed from its practical role as vehicle and completely transformed. While "Mustang Sally McBright" would certainly be chaotic as a car, it is completely organized as a work of art, for the shapes that compose it have been arranged in an organic unity. The sheen and coloration of its metal surfaces engage our eyes, which move around and over the work, following its lines and dented volumes. We visually feel each surface, comparing it and contrasting it with the surfaces around it.

All the parts of Chamberlain's sculpture have been arranged by the artist with patient care, and the result is a flowing symphony of bending, crunched, and puffed-out surfaces that stimulates our sense of touch. The visual order of its strong metal facets makes us aware that the artist can leave his imprint on any and every material he chooses.

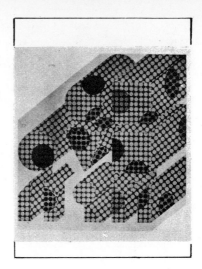

COLOR

"Geometry?" 1965, by Joe Tilson (British, b. 1928). Screen print. 27 x 39". Courtesy Marlborough Graphics Gallery, New York. Photo by O. E. Nelson.

The question mark in the title of this screen print is important because it pinpoints not only the artist's intention but much of our response to the work. We cannot look at the composition without wondering whether sections of it are really three dimensional. The complexities of the surface prompt us to explore it with our fingers.

Tilson toys with our perception in this ambiguous but calculated design. The overall pattern of blue polka dots in regular rows makes it, at first sight, entirely flat. Even the disks of different colors contribute to this impression, despite the fact that some have been cut and others seemingly distorted. But the polka-dot pattern remains regular, and we seem to be looking at pieces of cloth of the same design, but cut from bolts of different colors, lying flat on the flat yellow background. There is not a suggestion of shadow or modeling, no ripple in the cloth, and no depth.

But now we see how the artist simultaneously hints at three-dimensionality. He "cuts" into the blue polka-dotted area so that angles of yellow show, and he shifts sections of the surface so that the cut edges of the dots are displaced (as though the patterned cloth had been cut in pieces and put back together without matching the dots). The implied straight lines created between the unmatched dots, and the angles made by them and the yellow ground, form subtle, illusionary blocks; the implied curved lines suggest the ends of cylinders. These volumes cannot quite be resolved, however, and we are, as the artist intends, left to question the nature of this plane and solid geometry.

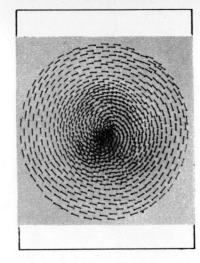

Surface

 COLOR

"Between," 1963, **by Alfonso Ossorio (U.S., b. 1916)**. Assemblage on composition board. 48 x 48". Collection The Whitney Museum of American Art, New York; gift of Howard and Jean Lipman.

No matter how much intrinsic interest an object has, when it becomes part of a conglomeration in which no part is given predominance, it becomes surface rather than shape. In this assemblage there is such an abundance of objects that the individual identity of each is less important than the tactile quality it contributes to the whole.

Despite the number and variety of the objects Ossorio assembles, there is a sense of underlying organization in the work. Shapes and colors are repeated. The parts seem to flow, but within definite areas of the surface. They make up a loose mosaic that constantly rearranges itself before our eyes, like some strange living organisms moving in a drop of water under a microscope.

We may try to concentrate on one fascinating object or another—we can discern a myriad of shiny round shapes (actually glass eyes used by taxidermists), buttons, beads, shells, fragments of mirror, gems from costume jewelry, feathers, and even a bone. But we are always conscious of the textures—smooth spots and rough passages —and we find, like children before a case of penny candy, that the multiplicity of choices will not let us stop at any one for long.

"Phantom," 1963, **by Günther Uecker (German, b. 1930)**. Masonite and nails. 60" (diameter). Courtesy The Howard Wise Gallery, New York. Photo by Sheldon Brody.

Although composed of hundreds of ordinary nails of identical design and size, this work provides as varied a visual experience as the conglomerate collection of Ossorio's "Between" **(Surface 3)**. The nails are arranged in a spiral design, and changing patterns of nails and shadows are formed with the slightest shift of the viewer's position or the lighting. Surprisingly, however, the nail-studded relief does not invite touch or evoke the strong tactile sensation that we might expect. Uecker's interest in surface is optical, and the orderly arrangement of nails actually reduces the feeling of texture.

The artist's concern here is the effect of movement on our visual perception. The mechanical structure of "Phantom," unlike Ossorio's brightly colored, free-flowing assemblage, is a controlled experiment. The movement we experience is coordinated, like that of iron filings manipulated with a magnet. The heads of the nails provide moving points, their lengths moving lines, and their shadows changing, sometimes vanishing variations. All work together with an almost mathematical severity, yet the configurations of form, light, and shadow are constantly new and constantly enticing to the eye.

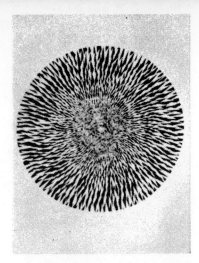

Surface

"Bombardment of the Optic Nerve II," 1963, by Miroslav Sutej (Yugoslav, b. 1936): Tempera and pencil on circular canvas. 79" (diameter). Collection The Museum of Modern Art, New York; Larry Aldrich Foundation Fund. © 1968 The Museum of Modern Art, New York. Photo by R. Petersen.

"Bombardment of the Optic Nerve II" is, like Uecker's "Phantom" **(Surface 4),** circular, and both works exemplify the Op artist's interest in perceptual movement. But as a result of different surface treatment, the two are extremely different in effect. While our eyes move in a spiral over the surface of "Phantom," here they are swept inward and out again. The three-dimensional relief by Uecker is flat compared to this two-dimensional painting, whose pulsations produce in us a hypnotic and disturbing sense of depth.

How does Sutej induce this optical illusion? He manipulates the triangle, the basic motif, to create seemingly solid forms. These then appear, according to our point of view, as a series of diminishing, elongated diamonds. In places—particularly at the bottom of the composition—they seem to disintegrate back to flat triangles, while at the top they stand out in sharp relief. As a simple experiment will show, the artist's treatment of the triangle is actually the same, and it is our own point of view that changes, our perception changing with it. Turn the work upside down and this phenomenon becomes clear. No matter how often "Phantom" is turned, in contrast, the depth relationships of the nails remain the same. Rapid changes of scale from the perimeter to the center take place here, and they are essential to the visual impact—the "bombardment"—that we experience.

Benin sculpture of a head, from Nigeria. Cast bronze. 10¾" high. Courtesy The Museum of Primitive Art, New York. Photo by Charles Uht.

Surface plays a dramatic part in this monumental bronze sculpture. With a simple, tubular element the artist creates rich and lively ornamentation. Strong as the visual impact of this texture is, its end effect is to clarify the volume of the head and emphasize the smooth surface and simple contours of the face.

The criss-cross pattern of the head covering gives fullness to the crown of the head; the ropelike verticals draw our eyes up and around the sculptural mass, and the high "collar" of horizontal detail emphasizes the roundness and three-dimensionality of the form. All the design of the decoration serves to frame and give importance to the face.

The face itself is a masterpiece of expressive form. It is modeled simply and naturalistically, its broad and curving planes set off by the strong surrounding textures. The graceful outline of the eyes, the flaring nostrils, full lips, and gentle, convex bulges of the cheeks are modeled with perfect clarity, and the careful avoidance of detail enhances the statement of mass. This compact work delights the eye and refreshes it and stands as a striking example of sculptured surface.

Surface

⑦

"Rasp File," 1967, photograph by Sheldon Brody. **The** Reinhold Visuals Collection.

This detail of a rasp file is not the work of a Pop artist, although the monumental size of the industrial product and the inclusion of the word "hi-test" might recall such works as Warhol's "200 Soup Cans" **(Organization 14)** or Lichtenstein's "Tire" **(Mass 19).** The rough surface of the file is an example of texture found in the environment—there are hundreds of objects, natural and man-made, that might be studied for the varieties of surface they present. The surface of the file is composed of small, three-dimensional cutting points designed exclusively to serve a practical purpose. Careful lighting and enlargement by the photographer reveal its remarkable aesthetic qualities.

It is interesting to compare the file with two works of Op art. The motif, like that of Sutej's "Bombardment of the Optic Nerve II" **(Surface 5),** is the triangle; the regular repetition of it in relief recalls Uecker's "Phantom" **(Surface 4)** and similarly produces changing visual patterns. The surface of the file, however, evokes a strong tactile sensation, and this is not entirely due to the viewer's knowledge of its function. The particular structure of the tool and the composition of the photograph together serve to intensify the feeling of roughness. The sharp points and edges of the teeth (as opposed to the flat heads and round shafts of Uecker's nails) contribute to this effect, and the serrated edges reinforce it, while the smooth-grained end, purposely included, provides emphasis by contrast.

⑧

"Cut Glass," 1967, photograph by Sheldon Brody. **The** Reinhold Visuals Collection.

The scintillating surface of a Victorian cut-glass bowl cannot quite be reproduced in a photograph, but this magnified detail makes a fascinating study. It is an unusual surface—precise, but in striking contrast to the functional precision of the rasp file **(Surface 7)**—and perhaps comparable only to the glittering surface of a jewel. Like a jewel, too, it is designed purely for decorative effect: its purpose is to please the eye.

The smooth, shiny hardness of the material gives this surface a pleasant tactile quality. Its waffled and starred lozenges and diamond-shapes are delightfully evocative of symmetrical forms in nature, for example, snowflakes and crystals and even living structures such as that of the pineapple. But the polished facets of the bowl are actually secondary: they exist above all as agents for the play of light. Light is a positive element—it is the sparkle of the surface that captures the eye.

The design of the surface is difficult to understand visually, for it challenges the viewer to understand the spatial relationships of its parts. The point at which surface ends and light- or shadow-filled space begins is unclear. This complex optical instability is created by the combination of light, material, and design. The surface is composed not of an applied, opaque "skin" with areas of light, highlight, and shadow, but of many little angled transparent surfaces, which both reflect light and transmit it from different levels of illumination.

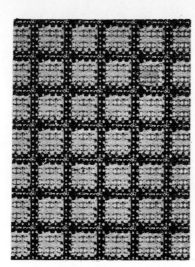

Surface

⑨ COLOR

Circuit chips of an IBM computer, System 360. (A group of experimental circuit chips photographed through a microscope. Each of these chips is 1/18″ square and contains 150 electronic elements making up sixteen circuits.) Courtesy The IBM Corporation.

Frosted windowpanes and the rippling sand of a beach are examples of surface in the environment that we commonly notice and appreciate, but the beauty of the world opened up by modern technology is still largely undiscovered or unrecorded. The bright pattern formed by these circuit chips—tiny components of a computer—is a new and exciting aesthetic experience.

The original purpose of this photograph was to provide technical information about the circuit chips, and therefore clarity was essential. Clarity is a part of what makes the composition visually satisfying: the surface is built up through simple repetition of a single motif. Mere repetition can be boring, but as dramatic lighting, enlargement, and contrast expand the visual opportunities of the surface of the rasp file **(Surface 7),** here other factors come into play and make the surface active and intriguing. The warmly brilliant, almost glowing color of the circuit chips stands out from the deep black background with the dynamic effect of electric lights against a night sky. Although all the circuit chips are exactly alike, their internal complexity fascinates the eye. While the overall grid arrangement of the units remains clear, the space between them takes on the mazelike quality of the network within, and we are unendingly stimulated to explore the intricate pathways of the surface.

⑩ COLOR

"Shipside," 1963, photograph by Sheldon Brody. The Reinhold Visuals Collection.

Color never exists alone in art, although artists have sometimes tried to isolate it. But its effect is always qualified by surface. Even if every irregularity of surface is systematically excluded so the color is completely flat, there will still be surface. A single color red, for example, stimulates our vision one way when it is shiny, another when it is mat. The artist must be as conscious of the surface he creates as he is of hue. For this reason painters often add substances such as sand to their paint, or make thick impasto strokes, or use varnish, or scratch and scrape to achieve other textural effects.

Brody was clearly aware of surface when he photographed this scene, for "Shipside" is a vivid catalog of its effect on color. There is "pure" color (in the bucket), color splattered in spots and rich wet patches, streaked, weathered, and pitted color. The range is as wide as on a painter's canvas, but with no reference to art. (A sailor is brushing rust arrester onto a ship's hull to protect the metal.)

The photograph, however, is a highly organized work of art. Each of the quadrants into which the composition is divided is different, but all are related as are variations on a theme in music. In terms of structure, therefore, the blue uniform of the sailor in the lower left quadrant provides a strong contrasting passage that is subtly echoed in the upper right; the bright orange-red splashes in the lower right quadrant are answered by the diffuse color of the upper left. The subject of "Shipside" is neither the sailor nor the ship: the theme is the visual elements of color and surface.

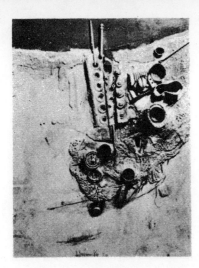

Surface

"Metallic **Grey," 1960, by Jaap Wagemaker (Dutch, b. 1906).** Wood panel with aluminum egg-slicer and scrap metal. 24 x 19⅝". Collection The Museum of Modern Art, New York; Philip C. Johnson Fund. © 1968 The Museum of Modern Art, New York. Photo by Soichi Sunami.

The assemblage, a combination of diverse objects into one work of art, opens up a whole new realm of surface possibilities for the artist to explore. It frees the painter from the strict two-dimensionality of traditional painting, where depth is created primarily by illusion. Wagemaker takes advantage of the freedom of this art form and pushes surface treatment to the extreme. Deep apertures gape in the built-up paint surface; heavy textures create a kind of geological topography, and sporelike growths multiply and spread menacingly. Even the comparatively quiet areas of this work are scarred, and the whole has an abrasiveness that may jar our ideas of what is aesthetic.

The violent contrasts of surface that mark "Metallic Grey" are the direct opposite of the regular pattern and formally organized surface of works such as the photograph of circuit chips **(Surface 9)** and the Chinese bronze vessel **(Surface 13).** Wagemaker's assemblage might well be considered an artistic reaction to the world of rational structure. But this is not an artistic "temper tantrum." The artist uses unusual materials in a free organization that grows out of the nature of the materials themselves. Found materials, unlike traditional art media, often have identities of their own so strong that they indicate directions in themselves, and so help to determine the final form of the work of art. "Metallic Grey" is a serious attempt on the part of an artist to express himself in the most vigorous and dynamic way possible, with no holds barred.

COLOR

"Pastry Case," 1962, by Claes Oldenburg (U.S., b. 1929). Assemblage. 20½ x 30 x 14". Photo courtesy The Jewish Museum, New York.

What, a startled viewer might wonder, is the purpose of taking an ice-cream sundae, a banana split, a wedge of pie, and other pastries—objects of absolutely no meaning except as food—as the subject matter for a work of art? What, indeed, have these inedible desserts, not even arranged in the familiar still-life grouping of the studio, to do with art?

A closer look at "Pastry Case" provides a clue, for a clear lacquer completely covers each and every object with an impossible, high sheen. Actually, this assemblage is a study in surface. The subject matter has not been changed in terms of its mass or organization, and the artist has relied solely on surface treatment (including intensified color) to make his point. In thus heightening the original identity of each object he discloses his Pop art intent, which is to glorify the ordinary—to show us pastry as we have never seen it and to make us think of it in an entirely new way, not as food, but as an object possessing unique form, color, and surface. Oldenburg puts his glamorized display in an authentic setting—a real pastry case—but with the whimsical touch of the half-eaten jelly apple, he gives us notice that he is also gently pulling our leg.

Surface

 COLOR

Chinese ritual vessel, early Chou Dynasty (1122-255 B C) Bronze. 9⅝" high. From The Sackler Collections. Photo by O. E. Nelson.

This Chinese bronze is a masterpiece of understatement and a remarkable example of the intensity of expression that can result from the perfect control of aesthetic elements. All of the drama of the vessel is created by its flaring shape, yet the utter simplicity of the curving lines is also the source of its elegance. More than half of the surface of the vessel is totally undecorated, but the effect of this restraint is to emphasize and thus allow us to savor the bronze's rich patina of iridescent blues, greens, and soft browns.

Our eyes travel slowly down the smooth surface to the decorative heart of the piece—the raised central band with its delicate fret pattern (symbolic, in ancient China, of clouds and thunder). The design is repeated on the base, providing weight to balance the smooth expanse of the upper surface, but it does not diminish the importance of the central band—the flare of the base is muted, and its curves lead the eye upward again The central band is empha-sized, too, by the two simple rings above and below that set it off, by its definite relief, and by the slight concavity of its surface, which subtly opposes the curves of the main shape.

The intricate surface of the fret pattern, complementing the smooth simplicity of the upper surface, gives the bronze its animation, but here too the artist uses restraint. Although the pattern is similar to that of the circuit chips **(Surface 9),** the effect is different. The nuances of cool color and slight variation of the basic motif here, together with the undramatic low relief, have quiet dignity. The purpose of this decoration is not to dominate the form, but to enhance it.

 COLOR

"Abalone Red," 1967, photograph by Sheldon Brody. The Reinhold Visuals Collection.

The lunar mountains, craters, and valleys we see here are not an artist's conception of the moon, but a photographic detail of the natural surface of an abalone shell, magnified to many times its actual size. Because the photographer concentrates on what is in reality a small part of the whole, eliminating the familiar outlines of the shell form, we are able to experience its surface in a purely tactile way. We understand and appreciate this natural surface as though we were actually running our fingers over it, but the sensation is heightened, for we are not distracted by specific subject matter. We become acutely aware of the visual elements that compose the surface: the varied shapes and nuances of color—countless irregularities that nevertheless relate harmoniously and give the impression of order and rhythm even though we can discern no obvious pattern

The intensity of sensation that we feel when presented with the stimulus of surface devoid of subject content acts as a catalyst to the imagination, evoking associations such as that of the lunar landscape; it can also make us feel a variety of emotions. Artists often use the sensory potential of surface to create specific feelings: Wagemaker, for example, in "Metallic Grey" **(Surface 11),** intentionally disturbs us with violent contrasts of texture. The nature of the surface determines the kind of associations and feelings evoked, and by his choice of effect, the artist manipulates our perceptions and response.

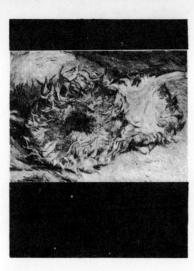

Surface

COLOR

"Sunflowers," 1887, by Vincent van Gogh (Dutch, b. 1853, d. 1890). Oil on canvas. 17 x 24". The Metropolitan Museum of Art, Rogers Fund, 1949.

The surface of "Sunflowers" is charged with intense emotion. Van Gogh felt passionately the beauty of all things created by God, even these tortured shapes of flowers gone to seed, and his conviction is revealed in his use of brush and paint. The stunning impact of this painting is due almost entirely to the direct, forceful treatment of surface, which brings to life not only the subject matter but the entire canvas.

Every part of the turbulent surface literally expresses the artist's burning feeling; every stroke he makes is the result of compelling emotion. The paint writhes, leaps, and twists like flames around the heads of the flowers. Jabs of the brush pull the paint up into spikes, and scoring breaks up and roughens the center of the larger flower; strokes with a fully loaded brush, dragged across the canvas, leave the imprint of the force of application on the other flower. We feel the organic mass of the flowers in the physical texture of the paint: it is piled so thick in places that it casts shadows; elsewhere the surface is scraped raw so the canvas shows through like an exposed nerve. The forms are infused with power, the whole surface charged with energy, as the path of the brush visibly changes direction, speed, color, shape. The rhythm of the surface is accelerated—our minds almost whirl with the intensity of the expression. Van Gogh does not make a botanist's scientific statement: using the full power of his palette and brush, he conveys an impassioned spiritual vision.

Helmet mask *(eharo),* from Melanesia, New Guinea. Bark cloth, paint, cane frame, and raffia. 28¾" high (with ruff, 37¾"). Courtesy The Museum of Primitive Art, New York. Photo by Charles Uht.

The design of this mask from New Guinea is stern and formal; it has a geometric precision that is diametrically opposed to the passion of Van Gogh's "Sunflowers" **(Surface 15).** Yet if the mask does not express the maker's state of mind and inflame the viewer's emotions, its effect is more deep and far-reaching than that of mere surface decoration. It has a cold, impersonal quality, a detacnment and impassivity that startle and awe—even frighten—the viewer.

The mask is shaped like a death's-head. The staring circles and holes that form the eyes and the gaping mouth with its misshapen teeth are contained within abstract shapes that are elongated into hornlike points; the nose, as in a skull, seems hardly to exist, yet rises to a bulbous mass. These disquieting features stand out with heightened strength against the chalky surface of the stretched bark cloth. The jagged ring of dagger-sharp points that surrounds the face emphasizes its air of menace and hostility as does the disheveled ruff—the crude brush of raffia accentuates the austerity and hardness of the mask's surface.

Surface

 "Shack," 1960, **photograph by Sheldon Brody.** The Reinhold Visuals Collection.

Wood is a material that is universally appreciated, and this is in large part due to the endless variety of surface effects it offers. The textural quality of wood grows out of the natural line and rhythm of its grain. This quality can be modified by the artist or craftsman: the surface can be cut with the grain or across it; it can be polished or rough-hewn. It can also, as in this photograph, be modified by weathering and the passage of time.

The crude door selected by the photographer is a study in wood surface. The exclusion of extraneous elements heightens our perception of variations in the grain of the wood and the rhythms created by the simple whorls and verticals of the boards. The gentle modulation of light and shadow helps us to see the detail of the grain, and our reaction is overwhelmingly tactile—we feel the rough, even splintery surface and sense its coarse solidness.

While the entire field of the photograph is wood, the picture has been carefully composed so that it is not monotonous. The slight projection of the door creates heavy shadows in the lower left-hand corner of the composition, giving depth to the picture plane. The diagonals that result from a slight tilt of the camera and the horizontal board at the bottom provide visual relief from the uniformity of the material, and the door latch and hinge make balanced, minor focal points—but texture remains the subject of the photograph.

 COLOR "The Studio (Landscape Painting)," 1963, by Jim Dine (U.S., b. 1935). Oil on canvas; glass, wood, and metal. 60 x 108". Collection Mr. and Mrs. Eugene Schwartz, New York. Photo courtesy The Sidney Janis Gallery, New York.

In a painter's studio we expect to find a whole world of surfaces and shapes: finished and unfinished canvases crowding the walls, paint tubes and brushes, rags and bottles, and a variety of fascinating junk the painter just likes to have around. This world is, in part, the subject of "The Studio (Landscape Painting)." We can recognize it in the objects on the tray attached to the front of the huge canvas—there are bottles and glasses, ashtrays and cups, which the artist seems to have just finished using. They are smeared with paint—the very colors of the painting (or is it six paintings?) itself. The whole work, then, represents in artistic form the working environment of the painter.

Within this symbolic studio, however, is the variegated canvas, and the meaning of its painted panels challenges us. The title of Dine's work is extremely helpful, for it tells us that the subject is also a landscape. But it is clear that the artist's interest is not in a particular scene, for there are no trees, no hills, no sky. Rather, he appears to be concerned with the elements that compose such scenes. What the artist in his studio uses to create a landscape—his artistic as well as his physical equipment—is presented here. We might say that this painting is a sensory inventory of a landscape. The elements are shown out of context, as though we had inquired what they were and the artist had simply pulled them out of his memory at random and lined them up for inspection. There is order in this painting, but it is the order of art, not of a landscape. Each color and surface is familiar, but its identity is universal, not specific. The landscape is an artist's creation—real and of the imagination at the same time.

Surface

Typing head **used in the IBM Selectric typewriter.** Courtesy The IBM Corporation.

This remarkable sculptured object was not designed to be looked at, nor is it sculpture. It is a working part of the IBM Selectric typewriter. It contains the same characters as the keys of an ordinary typewriter, and when the keyboard of the Selectric is struck, the typing head revolves to type the desired symbol. We become aware of it in aesthetic terms here because it is displayed in an objective context, without reference to its function, and we find that it holds its own as an organized, visually satisfying form.

As form, the typing head is the height of rationalism and control. It has a pleasing symmetry. Its wide, scalloped base gives it a feeling of stability even though the head appears suspended in midair, and provides a balanced contrast with the smooth curves of the top. Each raised character is allotted the same amount of surface; all are lined up precisely. The functional nature of the typing head, of course, requires this regularity of form, but a varied surface at the same time relieves it and stimulates the eye. The differences in size and shape of the characters are emphasized by the flat, blank background surface from which they rise, and the lighting gives them depth and softens their edges with shadow. Because they are reversed, the familiar symbols take on an abstract quality, which is heightened by the fact that we see them in increasing profile on the spherical head. They become elements of a harmonious design rather than letters, numbers, punctuation marks.

COLOR

"Lux 19," 1959, by Nicolas Schöffer (Hungarian, b. 1912). Brass and copper, motorized, with luminodynamic projections. 39⅜" x 2½'. Collection Denise René Gallery, Paris. Photo courtesy The Jewish Museum, New York.

This sculpture, which looks like a machine out of a science-fiction story, is an experiment in texture created by the active forces of movement, light, and space. Powered by a built-in motor, the metal construction revolves, reflecting one color, then another, as projected light sweeps across and through its cut-out surfaces. In a sense, Schöffer minimizes these primary planes, punching a variety of circles, squares, and rectangles out of them. As light passes through the apertures, changing patterns of shadow are cast on the sculpture itself and on the surrounding walls. Space, as well as solid surface, is thus a positive element.

The design of the overlaid planes and geometric silhouettes of "Lux 19" has a striking resemblance to that of Tilson's screen print, "Geometry?" **(Surface 2).** Tilson, however, makes use of optical movement to create ambiguous surface with his planes; Schöffer's planes actually occupy space and move in time. His construction is kinetic; the textures change constantly. We cannot take in its surfaces at leisure, as we can those of Chamberlain's "Mustang Sally McBright" **(Surface 1),** nor can we understand and appreciate them from a single point of view, as we can those of the Chinese ritual vessel **(Surface 13).** "Lux 19" must be explored from many points of view, over a period of time, if we are to experience the full measure of its textural richness.

Surface

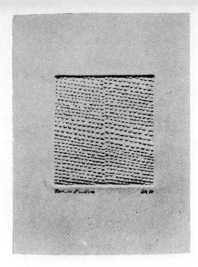

"Untitled" (marked artist's proof), 1961, by Hans Haacke (German, b. 1936). Uninked intaglio print. 12¹¹⁄₁₆ x 19¾" (sheet). Collection The Museum of Modern Art, New York; gift of Mr. and Mrs. Peter A. Rübel. © 1968 The Museum of Modern Art, New York. Photo by Soichi Sunami.

To make this intaglio print, Haacke took a dampened sheet of heavy, grainy paper with a rich texture of its own and, using a printmaker's press, forced it against a plate in which a series of tiny depressions had been made. As the press roller passed over the damp paper, it pushed the paper into the depressions. When the print was pulled from the press, the rectangle of raised texture that dominates the sheet appeared.

Straightforward and undramatic as this work is, it awakens in us the urge to run our fingers over an inviting surface. The organization of the raised dots, forming a single rectangle, is extremely simple—simpler, even than the grid of brightly colored circuit chips **(Surface 9).** But shadows and highlights make every bump here stand out in bold relief, and the effect produced is that of a cobblestone street, although the dots are raised only a fraction of an inch above the background. Subtle variations in the individual dots and rows become noticeable, and there is an active relationship between the central intaglio rectangle and the rest of the sheet of paper. Unlike the traditional printmaker who works with ink, Haacke uses only the natural tone of the paper. The elements of design are simplified to the bare minimum, in order to leave the artist free to explore the potentials of pure texture and surface sensation.

"Decalcomania" ("Décalcomanie sans objet"), 1936, by Oscar Dominguez (Spanish, b. 1905). Ink. 14⅛ x 11½". Collection The Museum of Modern Art, New York. © 1968 The Museum of Modern Art, New York. Photo by Soichi Sunami.

Since surface is one of the artist's primary means of expression, we expect that it will be the result of controlled steps toward some considered end. No one would doubt, for example, that Tilson, in his "Geometry?" **(Surface 2),** or the sculptor of the Chinese bronze **(Surface 13)** had not made every use of his artistic expertise to achieve the desired surface effect. In "Decalcomania" Dominguez creates surface in an entirely different way—he uses an "accidental" technique. The work is a monoprint, made by placing ink between two sheets of paper, pressing them together, and then peeling them apart. This technique produces one-of-a-kind prints of a distinctive character, for with it the artist introduces the element of chance and leaves the final nature of his work beyond his complete control.

To a great extent, of course, the outcome is influenced by the artist's exploration of the process and repeated experiments, so chance is qualified by experience as well as sensitivity. But although the surface of "Decalcomania" is not wholly accidental, it has an almost supernatural quality. Its inked texture seems almost three-dimensional, and its strange shapes evoke many fantastic images, much as clouds do. We may read in "Decalcomania" the grandeur of an oriental landscape, a snow-covered forest, lunar caverns, gigantic waterfalls—whatever scene our fancy dictates.

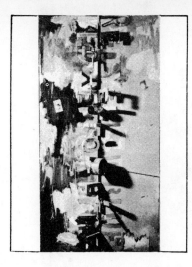

Surface

"Lettuce Coral," **1967, photograph by Sheldon Brody.** The Reinhold Visuals Collection.

The fantastic, orchid-like form of lettuce coral, actually rigid, appears to undulate and flow as though bending with currents in the sea from which it comes. Its natural surface, with all its complexities, is emphasized in this photograph because Brody shows us only a section of the coral. Context, which would indicate its size, and overall outline, by which its mass might be identified, have been eliminated.

The leafy structure of the lettuce coral seems free and unbridled, but close and careful examination would reveal that the parts are basically the same. There is no suggestion of regularity or mechanical repetition here, however, as in the photograph of circuit chips **(Surface 9)** or Haacke's intaglio print **(Surface 21)**, because the units are organized in deep space instead of moving across a plane. The play of light and shadow over them gives the feeling of motion and variety; lines of growth and ragged edges turn the sharp-edged, rigid shapes into ones that seem soft, lacy, and floating.

The convoluted surface of the lettuce coral may remind us of Dominguez' "Decalcomania" **(Surface 22)**, but its effect is significantly different. The underlying order of the shapes inhibits image-forming. We do not envision unworldly landscapes here, but take delight in the intricacies of natural surface.

COLOR

"Field Painting," 1964, by Jasper Johns (U.S., b. 1930). Oil on canvas with objects. 72 x 36¾". Collection of the artist. Photo courtesy The Jewish Museum, New York.

The surfaces of this painting-assemblage are so crazy that the artist has actually marked the corners "upper right," "lower left," etc.—yet even when the work is hung according to instructions, it has no apparent equilibrium. We usually rely on surface as an orientating element in art, but Johns shows us that it is merely a tool of the artist. We cannot depend upon established perceptual clues in this "field"—the horizon line is vertical; real and painted shadows make us uncertain what is flat and what three-dimensional; red exists both as color daubed on the canvas and in the form of the word "red" spelled out. Surfaces made of oil paint and canvas are interspersed with the surfaces of real objects—cans, a knife, a light switch (and the light turned on by the light switch causes yet another overturning of our perceptions as new shadows and surfaces are created).

By thus destroying the clarity of what is "real," what artistic "illusion," Johns demonstrates the relative nature of reality. In a sense his treatment of surface is more radical than that of Tilson in "Geometry?" **(Surface 2)** or Sutej in "Bombardment of the Optic Nerve II" **(Surface 5)** because once we catch on to the optical nature of the ambiguity in their works, we can comprehend the surface intellectually, even though we cannot resolve it. In "Field Painting," however, there *is* no system. Johns does not stick to the "rules"—he constantly disorients us and challenges us to accept the variety of experience offered by life and art.

Portfolio 5, Color

Color in Art

Of all the visual elements of art, color is the one that makes the most immediate impression on us, the one to which we respond most directly. It is also in many ways the most complex. Color is a sensation in the eye caused by light; the difference between colors is a matter of the wavelength and frequency of the light. The *pure* colors of the visible spectrum, seen by passing white light through a prism, range from red, with a long wave and low frequency, to violet, with a short wave and high frequency. With the three *primary* colors of light, we can create other pure colors; when the three are mixed, white light results. Actually, most of the color we see is reflected light. A red flower or pigment on the painter's canvas looks red because when it is illuminated, it reflects only red light, while it absorbs all other colors. When we mix the three primary colors of pigment, all color is absorbed and black results. To describe color, we speak of *hue* (the name of a color), *value* (its lightness or darkness), and *intensity* or saturation (its purity or the amount of gray in it).

The way in which we perceive color once light reaches the eye is not completely understood. But our perception of a color—and our reaction to it—are influenced by many factors. Colors are affected by the colors around them; complementaries interact one way, related colors another. The way in which color is applied (in dots or planes, flat or modulated, thick, textured, or transparent) as well as the kind of color used (oil or acrylic, shiny or mat) create an infinite variety of effects, subtle and dramatic. Colors may appear cool or warm; they may advance or recede or fluctuate; they may be symbolic or literal. Artists through the ages have explored the range of color as an expressive force; today, with the aid of modern technology, they are achieving results that yet again require us to expand our ideas about what color is and how it can be used.

Color

"Red Door," 1968, photograph by Sheldon Brody. The Reinhold Visuals Collection.

Color is all around us in the environment—natural and man-made, harmonious and clashing, bright and drab—and while we are not always aware of it, it makes an enduring impression on us. Our primary identification of objects is likely to be based on color rather than other attributes, because color has the most immediate sensory impact. But for its brilliant hues, the dilapidated entranceway shown in this photograph would no doubt stand unnoticed, an undistinguished element of an urban scene. Not only does color give it a special identity; it makes the peeling, battered facade demand our attention.

Color is used here in a decorative way. Although there has been no attempt to organize the space pictorially—to create a painting, as was done with the mural on the Job Lot Trading Company building **(Perception 1)**—the result is visually compelling, and the photographer's composition of his picture transforms the entranceway into an intriguing color field. The color has been applied in solid, interlocking blocks. These blocks of color divide the space in a way that is quite independent of the building structure; they exist as visual entities. The butting of vivid red again blue, red and blue against deep black, creates optical vibrancy, and the features of the building—door, transom, architectural ornament—become subordinate to the dominating interplay of the color-shapes.

"View from the Studio," 1967, by Morton Kaish (U.S.). Acrylic on canvas. 45 x 50". Courtesy Morgan Flagg. Photo courtesy The Staempfli Gallery, New York.

In "View from the Studio," the painter explores mass and space through the interpretive medium of color. For Kaish, the color of a thing is not an absolute property—it is determined by the light reflected to the eye. There is no black in his palette, therefore, because black is the absence of light. The dominant colors here are cool blues and warm, sunlit pinks; shadows are never gray but an intensification of the color seen in shadow. While Kaish and Monet both consider color as reflected light, their paintings are quite different. In the impressionist "The Poplars" **(Color 3)**, form dissolves into a composite of momentary sensations of color. Kaish, in contrast, applies his paint in planes of color, and it is by the arrangement of these planes that he builds up mass. The contrast of hues, the juxtaposition of intense colors and pale tints, the merging or butting of adjacent planes—these interrelationships create volume and solidity of form.

The traditional method of depicting space on a two-dimensional surface is perspective projection such as that used by Bosch in "Adoration of the Kings" **(Color 6)**. In this illusionistic space, forms recede in relation to a single point of view. Here, space is organized by several viewpoints. The planes of color are not fixed but appear now nearer, now farther away, simultaneously flat and deep. We look down at the still life under our eyes, out at the compressed view framed by the window, and far away through space filled with light and air. This shifting is like our actual experience—as objects in every part of space claim our attention, we constantly refocus our eyes.

"The Poplars," 1891, by Claude Monet (French, b. 1840, d. 1926). Oil on canvas. 32¼ x 32⅛". The Metropolitan Museum of Art. Bequest of Mrs. H. O. Havemeyer, 1929. The H. O. Havemeyer Collection.

Impressionist was originally a derisive term, meant to imply that the painters so named—of whom Monet is the most famous—had not bothered to give more than an impression of their subjects. The scornful critics, however, missed the point entirely. What Monet wanted was not to paint the landscape with illusionary verisimilitude, but to capture the quality of a visual experience at a particular moment, to depict images as we perceive them, in terms of light reflected from them to the eye. Color, which is reflected light, therefore was not a minor attribute of form; it was primary sensation. Thus, instead of modeling forms with light and shade, Monet painted them as colored light. The difference is seen if we compare the tree trunk in the foreground of Bosch's "Adoration of the Kings" **(Color 6)**, defined by shading from light to dark, with Monet's poplars. The light that bathes these trees dematerializes them; they are composed of equal values of blue, pink, green.

Monet realized that a brown tree trunk (for example) is not a solid color brown to the eye: it may contain colors reflected from the sky or foliage, or appear more or less intense depending on colors placed nearby; it may even be transformed, as in the distant trees, by light in the atmosphere, becoming the merest flicker of color. Instead of mixing his colors on the palette or blending them on the canvas, Monet applied them in dabs, to be mixed in the viewer's eye, as in reality they are. In this way, he translated visual experience into sense impression, conveying truly the scintillating effect of color as light.

"Door to the River," 1960, by Willem de Kooning (U.S., b. 1904). Oil on canvas. 80 x 70". Collection The Whitney Museum of American Art, New York.

If we were to enlarge a few square inches of Monet's "The Poplars" **(Color 3)** to the size of a small painting, the resulting work would have no subject in the traditional sense. We would seen only dashes and spots of color, the peaks and valleys of the paint, and the marks of the brush used to apply it. But these are the elements that add up to the expressive whole of "The Poplars," and so they are expressive in and of themselves. Wholly abstract, de Kooning's "Door to the River" illustrates this forcefully, that color and shape alone, independent of the visual reality of trees, figures, or other objects, have the ability to express feeling and evoke response.

We are free, in "Door to the River," to associate colors and shapes with specific images—the greenish-browns and warm yellows with nature and landscape, the strongly stated verticals and horizontals with the structure suggested by the title. But the impact of the painting is not in such imagery: it is in the emotion transmitted to us from the painter through his slashing attack on the canvas. What we see is feeling directly expressed in gesture. The brush, loaded with color, has been dragged across the surface with such vigor that splashes of paint are left in its wake. We can see clearly the path of each brushstroke, and in it the physical action and emotional heat that propelled the brush. The composition is spontaneous and unpremeditated, but it is neither formless nor unrestrained. The painter's hand and arm, in their sure control, move with the quick, decisive, and accurate reflex of the athlete, checking the momentum of the brush, changing its direction, scraping, mixing, and spreading the color with the understanding of the master painter.

Color

"Flowers," 1964, by Andy Warhol (U.S., date of birth not known). Acrylic and silk-screen enamel on canvas. 48 x 48". Courtesy The Leo Castelli Gallery, New York.

Although the starting point for this work was a photographic image from nature (which was transferred to the canvas by the silk-screen process) and we can easily identify flowers and grass as Warhol's subject matter, the forms have lost their natural color as well as their three-dimensional character. The artist leaves no doubt in our minds about the mechanical nature of his process—the color of the grass impinges on the blue of the flower petals, the blue on the green, as though out of register in printing. There is a feeling of detachment in this forthright acknowledgment of the picture surface, and it is emphasized by the treatment of the flowers, which are disembodied and lacking in detail like overexposed photographic images. The color is slightly streaked, reminding us that it is only paint, and in some areas the grain of the canvas shows through.

Warhol is not concerned with communicating a specific sensuous experience of color, as Monet was in "The Poplars" (Color 3). Yet the unusual quality of color in "Flowers" serves to intensify experience in another way. The flowers and grass here are transformed into the essence of flowers and grass on a beautiful day. The grass is more green than ever grass was—the color is almost artificially intense, as though we were seeing it through a green filter that deepens its color but obscures detail with shadow. The flowers, on the other hand, become windows: in them, or through them, we see the cool, transparent depth of a cloudless sky.

"Adoration of the Kings," center panel of an altarpiece, ca. 1495, by Hieronymus Bosch (Flemish, ca. 1450-1516). Oil on wood. 54⅜" x 28⅜". Courtesy The Prado, Madrid. Photo by David Manso Martín.

This painting does not depend on color for its effect—if we were to reproduce it in black and white, the main elements of the composition would still be clear. For Bosch, the representation of form in space is of primary importance, and it is light (and shadow) that reveals form. The effect of Monet's "The Poplars" (Color 3), in contrast, would be lost in black and white because for the impressionist, light means color. In "Adoration of the Kings" color is an attribute of objects—it describes them and enhances the illusion of their reality, but it does not define them. This is not to say, however, that color is unimportant in Bosch's painting.

The strongest colors in this painting are in the foreground, and they serve both to draw attention to the main subject of the work and to direct the eye through the scene. The most intense color, the blue of the Virgin's robe, makes a frame for the Child. Balance is provided by the white garb of the African King and the red cloak of the center figure, while the alternation of these three colors in minor accents creates visual rhythm within the tableau. While this sacred scene is depicted in emphatic colors, the ordinary world—the stable, the peasant folk, and the panorama of life beyond—is rendered in muted tones of brown, yellow, and green that dissolve into haze at the horizon. This fading of color in the distance (aerial perspective) establishes depth and, at the same time, underlines the meaning of Bosch's religious theme. In the contrast of color in foreground and background, the artist expresses the antithesis of the eternal reality and that which is human and transitory.

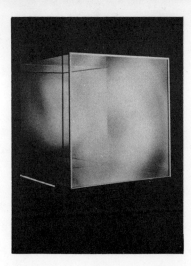

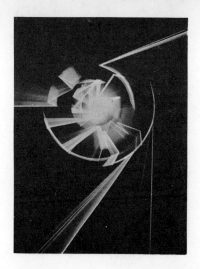

"Memories of Mike," 1967, by Larry Bell (U.S., b. 1939). Vacuum-plated glass and metal. 24 x 24 x 24″. Courtesy Mr. and Mrs. Arnold Glimcher. Photo by Ferdinand Boesch.

This extraordinary cube, which appears to be filled with rainbow-hued light, is composed of clear glass panels coated with vaporized crystals that reflect and refract light. It is an exploration of light as the source of color, and in this sense related to impressionist works such as Monet's "The Poplars" **(Color 3)**. But in contrast to Monet's use of color to reveal form, Bell is concerned with pure visual sensation. His object is to deal with light as directly as possible, without the distraction of form or the limitation of opaque paint. Bell's medium is light itself, and the form he employs is minimal—a basic geometric shape entirely devoid of subject-content.

The colored light produced by this iridescent box is more abstract, even, than that of Chryssa's "Fragment for the Gates to Times Square" **(Color 12)**, for the neon sculpture ultimately depends on form; we can trace its contours with our fingers as well as our eyes. Here the patterns of light defy any attempt to define their location or boundaries. At one moment light seems trapped, like a gas, within the confines of the cube, yet at another the light dissolves the glass walls; the colors shift and change with our every motion, threatening to disappear like the mirage-rainbows we see on wet or oil-slicked surfaces. In "Memories of Mike" we experience color as light-energy that is space-filling yet intangible, evanescent sensation that is no sooner felt than transmuted into new feeling—endless vistas to be remembered but not recaptured.

Photograph for an advertisement for Container Corporation of America, 1959, by Herbert Matter (U.S., b. 1907). Courtesy of the artist.

Light is a medium that is intangible and ephemeral. We cannot, for example, catch the reflected and refracted rays of which Bell's "Memories of Mike" **(Color 7)** is made and feel them with our fingers, nor can we preserve the changing patterns of color that they produce. But in this photograph created by Herbert Matter, we can in a sense see the physical impact of light rays striking against a surface, and the patterns produced by their impression are permanently recorded on color-sensitive film.

To make this photograph, the artist cut a number of narrow slits in a sheet of opaque black paper and rotated it between the lens of his camera and a light box set up to provide a source of changing colored light. Then, using multiple exposures and varying shutter speeds, he recorded this swirling color image. Of course, the kinetic iridescence of Bell's work, in which actual change takes place as we move, is different from this picture, which compresses a succession of sensations into a single visual experience. Moreover, if we were to stand in the camera's place and watch the colored light as it came through the apertures in the paper, we would not see what we see here. Matter's photograph is more than the sum total of sense-images recorded. We can discern in its pattern the kinetic nature of the artistic process as we can feel in paintings the force behind the brushstroke. But as the result of the brushstrokes is a unified whole, so this is a complete, coherent work produced by the controlled manipulation of color and light.

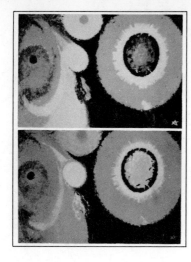

Color

"Three Muses," 1967, by Herb Aach (U.S., b. 1923). Acrylic polymer on canvas. 44 x 62". Courtesy of the artist.

We are hardly aware, in practical terms, of how light influences color. Every day changes in color take place before our eyes, but they are so gradual that we do not notice. A flower that is brilliant crimson in the morning, when the long, warm wavelengths of light predominate, appears increasingly darker as the day wears on and the short, cool wavelengths become dominant. In the nineteenth century scientific studies involving the effects of light modulation on color prompted painters to experiment and evolve a new mode of expression, exemplified by Monet's "The Poplars" **(Color 3).** In the same way, the technology of this century affords artists such as Herb Aach scope to explore still newer possibilities for expression.

Shown here are two views of the same painting. In the picture at top, the work is illuminated by ordinary gallery light, and we can recognize in the swirling, floating forms color derived from the traditional palette of the painter. In the second view, the work is seen under "black" light—ultraviolet rays that are a part of the spectrum but are not directly visible by the human eye. Although we cannot see ultraviolet as a color, we can see its effect: pigments that absorb it appear dark (as the room lit by black light does), while pigments that reflect its short wavelengths (the red end of the visible spectrum) are enhanced and transformed. A fiery, glowing intensity is attained, and we experience a new range of color. "Three Muses" is a forceful reminder that science continually provides art with avenues for exploration, and that traditional definitions must ever be expanded to accommodate the discoveries of the artist.

Staircase at The Electric Circus, 1967, painted by Louis and Janis Delsarte. Courtesy of The Electric Circus, New York.

The entrance to the Electric Circus, famous for its multi-media productions, appears to be illuminated by an intricate network of colored lights. Actually, it is decorated with a two-dimensional design in paint that glows in the dim fluorescence provided by fixtures suspended from the ceiling. Although for functional reasons the steps are defined by bright horizontal patterning and the handrails are discernible, the solidity of the architecture has been dissolved. Every surface is covered with fantastic images animated by energy-filled lines and densely packed dots so that the space of the entrance seems tenuously confined by an eerie, luminous veil beyond which stretches dark, undefinably deep space. The ceiling, like the walls, is obliterated, and the lights and spheres suspended from it merge with the painted design.

To fully appreciate the impact of this psychedelic setting, we must imagine ourselves ascending the bizarre staircase. We are transformed by the glow that tinges clothing and flesh with unearthly color, as well as enveloped by sensation. Our ears are barraged by the insistent volume of electronic music and weird sounds of a high-frequency oscillator, while our eyes are filled with phosphorescent visions of figures, flowers, mystical symbols, and a message of love. We are involved in a total environment—an "electric circus" of sight and sound.

"Luminous," 1965, by Richard Anuszkiewicz (U.S., b. 1930). Liquitex on board. 24 x 24". Courtesy The Sidney Janis Gallery, New York.

Color is the most relational of the visual elements. A strong color may appear weak, a dark color light, a bright color dull, or vice versa, depending on a variety of factors. Not only does the character of a color change according to the light under which it is seen, as in Aach's "Three Muses" **(Color 9)**, but it is affected by the colors around it. Thus, the squares of similar hue and gently gradated value in Albers' "White Line Squares" **(Color 16)** interact subtly, while the contrasting hues and sudden changes in intensity here have a dramatic effect on one another. It is through his use of color, primarily, that Anuszkiewicz "turns on" his painting.

If we stare at a red square for a few moments, then look away, a bright blue-green square—the afterimage—will shine before our eyes. In juxtaposing these complementary colors, therefore, Anuszkiewicz precipitates the phenomenon of "successive contrast": each is intensified by the afterimage of the other. Although only one red is used in this painting, its character changes as it interacts with the colors near it. In the central diamond of the composition, the warm yellow-green lines make the red seem warmer—almost orange—while in the surrounding diamonds, the cool blue produces the opposite effect. The tendency of the central diamond to advance is countered, however, by the multiple focal areas formed by converging lines—these dazzling points recede, pushing forward an illusory pattern of faceted shapes. No single sensation can dominate, and the result is a continuous optical disturbance—a perceptual assault that is almost painful in its intensity.

"Fragment for the Gates to Times Square II," 1966, by Chryssa (U.S., b. 1933). Neon and plexiglass. 43 x 34 1/16 x 27 1/16". Collection The Whitney Museum of American Art, New York. Gift of the Howard and Jean Lipman Foundation.

For Chryssa color and light are one and the same element, and colored light is the material as well as the subject of her sculpture. The blazing neon sign, with its message in insistent words and images, is a commonplace sight in our modern world and a symbol of commercialism and tawdry brilliance to many people. In conceiving this work as part of a monumental entrance to New York City's Times Square, Chryssa makes clear its origins in the dazzling extravaganza of neon that illuminates the heart of the city, but she finds in its flamboyance a source of color unmatched by any other medium.

Here neon light has been stripped of its advertising content; what remains in the precisely drawn, abstract curves of "Fragment" is pure, glowing electric color that possesses a unique and concentrated beauty. While transparent tubing physically contains the incandescent gas, and its curves provide the linear framework of the sculpture, the light that fills them spills out into the surrounding space and is reflected in the plexiglass cube that encloses the work. Subtle variations of color are created by the involutions of each tube and by the interweaving of yellow and green on one side, orange, deep pink, and blue on the other. The entire network, emanating a soft glow, seems to pulsate with color—color that gives visible form to the kinetic energy of an electric current.

Color

"Shin," 1968, by Anne Brody (U.S., b. 1932). Hooked wool. 7 x 7'. Tapestry commissioned by Gueron, Lepp and Associates, Architects, for the Manhattan Rehabilitation Center, New York State Narcotic Addiction Control Committee. Courtesy of the artist. Photo by Malcolm Varon.

This warm, richly textured hanging was designed for an inter-denominational chapel; the calligraphic image woven into it is the Hebrew letter *shin*, which symbolizes the Almighty. Although artists such as Anuszkiewicz, in "Luminous" **(Color 11)**, and Albers, in "White Line Squares" **(Color 16)**, carefully exclude specific subject matter from their work in order to concentrate on pure perceptual response to color, the designer of "Shin" closely approaches their intent, for the sensory experience offered by this work is of paramount importance. It is here rather than in the symbol that the religious nature of the piece resides.

"Shin" is optical art of a special kind, best illustrated by comparison with its opposite. Anuszkiewicz' "Luminous" is based on extreme contrasts that assault the senses; here there is almost no contrast at all. Instead of precision and flat, complementary colors, the soft wool creates nuances of texture and subtle transitions between colors that differ almost imperceptibly. The essence of the work is subtlety. The image barely elicits perceptual response: a quick glance yields no more than brilliant color. To experience the delicate tension of the minutely modulated colors, quiet and contemplation are required. In the depth of feeling that rewards the search, aesthetic and religious experience merge into one identity.

"Saint Ursula and Her Maidens," early 15th century, by an unknown Venetian painter. Tempera on wood. 37 x 31". The Metropolitan Museum of Art, Rogers Fund, 1923.

Although painted in the same century as Bosch's "Adoration of the Kings" **(Color 6)**, this sumptuous panel is the result of a totally different artistic outlook. While Bosch employed color to create a feeling of deep space and rounded form, the Venetian painter's object was to achieve the richest possible decorative effect. He was as unconcerned with representing space and mass realistically as with reproducing the "real" colors of things: there has never been a sky that possessed the rich red hue of the background here. Pure, brilliant color—red and deep blue, luminous pinks and greens, sparkling gold—was what the Venetian delighted in.

The painting is completely two-dimensional. The overlapping of the figures and a few formal drapery folds, schematic indications of depth, are overruled by the artist's use of color. Except for the modeling of the faces, the surface is composed of flat, precisely defined color-shapes that form an abstract pattern. The whole is welded together by the tight interlocking of these color-shapes, the symmetry of their arrangement, and the small repeated patterns that cover almost all the surface with a veil of delicate tracery. The painting is perfectly balanced but not static, because the opposing elements are subtly varied. For example, the related colors of pink and gray on the left interact differently and are different from the complementary green and pink on the right; it is in value that they balance. Although the focal point of the work is the saint's haloed head, the artist's real interest is not his religious theme, but the abstract design animated by the interaction of color-shapes.

"Ice," 1966, by Richard Lindner (U.S., b. 1901). Oil on canvas. 70 x 60". Collection The Whitney Museum of American Art, New York.

"Ice" is a frightening painting, and it is meant to be—its theme is the dehumanization of human beings in the modern world. The title, blocked out in bold letters across the canvas, is the artist's description of life in a totally mechanized world: it is cold and hard. This theme is stated in the complex imagery of the painting and dramatically and emotionally expressed in its color. The Indian head in a sharp-pointed star is the insignia of the motorcyclist, who represents man's fascination with mechanical speed, danger, and excitement. The goggles covering the figure's eyes, and the grotesque baring of her teeth and tongue, transform the face into a glaring, menacing mask. This woman is a mechanical object—a robot. Her hair, gauntlets and leggings, and even her flesh have a metallic glint, as does the ice cream, which here becomes a symbol of the pervasive coldness of life.

The grim figure is fixed within the central diamond shape of the painting as though frozen in a block of ice. In Lindner's controlled, symmetrical arrangement of flat color-shapes, his work is strikingly similar to the fifteenth-century "Saint Ursula and Her Maidens" **(Color 14)**, and a comparison of the two is telling. Here every area of color is bounded by knife-sharp edges. The austerity of the flat surface is unrelieved by decoration, by warmth or softness of tone. The colors have a synthetic, unwholesome quality. The blue is cold, not rich; the red is grayed and dull, not pure and clear. Instead of luminous color enlivened by the sparkle of gold, there is a deadened quality and a metallic sheen. The stark contrast of black and white is central here; cold and hard, it summarizes the painting's theme.

"White Line Squares," No. 7 (top) and No. 3, by Josef Albers (U.S., b. 1888). Two of a series of lithographs. 30¾ x 20¾". Printed by Gemini G. E. L., Los Angeles.

Each of these studies is composed of a series of precise squares, one within another; the squares are varied only in value, or relative lightness and darkness. The innermost square is darkest, the outermost square is lightest, and the middle square is intermediate in value. A "white line square" subdivides one square in each work. If we look quite carefully, we discover that this white line has a remarkable effect. In the top print, where the line cuts through the intermediate area, the color inside it (adjacent to the dark square) appears lighter; the color outside it (adjacent to the light square) appears darker. In the second print, where the line subdivides the center square, the color inside it seems more intense than the color outside it. In addition to these shifts in value, other changes occur. The color squares fluctuate, now moving backward, now forward, now expanding, now contracting.

Seemingly simple, Albers' squares are exceedingly complex. The moment two colors (or values of a color) are juxtaposed, they affect each other; a third creates still another relationship, and each new element sets in motion further actions and reactions. This interaction of color is the subject of Albers' studies. He purposely avoids the dramatic effects achieved by Anuszkiewicz in "Luminous" **(Color 11)**, concentrating instead on the most delicate and subtle relationships in order to show us how relative, how unpredictable, and how sensitive an element color is.

Color

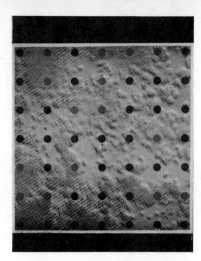

Lumagram from hand-painted projection slide for "Black Zero," multimedia theater production, 1965, by Aldo Tambellini (U.S., b. 1930). Courtesy of the artist.

Black and white are paradoxical quantities. We think of them as the opposite of each other, yet we also consider both the opposite of color—when we say an image is "in black and white" we mean that it has no color. Nevertheless, black and white *are* colors. Just as the chromatic colors—red, yellow, and the other hues in the spectrum—are visual sensations, so are black, white, and the range of grays in between. We call them achromatic or neutral colors, but in practical terms they are far from neutral. They can affect us as strongly as any hue, and sometimes even more strongly. With black and white we can achieve not only the most subtle gradations in the scale from light to dark, but also maximum contrast.

The kind of color an artist chooses to work with is therefore only a matter of the particular effect he wishes to achieve; like the shapes and structure he employs, color is a part of his mode of expression. Aldo Tambellini's lumagram—a hand-painted slide modified by the manipulation of light on a photographic emulsion—was created for use in a multimedia theater production in which the environment was transformed by projected images together with other visual and auditory stimuli. Black, in this context, is a positive element: it is not the absence of light but the counterforce to light. The energy contained in this image, which whirls in space like a miniature universe, is created by the interaction of two equally powerful visual sensations.

"Derrynan II," 1967, by Harold Cohen (British, b. 1928). One of a series of screen prints. 27 x 27". Courtesy The Marlborough Graphics Gallery, New York.

One of the most important properties of color is its ability to produce texture—that quality of a surface which relates to our sense of touch. By manipulating color, the artist can create the appearance of hardness or softness, smoothness or roughness, or any other texture, regardless of the actual surface. He may, like Bosch in "Adoration of the Kings" **(Color 6)**, simulate the textures of cloth, straw, wood, and other materials. Or, like de Kooning in "Door to the River" **(Color 4)**, he may emphasize the texture of the medium as part of his design. In "Derrynan II," the approach is still different. Cohen explores the textural potential of color for its own sake. The color is broken down into a system of dots that cannot be resolved into any recognizable object or material; they are pure visual stimuli.

The intial effect of "Derrynan II' is strongly tactile. The irregular pattern of small red and lavender dots produces the sensation of a rough surface such as that of cut velvet or flocked paper. But the flat green disks with their precise edges and regular placement insinuate their presence disconcertingly. At one moment they appear to float above the surface, at another to recede behind it (as though in a plane seen through holes in the surface). We begin to feel the flicker of afterimages, which are especially strong in the areas of complementary red. The surface of this screen print is ambiguous and kinetic. Color here is a physical experience, but one that is complex, relative, and variable.

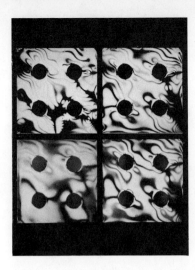

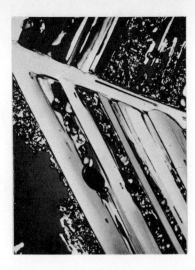

"Tension Picture No. 3," 1962-64, by Karl Gerstner (Swiss, b. 1930). Plastic lighted by polarized light. 28 x 28". Courtesy The Staempfli Gallery, New York.

The concept of the work of art as a "finished" object with immutable form and fixed meaning cannot be applied to the work of artists such as Karl Gerstner. He shares with many other contemporary artists a new appreciation of process as a vehicle for expression, and his "Tension Picture No. 3" depends on process. The squares of color shown here are four views of the same work at different moments. The construction consists of a block of plastic subjected to tension by clamps. The pressure creates an invisible field of force, which becomes visible when polarized light is channelled through it. The plastic is set in a box containing the lighting apparatus, which produces a changing flow of light.

Inactive when the light is turned off, the plastic is filled with kinetic energy when it is illuminated. Myriad patterns ripple around the four circular apertures in the material, providing an ever-changing drama. The fluid colors are independent of any object; they exist simply as visual sensation, as do the shifting values in Alber's "White Line Squares **(Color 16)** and the opalescent colors in Bell's "Memories of Mike" **(Color 7)**. In Albers' work the process involved is perceptual; in Bell's it is optical and activated by the movement of the viewer; but the change that takes place is nonetheless as real as the actual movement that we see here.

Radial section of European larch tree *(Larix europia)*, 1966, polarized light photomicrograph by Mortimer Abramowitz. Nikon EFM Microflex photomicrographic camera mounted on a Nikon S-Ke polarizing microscope. Kodachrome IIA film. Courtesy of the photographer.

The technique of the photomicrograph makes it possible for us to examine a natural structure that is not ordinarily visible by illuminating it with polarized light under a microscope. The stunning, jewel-like color we see here is not the color of the larch tree, but is produced by the reflection of the light from the tree section. The color in Gerstner's "Tension Picture No. 3" **(Color 19)** is also produced by polarized light. But in Gerstner's work, the patterns are planned by the artist—they are the result of induced tensions and programmed lighting. The colors in the photomicrograph, on the other hand, are determined by the structure of the tree—the scientist did not compose them.

We tend to think of art and science as representing opposite poles of man's endeavor, but they do not, and the interchange between them has always been fruitful. We might never have seen Monet's "The Poplars" **(Color 3)** if physicists had not studied the nature of light, nor been dazzled by Anuszkiewicz' "Luminous" **(Color 11)** if physiologists and psychologists had not been interested in the phenomena of perception. Science has not only provided artists with new materials and techniques for image-making; it has shown them new images of nature, as here in this radiant larch tree.

Color

"Laila Visiting Her Lover, Majnun, in the Desert," ca. 1720, Indian, Kulu School (Punjab Hills). Courtesy The Victoria and Albert Museum, London.

The design of this Indian painting is superbly simple and direct; its richness and life lie in the artist's use of color and pattern. Like the Venetian painter of "Saint Ursula and Her Maidens" **(Color 14)**, the Indian artist concentrates on the elaboration of the surface and is frankly unconcerned with depicting space realistically. In the Venetian work, however, pattern covers the entire surface. The painter's purpose was to honor the saint by the richness of the decoration, and the figures are generalized and symbolic. Here the figures are individuals, characters in a story, and areas of pattern are played against unembellished areas for narrative as well as aesthetic reasons.

The painting is divided into fields of color. Three horizontal bands compose a flat, stable framework. The intricately patterned carpet defines the specific location of the action; the broad expanse of yellow, made into a landscape by a single delicate flowering tree, describes the desert setting; and the narrow band of greenish-gray sky, echoing the color below, keeps the viewer's eye within the painting. The wide curtain of yellow fills the picture with the warmth of the desert sun and provides an undistracting backdrop for the princess and her lover. The curving contours of her rich black robe, set against the deep red, rounded cushion, describe the softness of her body. Opposite her is the ascetic, seated in a position of contemplation on the hard ground. His body, angular and unadorned, is rendered in natural white and browns. Thus, color and pattern tell the story: the reconciliation of the worldly—elegance, wealth, and luxury— with the spiritual—austerity, poverty, and simplicity.

"Japanese Girl," 1958, photograph by Sheldon Brody. The Reinhold Visuals Collection.

The young Japanese girl in this photograph is dressed for a part in a traditional dance. She wears a colorful decorated kimono, a wig and an elaborate headdress, and her face is made up as delicately as that of a doll. In Japan, as in many parts of the world, costume and cosmetics in life as well as the theater are determined by time-honored traditions, and color serves a special purpose. One of the most interesting aspects of color is its symbolic meaning. Not only do we react to color emotionally because it is bright or because it is muted (for example); we may also react to it because it "means" something to us. This meaning is often related to the use of color in dress.

Color has always played an important role in costume. The color of one's garments as well as the dye or paint applied directly to the body has historically been full of significance, magical, religious, and social. While most of us consider the color of our clothing and makeup merely a question of taste in personal adornment, many traditions continue to be operative today. Not only do members of tribal societies still decorate their bodies for identification or other purposes but, in our own society, religious and military figures are distinguished by the color of their vestments or uniforms. Other symbolic meanings of colors persist tenaciously: we associate purple with royalty, black with death, and white with marriage. In the Orient, however, yellow is the color of royalty, white of mourning, and red of marriage. Thus, the meaning of a color is not based on any innate quality of the color, but is connected with particular cultural practices, and colors may retain their meaning long after the customs on which they were based are obsolete.

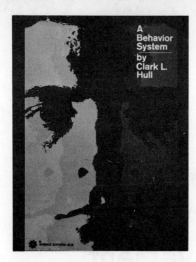

Book jacket, designed by Arnold Saks, for *A Behavior System,* by Clark L. Hull (John Wiley and Sons, Inc., Publishers). Courtesy Arnold Saks, Inc., New York.

A book jacket, like a poster or package, is an advertisement. It must tell us the title of the book and the name of the author—but the arrangement of these words is only a part of the designer's job. If we do not see the book on the shelf or in the window of the bookstore, we will not have an opportunity to read the words. Obviously, then, the cover must be eye-catching. The initial impact of Arnold Saks' design results from his choice of colors. The intensity of the individual colors is enhanced by the opposition of complementaries (red and green) as well as of "warm" and "cool" colors (pink and blue). These strong relationships make the cover visible from a distance; a subtle interaction—that of adjacent related hues—comes into play at closer range.

Once we have seen the book and come close enough to read the title, another problem arises: interpreting the words. "A Behavior System" may have quite different meanings for a biologist, a sociologist, a school teacher, or even a computer programmer! It is up to the designer to project what kind of behavior and what kind of system this particular book is about. Since it is a serious and scholarly work dealing with complex problems of human psychology, Saks has created a sophisticated image that is packed with specific meanings. At one and the same time the powerful colors form a human face, a Rorschach inkblot, and a diagram of a section of the nervous system. Each of these configurations represents an aspect of the subject matter. While the author can describe their relationship only by using thousands of words, the designer expresses it by fusing them into one clear and compelling graphic unit.

Circus poster, by Hubert Hilscher (Polish). Courtesy The Centaur Gallery, London.

The purpose of a poster is twofold: to attract attention and to communicate as much as possible about what it is advertising without requiring the viewer to spend too much time interpreting the "message." The designer of this gay poster for a circus has achieved both ends with impressive economy of graphic means. His statement is direct and simple, and it embodies the spirit of the entertainment. The dominant color, bright fire-engine red, appeals forcefully to the eye, while the bold black outlining of the lion proclaims the character of a star performer.

No attempt has been made to picture the lion realistically; on the contrary, he is drawn like an animal in a coloring book. His glaring eyes and ferocious teeth are rendered unintimidating by the fanciful blue and green curls of his mane as well as by the two-dimensionality of his body, which is depicted in a flat, frontal view (we cannot even see his hind legs!) and clearly painted in. This rather charming king of the beasts balances precariously on a unicycle, evoking images of performing animals, acrobats, and other circus attractions. The visual tension set up by balancing the bulk of the design on the fulcrum of the small word "Cyrk" (circus) draws attention to the single verbal element in the poster, and heightens the excitement provided by the strong color of the background. Unsophisticated in its directness, the poster is calculated to catch the interest of children, but the subtle wittiness of its execution implies that *this* circus will be entertaining for adults too.

Portfolio 6, Movement

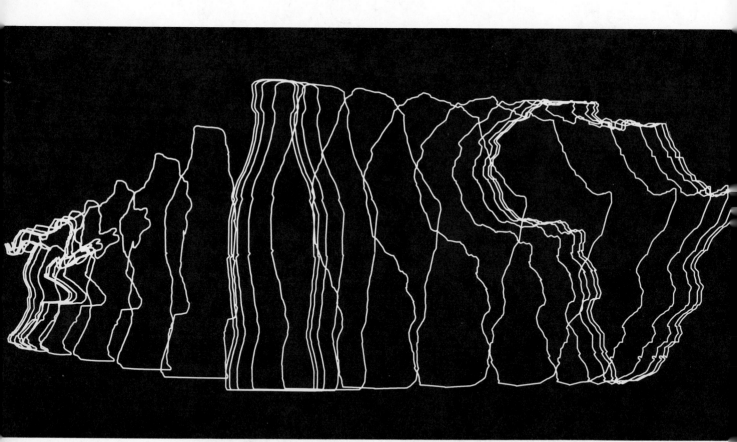

Movement in Art

Art, like nature, is never static. Just as movement is the sign of life and energy in nature, so it is the element that confers vitality in a work of art. Movement in art may be kinetic—actual physical motion through space—or it may be apparent—motion perceived by the eye and mind of the viewer. It may also be suggested—that is, an image may evoke a sense of motion. In addition, the viewer himself moves in a way that affects the work of art. Our eyes cannot remain fixed on any given area for very long; thus, the route they follow in moving over the surface of a canvas, a sculpture, or a building plays an important part in determining our response to it.

To a greater or lesser degree, depending on his objective, the artist must control all these forms of movement. Some artists, for example, deploy the elements of their composition to entice us to fix our gaze on one particular image, and thereby activate a multitude of unusual effects such as optical pulsation and afterimages. Other artists make it almost impossible for us to concentrate on any single image, and bring different reactions into play; while still others organize their work in such a way that our attention is directed from one point to another in a certain order.

The rhythm of a work of art is of primary importance to the expression of idea and feeling the artist wishes to create. His forms may be packed with energy or languid, floating or whirling, calm or excited. Whether real or apparent, explicit or implicit, movement is what gives a work of art its life and its power.

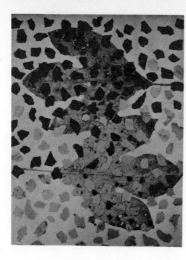

Movement

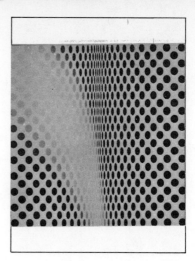

 Color

"Falling Leaves," 1955, by Anne Brody (U.S., b. 1932). Collage of paper and leaves. 11 5/16 x 8 11/16". Courtesy of the artist.

In this age when much art is abstract, mechanical, and hard-edged, the endlessly varied elements of nature provide a rich source of softness, of pleasing forms on the human scale. Nature is in constant motion. All living things change, or grow, and inanimate things too are moved by natural forces. The earth revolves, water flows, snow drifts, and leaves fall—nothing in the world, no matter how small or large, is really static.

This collage is a little piece of an autumn landscape, an artist's tranquil vision of nature and a particular aspect of motion in nature. Two real leaves in warm autumn colors are the main compositional elements. They have been arranged with neat symmetry in a relatively stable horizontal position, and they are placed compactly in terms of each other and the frame, like butterfly specimens in a case. This careful structure not only accentuates the resemblance of the leaves to the streamlined contours of birds, or even airplanes, in flight—it also serves as counterpoint. What imparts the quality of motion to the collage is the artist's use of paper against the natural forms. She has torn it into small fragments, irregular but related in shape, and superimposed them on leaves and background, creating three levels of depth on a basically flat surface. Scattered rhythmically over the composition, the bits of paper dance like leaves outside the window on a gusty fall day. Dark in color at the top, dark and light mingled in the center, and light at the bottom, they seem to float gently downward without ever coming to rest.

 "Loss," 1964, by Bridget Riley (British, b. 1931). Emulsion on board. 46¼ x 46¼". The Harry N. Abrams Family Collection, New York. Photo by Geoffrey Clements, courtesy The Richard Feigen Gallery, New York.

It is very difficult—perhaps impossible—to create a work of art that is completely static. Movement is so integral to life, so much a part of our surroundings, that we tend to interpret the slightest clue as signifying motion. Bridget Riley, like many other Op artists, is concerned with such perceptual, or apparent, movement. As illustrated by this painting, the illusion can be extremely convincing and powerful. Although "Loss" is painted on a flat surface, we immediately succumb to the illusion of movement in space. The relationship of each element to the next and of each to the whole is one of change, and we perceptually equate change with movement.

First, there is a gradual shift of shape from the full circles at far left and right to the narrow ellipses in the center of the painting. Simultaneously, the intervals between the shapes decrease. The circles appear to be turning slowly on edge, like rotating disks. In addition, a gradual shift of value takes place. Along a curving swath that stretches from the upper left part of the work to the middle of the bottom edge, the black circles become gray, and the gray circles become progressively lighter gray ellipses. This gradation suggests recession into space; it warps the surface of the painting. As we continue to look, afterimages appear and set the black shapes into vibration, and the two sides of the work seem to move independently, like drums revolving into the center.

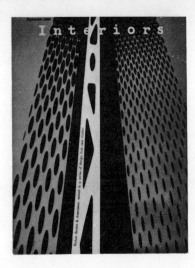

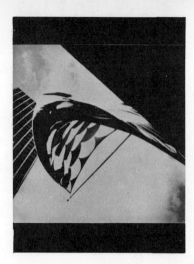

 Color

Cover of *Interiors* magazine, September, 1959, designed by Arnold Saks with Louis Klein. Courtesy Arnold Saks, Inc., New York.

The ellipse, used with striking effect in Bridget Riley's "Loss" **(Movement 2)**, is also a dominant motif in this magazine cover design. Riley, an Op artist, concentrates on the phenomena that cause us to perceive motion on a stationary surface and avoids suggestive form in order to isolate the perceptual experience. Arnold Saks' purpose, in contrast, is to communicate a particular idea. But he did not choose abstract forms arbitrarily; rather, they have a powerful expressive function. They have been composed in such a way that they produce both illusion and allusion: we do not need to read the lettering to recognize the reference to architecture.

In Anne Brody's "Falling Leaves" **(Movement 1)**, the elements move downward as though floating, and in Bridget Riley's painting the surface vibrates and turns inward. Here, the movement is upward—it has the soaring thrust of a skyscraper. Instead of covering the surface uniformly with pattern, Saks creates diagonal lines of force that draw the eye to the top of the composition. He controls the size of the ellipses and their proximity to one another, thereby slowing movement (on the left) and accelerating it (on the right) and giving a sense of height and distance (at the top). The white, girder-like upright and the black shaft that contains it echo the upward sweep. Color, too, reinforces the design. The wedges of solid red and blue in the upper corners emphasize the diagonal framework of the composition, while the opposition of black and white, red and blue, give it dramatic support.

 Color

"Street Banner," 1968, photograph by Sheldon Brody. Flag designed by Thomas Isabell, 1967, for Georg Jensen, Inc., New York. The Reinhold Visuals Collection.

Whether floating sleepily on a soft breeze, snapping crisply to a rising wind, straining at its ropes in a wintry gust, a flying flag is an embodiment of movement. Reflecting the slightest change in its environment, it gives visible form to the invisible element that surrounds us. Flags, banners, pennants, streamers—these bits of fabric catch the eye and the imagination. We even attach emotional significance to flags: a drooping flag seems to express dejection, a waving flag exuberance. They have diverse meanings: many still serve their original purpose of identification; some have become symbols of national pride; some are purely decorative.

The buoyant flag shown here is like a piece of moving sculpture. The photographer has captured only one of an endless succession of beautifully fluid shapes, but in this instant we can see all the potential of its furling form. Puffed out with air, the handsome banner resembles a colorful bird on the wing. Its dynamic shape echoes the pattern of the fabric. The geometric design of red and green is optically active in itself, further enhancing the sense of movement and ensuring a vibrant effect even if the day is calm. In this photograph, however, every element contributes to the expression of movement. The brilliant colors and curving shapes of the flag are set off against the structural grid of the building at the left and the triangle of solid black (made by the building from which the flag flies), and the slender flagpole seems barely to hold the surging, swelling form in check.

Movement

 Color

Detail of "Star Tree," 1965-67, by Preston McClanahan (U.S., b. 1933). Acrylic rods with electromechanical components (motors, pulleys, fluorescent tubes). 10′ (total diameter) x 3′ (height from base). Courtesy The Howard Wise Gallery, New York. Photos by the artist.

Motion is the life of "Star Tree"—not implied motion but real motion through space and time. In physical construction, the sculpture consists of three "branches," each a hollow shaft from which hundreds of plastic rods radiate. When the work is electrified, the rods transmit light from a fluorescent tube within each shaft. The light may be the regular fluorescent white or, as shown here, variegated (to produce this effect, a translucent cylinder of several colors is placed over the fluorescent tube in each branch). Each branch has its own motor and revolves at a rate of speed and in a direction determined by the artist.

The structure of "Star Tree" is a technical device, a means to an end. When lighted (as in the top picture), the simple linear components make a decorative, Christmas-lights pattern. But we cannot begin to understand the nature of the sculpture until it is set in motion, because only then is the artist's objective— a kinetic light environment—realized. The precise, machined quality of the work disappears, and it becomes a complex starburst of colored lights that constantly shift and merge into new wholes. There are no boundary lines or confines, no stationary points. The man-made materials of "Star Tree" compose a galaxy of changing patterns, radiant images, glowing rays, and dashes of illumination. The effects are multiplied by reflections on walls, floor, and ceiling, and the viewer is enveloped by a scintillating display of light energy.

Pole vaulter, 1964, photograph by Harold E. Edgerton. Multiflash photograph using two lamps with 20° beam at 25′. Alphax hand-operated shutter, 6″ focal length lens at f6.3. Kodak Plus-X film. Courtesy of Dr. Edgerton, Massachusetts Institute of Technology.

This dramatic picture was taken with strobe photography, which records the image by flashes of brilliant light rather than the opening and closing of the camera shutter. A scientific analysis of movement, it has the fascination of slow-motion film. It reveals, with beautiful precision, action too rapid for the eye to grasp, and it shows us the grace and skill of the athlete, who seems to float effortlessly through space.

In a stationary, two-dimensional work such as a painting or photograph, obviously, no actual movement takes place. What we perceive may be the result of illusion, as in Bridget Riley's "Loss" **(Movement 2)**, or of suggestion, as in the second photograph of McClanahan's "Star Tree" **(Movement 5)**, or of both. In "Star Tree," the artist used a long exposure to produce the blurred images of light dragged across his film. In Brody's "Street Banner" **(Movement 4)**, movement is also expressed by suggestion; that is, we relate the image to our experience of billowing flags. In this photograph, instead of the single, frozen instant, we see a series of instants that allow us to follow the event in time—without any distortion of the moving object. The forceful angle of the vaulter's path through space, emphasized by the string of lights across the top and the uprights of the hurdle, intensifies the action, as does the strong contrast of light and shadow. Each image is so clear and self-contained that the vaulter hardly seems to exert himself—but his flexed muscles and twisting body, the tension of the pole's curve, and the earthbound stability of the onlookers vividly underline the inner energy of his leap.

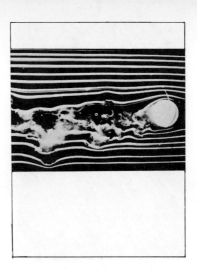

"Stichwen Tackled," 1963-64, by Kendall Shaw (U.S., b. 1924). Liquitex on canvas. 68 x 96". Courtesy The Tibor de Nagy Gallery, New York. Photo by Eric Pollitzer.

The subject matter of "Stichwen Tackled" is similar to that of Edgerton's pole vault photograph **(Movement 6)**—in both, action-packed sports events are depicted through multiple images in black and white. The photograph, however, is a scientifically accurate record. Its aesthetic qualities are incidental to the researcher's interest in the dynamics of pole vaulting. As a painter, Shaw is directly concerned with the aesthetics of action; he consciously manipulates the objective facts of the situation to reveal its beauty.

The football players' images lack sequential relation—the natural order of movement in time shown by the camera. We cannot reconstruct exactly "what happened"—yet the painting is imbued with the sense of movement, of action happening. The crisp negative-positive composition has a cinematic quality, but Shaw carefully omits all realistic detail (except for the decorative numerals). Our attention is concentrated on the interaction of form with form and form with space. The reduction of the figures to stark black and white silhouettes intensifies the implied impact by obscuring relationships of overlapping and depth and produces optical vibrancy, as hard-edge positive shape butts against hard-edge negative space. The reversal of positive and negative in the two "frames" creates still another level of dynamic tension: left and right are at once opposed by contrast and linked by the suggested continuation, across the center, of the figure with the numerals. The muscular contours and solid planes of the players give the impression of power, while their stances—head-on charge, sprawling fall, and upflung limbs—project the excitement and energy exploding in the tackle.

Spinning baseball, photograph by F. N. M. Brown. High-speed electronic flash photograph, 1/50,000 second. Courtesy Professor Brown, University of Notre Dame.

Pitchers and batters know very well that more happens to a baseball between the mound and home plate than meets the eye, but even they would surely be astonished to see in these graphic terms the turbulence and complex air displacement that a spinning ball initiates in its flight. This, approximately, is what is shown here. The phenomenon is not visible to the eye, or even to the camera under ordinary conditions: to make this photograph, a baseball was projected through a smoke-filled wind tunnel in a laboratory.

The purpose of the aerospace engineering researcher who made this remarkable picture of motion was to study the pattern made by the air surrounding a projectile. Specifically, this photograph illustrates the Magnus effect, which is the sideways force on a rotating cylinder (the baseball) placed with its axis perpendicular to a current of air (the smoke)—the thrust produced is used to propel ships and lift airplanes off the ground.

One of the most fascinating lessons of modern technology, as it reveals to us hitherto uncharted, invisible scenes, is that art is not a closed category, separate from life and the laws of nature. This photograph, though a scientific document, is composed of the same visual elements that artists have used intuitively to express velocity. The sharply defined leading edge of the baseball indicates the direction of movement; its pulsating energy is implied by the biting imprints left on the calm horizontal lines of smoke, and the cloudy trail in its wake constitutes a path of excitement through the pictorial field.

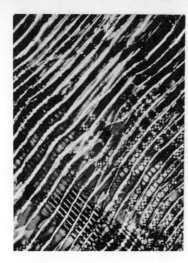

Movement

Color

Urea (carbamide) crystals, 1967, polarized light photomicrograph by Mortimer Abramowitz. Nikon EFM Microflex photomicrographic camera mounted on a Nikon S-Ke polarizing microscope. Kodachrome IIA film. Courtesy of the photographer.

Through extreme magnification and the use of polarized light, this photomicrograph discloses the structure of urea, a crystalline substance that is found in the natural world and in the human body. To the scientist, with his trained eye, the pattern produced when the light passes through the crystals is the key to their structure. Our experience, on the other hand, is quite different. We react in a direct, visual way. Unlike the strobe photograph of a pole vaulter **(Movement 6)** and the study of a spinning baseball produced by high-speed electronic flash **(Movement 8)**, here there is no familiar object to convey a hint of the subject to the layman. The image offered to us is not literal but poetic.

The photomicrograph affords us a unique and penetrating vision of the "invisible" physical world. Instead of the rigid structure associated with crystals, we discover an abstract play of colored light. Only its gemlike brilliance gives a suggestion of the material, but there is no sense of hardness or solidity. The luminous ribbons that flow diagonally across the surface create an illusion of movement like the rippling of a lake in a gentle breeze, and, as though the water were reflecting lights from the shore at night, blue, green, and red lights glow and shimmer.

Color

"Traffic Trails," 1968, photograph by Sheldon Brody. The Reinhold Visuals Collection.

In a sense, this composition was painted by moving light. The photographer manipulated the shutter of his camera to record not images suspended in time, but images changing in time. Instead of a progression of individual automobiles in sequential positions dictated by their motion, we see the continuous streaks of headlights and taillights as traffic speeds along the highway. In contrast to Edgerton, who used a camera far faster than the naked eye to produce his photograph of a pole vaulter **(Movement 6)**, Brody's camera was set at a speed slower than that of normal vision. While the strobe technique creates a picture that is an undistorted report of movement, "Traffic Trails" is *visually* more true to life. We cannot understand the pole vaulter's action until we deduce the meaning of the simultaneous images, but we know from experience that moving objects appear blurred to our eyes, and the faster they move, the more blurred they appear. Thus, as in the photograph of McLanahan's kinetic "Star Tree" **(Movement 5)**, we perceive movement here without hesitation—even though we cannot see the moving object itself.

The movement portrayed in "Traffic Trails" is, however, quite different from that in "Star Tree." We can make an interesting comparison, too, with Saks' cover design of a skyscraper in perspective **(Movement 3)**. Similar diagonals here imply movement in space, but the sharpness of their convergence suggests movement that is much more swift—the flashing approach and recession of automobiles. Instead of drawing the eye upward, this composition pulls us into the distance, past the stationary lights of the buildings at the right, under the night-haloed highway lights, and far away over the horizon.

Color

Showroom exhibition introducing IBM System/360 computer, 1965, designed by Arnold Saks and James S. Ward. Courtesy Arnold Saks, Inc., New York.

In the spirit of a child with a wonderful new writing implement and a clean expanse of wall, the designers of this window display have scribbled a delightful, luminous tangle of line along the length of the computer center's facade. The electric calligraphy of the neon tubing seems simple and ingenuous, and unmindful of the massive electronic equipment over which it plays, yet in the very freedom and spontaneity of its design lies its sophistication, its effectiveness, and its magic.

The familiar medium of banal commercial messages has been transformed here into a fluid sculpture. Instead of spelling out its purpose in words to be read and passed by, its brilliant lines entice the viewer to trace their movement from side to side and back again, to become involved in the labyrinth of loops and swirls that seem to have no beginning and no end.

As we are drawn into the environment of the display, the richness of its conception begins to emerge. In the top photograph we see the economy of the glowing sculptural line set against the flat expanse of the interior red wall, and its open flourishes in contrast with the solid blue-gray severity of the computers and structural columns. But the essence of the work is its movement. The free-flowing lines sweep gracefully through space, treating us to a visual roller-coaster ride. No matter what our point of view or distance, the undulations of the design carry our eyes along broad, measured curves and accelerate with ever more rapid and involuted swings in a crescendo of linear complexity.

Color

"Study in Motion," 1956, photograph by Herbert Matter (U.S., b. 1907). Courtesy of the artist.

Our eyes are capable of analyzing movement only within certain limits of speed. If an object moves too quickly, we may see it as a blur, or not at all. Modern photographic techniques have made it possible to record with accuracy things moving too fast for the eye to perceive—for instance, the spinning baseball **(Movement 8)**. If, however, the camera is not adjusted for the speed of the object photographed, it records a blurred picture similar to that seen by the eye. Since the photographer knows that we tend to interpret a blurred image as being in motion, he may choose purposely to distort his picture. Thus, in "Traffic Trails" **(Movement 10)**, Brody exaggerates the feeling of movement by keeping the shutter of his camera open.

Like a painter manipulating his brush and paint, the photographer controls his medium in order to achieve the effects he desires. Matter's "Study in Motion" is really an experiment in illusion. The delicate mobile of wire coils illuminated by beams of colored light was completely stationary when the photograph was made. Yet the sensation of movement is very strong. The apparent motion of the sculpture was created by strictly limiting the depth of focus of the camera lens. Thus, only parts of the mobile are seen in sharp detail: as the wires extend closer to or farther away from the camera, they fade out of focus and become increasingly indistinct. By suspending the mobile in complete blackness, Matter prevents us from using other clues to interpret the image, and so emphasizes the illusion. So forceful is the technique that we even lose the feeling of tangible material: the image appears to be made of light energy that vibrates and whirls in space.

Movement

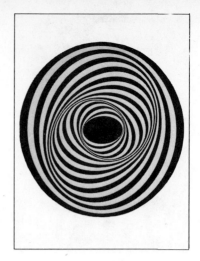

"Black Zero," by Aldo Tambellini (U.S., b. 1930). Calo Scott, cellist, in multimedia theater production; graphics by Aaron Rose. Photo by George Ehrlich, courtesy of Aldo Tambellini.

A musician moves at will around the stage; he carries his cello and plays improvisationally from time to time. Projected images and patterns of light sweep unpredictably over the stage. Other sounds are heard. A large inflated plastic sphere swells and shrinks with a hiss (as air is pumped in and out of it), roughly marking time for the music and for other events that may take place.

Only a fragment of this multimedia performance is shown here. The cellist, temporarily seated, is in the act of playing. Rings of light swirl dramatically over and around him, his instrument, and the puffed out sphere that is behind him, framing his bow hand. Everything in this happening is active and moving constantly. The choreography is spontaneous, and each sound and image contributes equally to the kinetic environment. The spectator is surrounded with sensations—no single element dominates, but movement infuses all. Forms seem to dematerialize, to be drawn into and become part of the eddying light. The cellist, the cello, the bow, all are dissolved into curves that circle and flow without regard for boundaries of mass and space into the dynamic center of brightness.

"Kinetic Painting," 1967, by Francis Celentano (U.S.). Black and white lacquer on masonite. 48″ (diameter). Courtesy The Howard Wise Gallery, New York. Photo by Geoffrey Clements.

The movement we feel in "Kinetic Painting" is illusory, but it is overwhelming—we cannot stop it or escape it. As in all painting in which the surface is optically activated, the two-dimensionality of the work is quickly destroyed. The feeling of depth is so intense that we may be physically affected. We experience a whirling movement similar in shape and direction to that of Tambellini's "Black Zero" production **(Movement 13)**, but it is more dizzying. Instead of surrounding the viewer with a multitude of sensations, as the theatrical artist does, Celantano employs a minimum number of stimuli. His only compositional element is the circle, and his palette is limited to black and white. But he endows these simple components with concentrated energy.

The painting is based on a perfect circle; inside it, concentric rings are progressively distorted through gradual widening and narrowing until, at the center, the circle has become an oval. So forceful is this distortion that it overrules the outer circumference of the painting and causes it to appear oval or lopsided. More important, this distortion makes the concentric rings appear to spiral continuously in toward the center of the painting. As we look, the movement accelerates, and our eyes are sucked into the dark vortex as into a tunnel. The whole stuff of the work seems to empty out, yet the strong black and white bands are not used up. Each time we pull our gaze out of the spinning center, it is immediately drawn back—the painting has the compelling attraction of a huge and devilish pinwheel.

Kite-flying. Photograph courtesy Kenmochi Isamu Design Associates, Tokyo, Japan, and James Wagenvoord.

Even in this age of space conquest, flight is a form of movement that has a special fascination and excitement for most people, and things that fly—both the creations of nature and of man—have a special and unique kind of beauty. This beauty, shared by birds, airplanes, and all forms designed to triumph over the invisible and contrary forces of wind and air, resides in the fluid lines and uncluttered, functional structure they invariably possess.

Kites are perhaps the oldest of man-made flying machines, and the feeling of delight that anyone who has ever coaxed one aloft can recall is ready evidence of the satisfaction we derive from controlling the forces of movement in nature. The simplest, most rudimentary kite is a familiar and pleasing example of aerodynamic form. But the design of kites has been a serious pastime in Japan for centuries, and the delicate structures shown in this photograph demonstrate the variety and complexity of form that can be obtained: the curved-wing, windmill shape of the kite at far left; the shell-like spiral of the one in the center; the intricate geometric constructions on the right. Straining against their strings, the kites have a light grace and airy symmetry that make their human masters seem awkward and earthbound. Soaring aloft, inbued with kinetic energy, each of these kites is an aerial sculpture.

Color
"White Whale," 1968, photograph by Sheldon Brody. The Reinhold Visuals Collection.

This white whale weighs well over a ton, yet it cuts through the water with awesome speed and grace because its immense form has been designed by nature for this particular type of locomotion. While a closer, straightforward view of the whale might provide us with more detailed information about the structure of this extraordinary self-propelling, living machine, half a dozen anatomical pictures could not communicate its dynamic character in the clear and forceful visual terms of this single photograph.

Not only does the photographer show us the whale in water, its natural element, but at a moment when the animal's form most graphically expresses its capacity for swift movement and smooth, seemingly effortless maneuvering. The whale is in the action of turning, and the camera allows us to see each part of its body in a position that perfectly describes its function in relation to the movement: the snub leading shape of the head; the compact, streamlined mass of the torso flowing smoothly into the powerful tail; the flattened, winglike fins. The whole body of the whale is articulated in a tension-filled curve that is emphasized by contrast with the straight aquarium wall at left and the flat floor below. Despite the whale's solidity and weight, it seems to navigate the water from sparkling surface to dark depth as lightly as a bird the air.

Movement

"Indian Dancer: Study in Motion," 1948, photograph by Herbert Matter (U.S., b. 1907). Courtesy of the artist.

The artist who seeks to interpret movement in space through a two-dimensional medium such as a painting or photograph deals, necessarily, in illusion of some kind: his subject must *seem* to move or *suggest* movement, since it is actually flat and stationary. This photograph by Herbert Matter resembles Edgerton's study of a pole vaulter **(Movement 6)** in that it shows sequential images to denote motion, and it is similar to Brody's "Traffic Trails" **(Movement 10)** in utilizing time exposure to trace an ongoing path of motion. Edgerton, however, is interested in seeing how the posture of the vaulter changes, and the relationship between the images is only implied; in "Traffic Trails" the moving object itself has disappeared in order to emphasize the continuity of the movement. Matter, in contrast, retains both elements—the dancer and the dance.

Matter is concerned with the total experience of the human figure in motion. His photographic composition has a painterly quality: the camera is a tool for discovering the essence of the subject. He concentrates on expressive movement, cutting out all that is superfluous—background and even physical detail. Dancer and dance are rendered with impressionistic softness, the lithe figure and graceful gestures dissolving into the rhythmic pattern of the movement.

Color

Detail from "The Harvesters," 1565, by Pieter Bruegel the Elder (Flemish, b. 1520?, d. 1569). Oil on wood. 46½ x 63¼" (overall). The Metropolitan Museum of Art, Rogers Fund, 1919.

In this painting, movement is used as a narrative device. Bruegel presents his subject matter—the harvest—through a composite of actions, each of which tells us a part of the story. Thus, one peasant cuts the wheat with a scythe, another rakes the fallen stalks into sheaves, while a third trudges toward them with a jug, perhaps bringing them refreshment. Each of these main actions is clarified by the isolation of the men, their stocky bodies framed by the richly textured backdrop of uncut grain, and by the characteristic way each strains at his task, so that the motion of cutting is different from that of carrying water. In addition, the various actions are carefully ordered within the painting so that our eyes are guided along a specific route— from the main scene in the foreground, down the narrow path at the right, and off to the left, where other peasants carry the wheat to a distant cart. Two complementary kinds of movements are thus taking place: one is descriptive; the other advances the narrative.

"The Harvesters" is crammed full of marvelous details that not only show us the outward appearance of a sixteenth-century harvest but also express the quality of the peasants' life. The toiling harvesters are locked visually into place by the tall wheat still to be cut. The hunched shoulders of the peasants, like the posture of the ox pulling at the laden cart, indicate how strenuous their labor is; the slow progress of the figures who bear the bundles of wheat away is emphasized by the free flight of two birds over the field, and the little scenes of rest and play in the distant meadows provide poignant contrast to the work at hand.

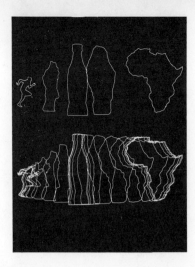

 Color

"Birthday," 1915-23, by Marc Chagall (French, b. 1887). Oil on canvas. 31⅞ x 39⅝". The Solomon R. Guggenheim Museum Collection.

There is magic and wry humor in this painting of a couple who levitate as they kiss. The movement of the man who rises several feet in the air, stretching his neck in an impossibly graceful contortion, is pure fantasy, yet it is set in a believable situation and thereby becomes both extraordinary and natural at once.

With a childlike feeling for reality in the midst of fantasy, Chagall includes such everyday details as the knife and plate on the table and the sentimental bouquet of flowers, which give poignancy and comfortable warmth to the scene. At the same time, however, he accentuates the magical motion of the main figures. The rippling contours of their clothes and their gravity-defying tilt lend credibility to their buoyancy. The front of the woman's dress unexpectedly blurs, with the effect of making her float gently forward, and the position of her feet in relation to the floor is ambiguous: she might be balanced lightly on her toes or not touching the ground at all. Of her husband's state there is no doubt at all—his feet are nowhere near the earth, and the sudden dissolution of the line between wall and floor beneath him assures us that he has been lifted into the air. Both in the spatial location of the figures and the gay, festive colors of the setting, "Birthday" makes a rich contrast to "The Harvesters" of Bruegel **(Movement 18)**. There the tones are muted and the peasants' feet are planted securely and stolidly on the ground—the mood is workaday and real, not holiday and delight. Chagall's use of motion is metaphorical: it expresses with gentle whimsy emotion that sweeps his protagonists off their feet.

"Running Cola Is Africa," 1967-68. Computer graphic by Computer Technique Group, Japan, programmed in Fortran IV on IBM 7090 and drawn on Calcomp 563 plotter. Design idea by Masao Komura, data by Makoto Ohtake, programming by Koji Fujino. Courtesy of The Institute of Contemporary Arts, London, and Motif Editions, London.

A running man becomes a bottle of cola becomes Africa, or, in computer language, the outline of a running man is algorithmically converted into the outline of a bottle of cola and thence into the outline of a map of Africa. The images in the top section help to explain how the transformation is achieved by showing us selected intermediate steps. This simplified progression has visual movement, but only in the second version does the nature of the movement become clear: with the inclusion of many more steps overlapping appears, and the continuity of the process emerges.

This computer print-out is an exciting visual representation of an activity we do not ordinarily think of as movement—it is conceptual, not physical. It is unfamiliar-looking, even funny, but it affords us a brand-new insight into the relationship of things. The running man, the bottle of cola, and Africa do, it turns out, have something in common. It is important to realize that this is an *artistic* insight: it translates thought into image and distills the essence of form in an ordered manner.

Computer technology has given us a whole new range of ways to express ideas and feelings. Cybernetic art is revolutionary—we are accustomed to art that bears the imprint of the craftsman's hands. Men and machines collaborated to produce "Running Cola Is Africa," and the result is strange to our eyes, but it is a meaningful and engrossing reflection of our time.

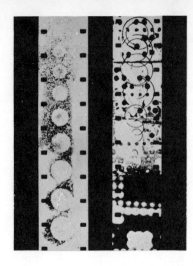

Movement

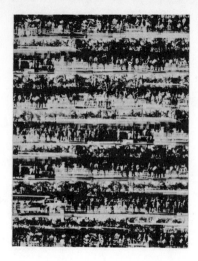

Film clips from "Blackout," 1965-66, motion picture by Aldo Tambellini (U.S., b. 1930). Printing assistance by Aaron Rose. Courtesy of the artist.

The movement that we see when we look at motion pictures is illusory, but the illusion is produced by actual movement in space and time—the passage of stationary film images through the projector. Although the images on the film are not intended to be seen individually, they nevertheless have intrinsic interest because they determine the character of the new whole created when they flicker past in rapid succession.

The two clips from "Blackout" shown here are especially interesting because Tambellini's movie was not made in the traditional way. Instead of exposing his film with a camera trained on moving objects, the artist worked inch by inch along thousands of feet of 16mm film and created the images directly by scratching the acetate and etching it with acid. Inspired by the electric-power failure in the northeastern United States in 1965, "Blackout" is a direct and personal expression of feeling.

While movement is implied by the sequential changes that take place in these clips, we can only imagine the actual effect when they are run through the projector. What we see as multiple circles of increasing size, for instance, will appear as a single, continuously expanding circle. Similarly, Tambellini had to envision the result of his work as he composed it. There were no predetermined graphic elements or patterns: the shapes, lines, and textures developed as he proceeded, and only movement completes the work and gives the images their final rhythmic form.

Detail of "Trolley Stop," 1966, photographed by Ray K. Metzker (U.S., b. 1931). Collection The Museum of Modern Art, New York.

In "Trolley Stop" overlapping photographs assembled into a montage compress moments of human activity over a period of time into one complex image. Only a portion of the full work is shown here: the figurative material is even more densely packed in the full version, but this detail has been enlarged to facilitate analysis. Metzker crowds time-organized images into one format so that we can experience them as a unified whole— not in a chronological organization but in an order that permits us to study their interrelationships from a new point of view not limited by the natural sequence of events.

"Trolley Stop" is about urban life; it both reflects the impersonal monotony of movement in the city and uses it as the basis for a rhythmic composition. Because of the open-ended technique he uses, Metzker can make any juxtaposition of elements he wishes to build up a pattern of sensation. The images of the vehicles suggest directional movement, but we soon realize that they are not "going anywhere"—they contribute only abstract energy to the work. There is optical movement in the articulation of the black and white shapes, and a strong left-right movement is emphasized by the horizontal tops of the trolleys and pavement lines, which are played against the subtle verticals of the upright figures. Shifts in placement and staccato recurrence of forms, plus the layering and overlapping of images, give an overall impression of two-dimensional kinetic texture. Metzker shows us the visual dynamics of a commonplace scene of little dramatic consequence, and it takes on haunting, almost ghostly, overtones.

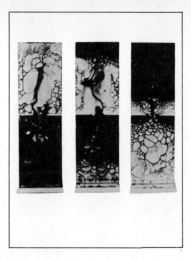

Movement

Color

Citric acid crystals, 1967, polarized light photomicrograph by Mortimer Abramowitz. Nikon EFM Microflex photomicrographic camera mounted on a Nikon S-Ke polarizing microscope. Kodachrome IIA film. Courtesy of the photographer.

Like the photomicrograph of urea crystals **(Movement 9)**, this study by the same photographer conjures up a fantastic landscape rather than giving us a literal, diagrammatic view of crystalline structure. Although we may not understand the scientific meaning of the patterns made by polarized light, a comparison of the photomicrographs makes it clear that the two substances have very different structures, for the images they evoke are widely diverse.

While the structure of the urea crystals suggests the gentle motion of rippling water, that of the citric acid crystals produces a composition with a feeling of intense force. The design resembles a configuration that might result if brilliantly colored shapes were attracted and held in tension by a powerful magnetic field, or were hurled outward from the center of a tremendous explosion. This dynamic quality is created by the strong focal point toward which every visual element leads (or from which all color and form radiate). Like the central shape in Celentano's "Kinetic Painting" **(Movement 14)**, the point forms a vortex. Here, however, the eye is pulled directly inward and outward along sharp diagonal lines of force; the absence of circular movement diminishes the sense of depth but increases the apparent speed.

"Scylla and Charybdis," 1964-65, by Hans Haacke (German, b. 1936). Clear Lucite and colored liquid. 24 x 7¾ x ⅞". Courtesy The Howard Wise Gallery, New York.

"Scylla and Charybdis," the title borrowed from Greek mythology for this unusual work, suggests a choice between two equally hazardous alternatives. On first consideration, no ready explanation for the reference is presented. Haacke's "flow-through" construction is a completely clear Lucite box, partially filled with a colored fluid, that is divided into two compartments by a gateway arrangement through which the fluid can pass. If we jiggle or shake the box, the fluid is set in motion, forming myriad patterns of bubbles. When we invert the box, the bubbling liquid flows gradually into the lower section, as the three views shown here illustrate.

This highly imaginative work can be enjoyed on a variety of levels. As an object that requires the viewer's physical participation, it affords the kind of pleasure we derive from play; indeed, it is an aesthetic toy. It has no function other than to be manipulated and contemplated: each time it is moved, a new abstract drama of gravity-density movement begins. We may influence the pattern of the drama by agitating the fluid, turning the box slowly end over end, setting it on its side, and so on—but we cannot call a halt to it once we have begun it; we can only wait for the conclusion. The inevitable and unpredictable character of the movement pattern, we may speculate, symbolizes the complexity of life (the mysterious fluid has a pronounced biological quality), which unleashes a chain of infinite possibilities. The course of events may be altered, but the element of chance presents us with ever-changing and unforeseeable vistas.

Portfolio 7, Perception

Perception in Art

Our response to a work of art depends not just on its subject matter and the artist's organization of formal elements such as line and color, but on the much more complex problem of how we perceive, or interpret, these things. Perception is defined as awareness of the environment through sensory stimuli—sight, sound, touch, taste, and smell. We are concerned primarily with the sense of sight, since we are dealing with visual art, but it is important to remember that other sensations constantly impinge on and influence our reactions to visual stimuli.

All artists must be concerned with perception to some extent, because perception shapes the images they create and our response to them. There has even developed an important and vital movement—optical art—to investigate perception and perceptual phenomena. Scientists as well as artists have studied the subject, yet the dynamics of perception are still not fully understood. It involves both physiological and psychological factors; for example, afterimages are illusions partly accounted for by actual changes in the eye. Moreover, we continuously interpret stimuli on the basis of incomplete information. Given only the most basic clues, we will attribute such qualities as unity and three-dimensionality to images that are divided and flat; we will judge relative size and distance with no more evidence than color and direction. To further complicate the matter, perception is not always fixed and definitive: we can interpret the same stimuli quite differently at different moments. The mechanical act of looking is only the beginning of the perceptual experience. It is empty unless subjective interaction with what we see follows: this is the source of the rich variety of perception.

Perception

Color

Job Lot Trading Company mural, 1967, by Jason Crum. Photo by Sheldon Brody. The Reinhold Visuals Collection.

The corner on which the Job Lot Trading Company stands was a typical run-down commercial neighborhood of dingy buildings and blank, peeling billboards until the management of the store commissioned Jason Crum to paint a mural on the flat expanse of wall above the display windows. The artist transformed the atmosphere of the block, gave the store a dramatic identity, and created a work of art that involves the visual perception of every passer-by. The bold geometric pattern is meant to challenge the eye, not to "tell a story" or evoke specific emotions. This is what makes the painting optical art. Some Op art is extremely subtle and requires us to concentrate intently. Other Op works, like this one, are more direct in their impact. The punch-in-the-eye approach is necessary here because the mural cannot be contemplated in the peaceful surroundings of a museum but must work upon the perceptions of passers-by in a busy commercial environment.

The painting is so bold that it takes only a few moments to notice how it plays with our perceptions. At first glance it may seem like varicolored strips of paper folded across themselves and woven together so that each emerges, disappears, emerges again, and again disappears. Another look reveals right-angle triangles of color neatly fitted together to form squares. Although the same simple geometric shapes are repeated over and over in a regular pattern, the colors are purposely varied. They may appear systematically arranged at first, but we soon realize that the organization is more complicated than our immediate impression indicates. The relationships of intense colors and pale ones, complementaries and related hues, the surprising stripes at the right, all add up to a multiplicity of visual possibilities—as many as and more than the viewer has time to investigate.

"The Wall of Respect," 1968, photograph by Michael Mauney. Courtesy Black Star.

This mural, known as "The Wall of Respect," was painted on the wall of a ghetto building by members of the community. The environment has been transformed through the decoration of an ugly exterior building surface, as in the case of the Job Lot Trading Company mural **(Perception 1)**, but the motivation, method of expression, and result are totally different.

The Job Lot Trading Company mural is a highly successful adventure in bringing a sophisticated and controlled art form out of the museum into the street. In executing it, the artist employed his knowledge of the principles of Op art. Its impact depends on the viewer's active participation—his perceptual response to color and other optical stimuli. "The Wall of Respect," in contrast, is the result of free and spontaneous folk expression. It involves our perception in its direct appeal to feeling, and its power stems from the depth of emotion conveyed by the images we see, not from the images themselves. Knowing the identity of the black leaders who are portrayed may add to our interest, but we do not need this information to feel the meaning of the work. (The figures are Claudia McNeil, Ruby Dee, Cicely Tyson, Ossie Davis, Oscar Brown Jr., Sidney Poitier, James Earl Jones, and LeRoi Jones.) "The Wall of Respect" is an effective work of art because the artists who created it used compelling techniques, forms, and structure instinctively. The crude realism of the portraits is set off by the inclusion of a photographic image and explicit, scrawled words. The window aperture is used as a frame for the heroic head that becomes the focal area of the composition; the sharp changes in scale are ordered by the balance of rectangular areas of wall space; and the underlying brick gives an organic unity to the whole.

Perception

''Opmobile,'' 1968, photograph by Sheldon Brody. The Reinhold Visuals Collection.

The automobile has become far more than a means of transportation: to many people it is a highly expressive symbol of the technological age. Its design, the result of a staggering annual expenditure of time and money, is intended to satisfy a great many requirements, both practical and aesthetic. The monotony of its assembly-line form, as well as its chrome and metal flashiness, have been glorified by Pop artists in paintings such as Rosenquist's ''Ultraviolet Cars'' **(Mass 18)** and Lichtenstein's ''Tire'' **(Mass 19)**, and in sculpture such as Chamberlain's crushed-car work, ''Mustang Sally McBright'' **(Surface 1)**. The owner of the ''Opmobile,'' with satiric irreverence toward the automobile industry and the Op art movement alike, has made his car the vehicle for an experiment in perception.

As in Komodore's painting ''Sun City'' **(Perception 17)**, line is the only visual element used. But the linear pattern of ''Sun City'' is confined by the strict boundary of a frame, and the optical movement it produces is experienced by the viewer in the controlled environment of the art gallery. Here, in contrast, the lines have been applied to a functioning machine, and the viewer encounters it parked at the curb or in the even more optically dazzling condition of moving down the street. There has been no attempt to mask the mechanical nature of the car; on the contrary, the painted lines emphasize the contours of hood, fenders, wheels. Despite the unorthodox combination of function (the vehicle) and form (Op art), the ''Opmobile'' is a successful synthesis—the actual kinetic character of the one plays against and reinforces the perceptual movement created by the other.

''Details of Portrait of Isako Yanaiahara,'' 1960, by Alberto Giacometti (Swiss, b. 1901, d. 1966). Oil on canvas. 32¾ x 28½''. Photographed by Herbert Matter on August 9, 10, 11, and 12, 1960. Courtesy Herbert Matter.

We are privileged usually to see only the final result of the artist's labor, and we consequently tend to assume that a work of art springs into being fully formed. Perhaps—we think—the painter may make a few preliminary sketches, but once he picks up his brush, surely all he needs to do is use his technical ability to transfer the image onto the canvas. Alberto Giacometti is a renowned artist, and we may be certain that he had technical command of his brush. Moreover, we can see that power to wield it with force and meaning is not lacking in any of the four versions of the portrait shown here. Yet these pictures are different stages of the same work, photographed on four successive days. They document the complex and mysterious changes which took place within that short space of time.

What changed, of course, was not the physical appearance of the sitter, but the vision of the artist. Perception is not a single cognitive act: the eye and mind do not function like a camera, recording appearance once and for all. Whatever the painter's purpose—to render a likeness of the sitter's character and physical characteristics, to explore form, express feeling, evoke mood—the very process of translating these intangible but perceived qualities into shape and color affects his interpretation of what he sees. The artist interacts, too, with the sitter and with the paint on the canvas, and this triggers the development of awareness. The changes that we see are subtle, but they signify the discovery of new meanings, the growth of insight, and the refinement of perceptual truth.

Perception

Color

"Rock," 1967, photograph by Jay Verhulst. Courtesy The Electric Circus, New York.

Perception is a constant and continuous process, as innate and vital a function as breathing. Even when we are asleep, we respond to sensory stimuli; when we are awake and alert, we are sensitive to an endless variety of sensations through which we perceive the elements of our environment. It is impossible for us to shut out all sensations entirely, yet we continually screen them, concentrating on those that are important to our purpose at any given moment and minimizing those that distract from it. This is why many people close their eyes when they listen to music, and why Op artists use simple geometric shapes and flat colors. The experiences of "pure" sound and "pure" sight are their respective goals. Other artists are concerned with the perception of as many stimuli as possible. It is as impossible to give all sensations equal attention as it is to shut them all out, but it is possible to bombard our perceptions to a mind-reeling degree.

The multimedia performance of the Circus Maximus group is designed to achieve just this end, and the photographer has attempted to communicate the nature of the experience. He cannot literally record sounds, smells, movement in space and time, actual textures, or temperature, but he is able, through control of his art, to evoke almost all these sensations with visual imagery alone. For example, he has used a prismatic lens to create overlapping multiple images with blurred contours, which we interpret as movement, while the cramped arrangement of the images gives us the feeling of being crowded. The repetition of shapes suggests the pounding rhythm of the music the intense red light, heat and excitement. These effects overload the senses, and the result is a bewildering loss of orientation.

Color

"Richard IV," 1967, by Harold Cohen (British, b. 1928). One of a series of screen prints. 27 x 30½". Courtesy The Marlborough Graphics Gallery, New York. Photo by Malcolm Varon.

We can still see, although in generalized terms, the image on which this portrait is based. "Richard IV" (one of a series shown in its entirety in **Perception 7**) is far removed from traditional portraiture. The object of the artist is not to create a likeness that expresses the character of his subject in emotional terms. Here there is nothing sentimental or romantic, and little that is personal. Like many artists today, Cohen is interested not in the details of what we see but in the mechanisms of perception—how we see it.

This portrait consists only of dots, yet we perceive the image quite clearly (if not in detail). Cohen has employed, in exaggerated form, a method of reproduction with which we are all familiar. We see it daily in book and magazine illustrations and newspaper photographs. These reproductions, called halftones, are, to all intents and purposes, clear-cut, informative pictures we easily comprehend. They are produced by a mechanical process. The original image is photographed through a screen, which breaks it down into a pattern of dots. The relative size and proximity of these dots (determined by the amount of light reflected by the image) spell out the details of the image. Obviously, the basis of these reproductions is a visual illusion, a phenomenon of perception. Their success depends on our tendency to group, or interpret as a continuous whole, discontinuous things that are similar and close together. This is how we react to "Richard IV." But Cohen has magnified the dots and given them blatantly artificial color. This emphasis reduces their image value and, in a striking reversal of the usual optical effect, we become aware of them as independent elements of design.

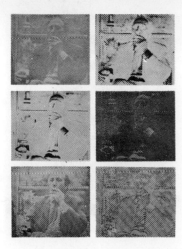

Color

"Richard Hamilton 1967," by Harold Cohen (British, b. 1928). A series of screen prints. 27 x 30½" (each). *Top left:* "Richard H," *right:* "Richard I." *Middle left:* "Richard II," *right:* "Richard III." *Bottom left:* "Richard IV," *right:* "Richard V." Courtesy The Marlborough Graphics Gallery, New York. Photo by Malcolm Varon.

This series of portraits is neither Pop art nor Op art entirely, but it bridges the two movements in a way that is most appropriate, since the artist is concerned primarily with perceptual phenomena, while his subject is a Pop artist. The starting point for the series is a photograph. The bare, untouched photograph, however, is not a portrait—it is merely a record of fact. The first portrait, "Richard H," shows the intervention of the artist. He has enlarged the photograph and printed on it a pattern of tiny silver-gray dots, producing the effect of a somewhat muted newspaper photograph. This allusion to the process of reproduction commonly used by the mass media (as described in **Perception 6**) is Cohen's method of expressing the character of his sitter, since Pop painters frequently use mechanically produced dots in their work.

The disintegration of the image into patterns of dots recurs in each of the "Richard Hamilton" portraits; each of the five following prints is a variation on the theme. Unlike the four stages of the portrait of Isako Yanaiahara by Giacometti **(Perception 4)**, these are all finished works. Each one is a study in color and surface. In true optical art the image is always abstract and geometric: the object is to sensitize our vision, to appeal directly to the senses without the intermediary of traditional subject matter. Cohen retains a specific subject here, but he subordinates it to the process through which we perceive it. The image has become a set of stimuli, the eye a computer, and the portraits graphic evidence of the varied and complex way in which we analyze and interpret visual data.

Color

Watercolor, 1968, by Milton Glaser (U.S., b. 1929). Illustration for "The Perfect Wife," *McCall's Magazine* (May, 1968). Courtesy Push Pin Studios, Inc.

Past experience as well as physical sensations shape our reactions to what we see. To put it another way, perception is influenced—and to an extraordinary degree—by memories and emotions, factors quite external to the object of perception. By the process known as "association," we bring a rich fund of personal meanings to the interpretation of sensory stimuli. A classic example of this is the well-known Rorschach test, which consists of a set of inkblot designs. The symmetry of these figures gives us the feeling of completeness, but their abstract form and complexity make them highly evocative. They activate our imagination as we seek to organize meaningfully what we see.

Artists make use of our tendency to associate in a variety of ways, depending upon their purpose. Op artists, for example, attempt to suppress the process as completely as possible; thus, they choose for their subject matter the spare forms of geometry—circles, squares, triangles. These forms, executed with hard-edged precision, do not "remind" us of anything; they remain abstract and serve to set optical phenomena into motion. Other artists, in contrast, intentionally use forms that provoke associations, some specific, some ambiguous. It is obvious that Milton Glaser has drawn directly upon the imagery of the Rorschach in creating this watercolor illustration. But the Rorschach images are completely abstract, while recognizable form—a profile—grows mysteriously out of Glaser's "inkblot." It becomes a Janus-like head, a haunting and undefinable image. What is the strange relation between the faces? Are they mirror images of one face, or two entities? They cannot be wholly merged or parted; they are joined at the seat of thoughts and of dreams, and they carry us into the realm of fantasy.

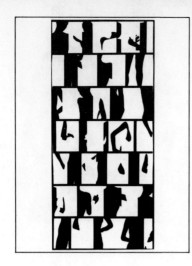

Perception

"Untitled," 1966, by Ray K. Metzker (U.S., b. 1931). Photograph. Courtesy of the artist.

Not surprisingly, artists have always been fascinated by the human figure. Sometimes the main object of their concern is its literal appearance; sometimes its abstract qualities become primary. Whatever expressive use is made of its form, however, the artist translates the facts of perception into aesthetic statement. Thus, Metzker uses a contemporary tool, the camera, not to report photographically how the human figure looks but to explore the essence of its form.

This photomontage was created by cutting up photographs of a model and rearranging the pieces. The figure is exploded into a variety of shapes, no two of which are exactly alike. Because we recognize parts of the figure, we are perceptually prompted to complete the image—to supply with our mind the continuity denied to the eye. Similarly, the sequential arrangement of the shapes, which gives the composition a movie-like character, indicates movement. But other elements contradict these interpretations. The shapes that should add up to the figure are dispersed. The contrast of values is heightened so that practically all modeling of form disappears, and only black and white remain. The relationship of these anonymous, two-dimensional elements—positive and negative—is such that we cannot sustain our original interpretation: figure and ground become ambiguous and reversible. The areas of white emerge as positive shapes in dynamic equilibrium with the black.

By denying us the complete visual existence of the figure, Metzker gives us new insight into its form. We perceive it here as pure pattern, a composite of varied shapes with unsuspected negative-positive possibilities.

"Walksleeper," 1967, photograph by Sheldon Brody. The Reinhold Visuals Collection.

Of all our senses, sight is the one on which we most rely. We know, of course, that our perception is influenced by our other faculties—sound, smell, taste, and touch—but we trust our eyes to tell us the truth. How many phrases and figures of speech reflect this: "Seeing is believing," "I see what you mean," "I get the picture," "I couldn't believe my eyes," and so on!

The photographer who took this picture was not only alert to his surroundings but also keenly aware of the vagaries of perception. With split-second reaction, he recognized in the scene a typical example of the kind of tricks played on us daily by our eyes. We seldom realize how often they play us false, because perception is also influenced by logic and reason—we are constantly, and unconsciously, adjusting our interpretation of what we see according to what we know. Thus, we *know*, as we pass by, that someone is walking on the other side of the truck, and the momentary juxtaposition goes unnoticed. The photographer's art, here, is in capturing the moment of visual absurdity.

There is nothing obscure about the scene—with a quick look we can "explain" the incongruity. But "Walksleeper" is more than an entertaining joke. It is able to sustain our interest because in it the photographer exposes the mechanisms of perception for our appreciation.

"Standing Man," 1967, by Michelangelo Pistoletto (Italian, b. 1933). Painted paper on polished steel. 86 x 48". Courtesy The Kornblee Gallery, New York. Photo by Burt L. Stern.

Exploring the subject of perception inevitably involves, at some point, exploring the nature of reality. As optical illusions demonstrate, we often cannot distinguish perceptually between the actual and the apparent. Pistoletto's "Standing Man" is one artist's approach to the complicated question—our first impulse is to discover what, exactly, is real and what is not in this composition.

Examination reveals that the "real" background (that is, the one created by the artist) consists of a sheet of polished steel. The figure, painted on tracing paper, cut out, and pasted on the reflecting surface of the steel, is similarly "real" and remarkably realistic (that is, it looks like a "real" person), even to the shadow it appears to cast on the floor. Everything else we see does not exist in the artist's work. Yet everything else is, in fact, real—or, more accurately, the reflection of a real thing. These real things, however, are all distorted by the reflecting surface, which is skewed like mirrors in a fun house, and they shift and change if we move so much as a step. Only the painted man remains stable. With this work Pistoletto takes us, like Alice, into the world of the looking glass, where reality is relative, depending upon one's point of view. He invites us, too, to take a hand in the picture-making process. By moving, by placing objects in front of the composition, by standing so that our own image is reflected, we become a part of the schema and, like the artist, manipulators of reality.

Color

"Roman Mirrors," 1964, photograph by Sheldon Brody. The Reinhold Visuals Collection.

Even in this miraculous age of technology, when the exact replication of images is a commonplace feat, the mirror and the mirror image remain a source of fascination. The reflected image has a peculiar and special relationship to the original. It exists simultaneously and changes simultaneously, implying identity, but it is intangible, temporary, and always in reverse—a step removed from the original. Reflections, thus, provide us with an avenue of perception different from any other; neither the eye, looking directly, nor the still or moving camera yields exactly the same experience.

Brody's "Roman Mirrors" prompts us to wonder whether the mirrors themselves (on sale in Rome's Flea Market) or the images reflected in them are the principal subject matter of the photograph. The composition has a natural order and balance, and its varied shapes and surfaces are unified by the low-keyed blue light suffusing the whole. The reflections, however, are more interesting: they reveal fragments of a scene that can be completed only in our imagination. Perception works something like this, although in less exaggerated fashion. When we look around us, dozen of sensations demand attention; we cannot possibly register every one. From the fragments actually seen, however, we construct—perceive—a coherent picture.

Perception

Color

Photograph for Wyandotte Chemicals Corporation, 1962, by Herbert Matter (U.S., b. 1907). Courtesy of the artist.

The ingenious way in which the property of reflection has been utilized to make this photograph is an indication of how varied are the means of expression available to the artist. Pistoletto's "Standing Man" **(Perception 11)**, Brody's "Roman Mirrors" **(Perception 12)**, and Herbert Matter's photograph here all incorporate reflected images, yet in each case the artist's purpose, technique, and result are totally different .

Matter was commissioned to create an illustration for an advertisement; the subject was the petroleum industry. The photographer went to a refinery, placed a drop of oil on a sheet of glass, and coaxed it into a desired shape. He then set the glass upright and took this picture. In it are captured a crystal-clear image of refining machinery reflected in the drop of oil and a hazy view of other parts of the refinery seen through the glass.

The photograph is a unique synthesis of artistic sensibility and technical expertise. Matter reveals to us a landscape of extra-ordinary beauty, a scene that cannot be perceived with the unaided eye. A literal statement of what a refinery looks like would tell us little we did not know. Matter transports us into the very midst of a new world of color and light. The machinery is still there, but we see more. And we see it through the material that is both product and symbol of this world—oil.

Color

"Music and Good Luck," 1888, by William Michael Harnett (U.S., b. 1848, d. 1892). Oil on canvas. 40 x 30". The Metropolitan Museum of Art, Wolfe Fund, 1963.

It is difficult to believe that "Music and Good Luck" is painted on canvas. Picture frame, cupboard door, sheet music, shadows —all are painted. This work is an example of what is probably the most ancient artistic experiment in visual perception, the technique of *trompe l'oeil*. Literally, this French phrase means "deceive the eye." Such optical illusionism, which can fool us into taking the picture for the "real thing," represents an extreme in art: we cannot go further than this in the depiction of exterior reality.

Just to imitate reality so successfully does not, of course, make a good work of art. We may admire the virtuosity of the painter, but there is more to art than technical proficiency. To begin with, Harnett chose a theme. He brought together objects with a particular unity, not only of subject but of textures and colors, to express a particular feeling, warm and nostalgic. The disposition of them on the canvas is not the result of chance but of careful organization. This analysis of the formal elements of "Music and Good Luck" is useful, but it is not a satisfactory explanation of Harnett's painting. Other artists, taking the same physical scene, would not render it so literally. *Trompe l'oeil* is not only a clever trick—it is a way of perceiving the world of forms around us. By employing this technique, Harnett shows us the complex nature of perception, and of reality. He knows perfectly well that if we get close enough we will discover the illusion—and it is essential that we do. Only then can we begin to experience the expansion of perception that the artist intended.

Color

"Performing KK No. 2 (Sunday Edition)," 1964, by Oyvind Fahlström (Swedish, b. 1928). Tempera on paper and canvas. 52 x 34". Courtesy Mr. Frederick Ossorio.

Krazy Kat was the Charlie Brown of his day (1911-1944). The hapless Kat rarely came out ahead, and when he did, there was always a twist; nonetheless, he was the "hero" of the comic strip. This remarkable painting looks exactly like an episode from George Herriman's Krazy Kat—until we look more closely. We do not need to have seen the real Krazy Kat to know that this is not an ordinary comic strip. The characters look right, the words sound right, even the situation of pursuit and revenge appears to make sense, but when we add the elements up at the end, it is nonsense. There is too much that we cannot make out. The props are vaguely suggestive, but finally strange, disquieting, and inexplicable—and all comic strips are simple, concrete, and self-explanatory.

The comic strip is popular art in the literal sense: it has mass appeal because everyone can understand it. It expresses in simple form fantasies shared by everyone—to be as strong as Superman; to enjoy Charlie Brown's moral triumphs over adversity. We enjoy the adventures of these characters without the intervention of intellectual analysis—our perception of the underlying meaning is quite unconscious. Fahlström has purposely borrowed the comic-strip form to jolt us into awareness of this deeper level of perception. "Performing KK No. 2" is a surrealist comic strip; that is, it is concerned with irrational fantasy. It evokes the strange, disquieting world of dreams, which has an inner logic but cannot be explained in rational terms. Confronted with these images, we must delve below the surface reality.

"Black Video #1," 1967/68, by Aldo Tambellini (U.S., b. 1930). Part of a multi-screen light environment displayed at The Howard Wise Gallery, New York. Courtesy of the artist. Photo by Martin Decker.

Television generally has been used as an extension of narrative exposition— a pictorial story-telling medium that is related to the comic strip and the traditional movie. Only recently have artists begun to explore seriously the potential of electronic devices for creative expression; that is, as a means of creating images rather than transmitting them. In Tambellini's "Black Video #1," television becomes the "electromedium" for a kinetic light environment.

To produce the environment, the artist records on videotape moving images of light that is both projected and shown directly to the camera. Sound, feedback from the microphone, is recorded simultaneously. The videotape is then run to multiple television sets, and the reception on each screen is regulated by the artist (and the viewer). Depending upon the adjustment of the set, the moving images may be the same on all screens, or different, as shown here.

Thus, Tambellini uses the electronic system to compose an abstract drama of swiftly changing light sensations accompanied by sound that is integral to the medium. Electronic energy, including what we usually consider "interference" or "distortion," is the material for an audiovisual kaleidoscope. Across the television "canvases" flicker myriad patterns, transitory images that vanish, like the notes of music, into time and memory.

Perception

"Sun City," 1965, by Bill Komodore (U.S., b. 1932). Acrylic on canvas. 72 x 64½". Courtesy The Howard Wise Gallery, New York.

The optical effects induced by "Sun City" throw us into a state of perceptual disorientation as soon as we look at the painting. So disturbing is the immediate impact that our first instinct is to look away, but if we continue to gaze at the work, we experience an expanding range of perceptual phenomena. Our eyes unfocus, swinging back and forth in the search for a center point or coherent structure, but our attempts to unify the field are frustrated. The surface begins to ripple and pulsate. The lines become charged with energy, shift, and produce a blinding glare; ephemeral images of color emerge and dissolve. If we look away, an afterimage glows before our eyes. Prolonged fixation on the painting makes the head swim!

All the dizzying, dazzling sensations we feel are illusory and depend upon our participation in the experiment set up by Komodore. The painting itself is composed merely of fixed, painted lines that move only in our eyes; only flat black and white exist where we perceive flickering color and light. The effects are not accidental, however; they are the result of careful planning. The artist has chosen precise, hard-edged lines as his subject and organized them in a pattern that allows no association with any scene or recognizable object. He also prevents us from making a sure interpretation of the pictorial space. The lines have no definite points of origin or termination within the visual field. Their dominant movement is from side to side, so the surface seems flat and two-dimensional, but diagonal movement bends it. In addition, Komodore confronts us with the ultimate in contrast—black and white. Distributed evenly over the surface, neither can dominate. The result is perceptual vacillation and illusory radiance.

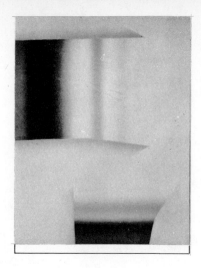

Color

"Stillness and Speed," 1968, by Louis Jaque (Canadian). Oil on canvas. 39½ x 32". Courtesy Spectrum Gallery, New York. Photo by Gabor Szilasi.

In "Stillness and Speed" such traditional devices as cast shadow, tone modulation, and color contrast create the initial impression of an originally flat shape cut from shiny sheet metal and then sprung to produce a sculptural form in low relief. However, what first appear as definitive clues to three-dimensionality give way to equally convincing evidence of flatness. We interpret the sharp-edged areas as being closer to us than the delicately toned "background" area, transferring to this situation the experience that objects that are near to us appear in sharper focus than those that are in the distance. In a similar way, we interpret the modulation of tone as defining three-dimensional form, the dark areas appearing closer than the light ones. Jaque has used these perceptual clues to establish the illusion of depth, while he simultaneously opposes them with highlights that merge into the background and edges that slip away.

Jaque poses a problem in sense experience quite different from that of Komodore's "Sun City" **(Perception 17)**. Here we can discern a figure—the cool, precise curves are strong and coherent forms. But their unrealizable three-dimensionality is a paradox that our perception cannot resolve. Instead of bombarding the eye with energy, "Stillness and Speed" draws its power from the subtle tension of ambiguity.

Trademark for Steel Properties, designed by Arnold Saks (U.S., b. 1931). Courtesy Arnold Saks, Inc., New York.

A trademark is a kind of visual shorthand, a modern heraldic symbol, the purpose of which is to identify. It must serve this purpose in the most direct and immediate way possible; if we have to stop and ponder it, it is useless. It must work when applied to products, packages, stationery, advertisements, and even architecture; it must be distinctive and legible whether it is reproduced a half-inch square or billboard size. Finally, a trademark is itself a form of advertisement. The better it expresses the identity of the owner, and the more visually compelling it is, the more effective it will be.

The emblem created for a construction company by Arnold Saks is an admirable example of graphic design. The actual figure consists of nothing more than four black chevron-like shapes on a white ground. It can be reproduced readily and in any size, and is instantly recognizable. Despite its stark simplicity, however, it is an image that demands further attention. It is optically active, because, like an Op artist, the designer has utilized the phenomena of perception to engage us in an exploration of what we see and how we see it. It is almost impossible to see this image as depicting two-dimensional shapes. We perceive it first as a set of cubes (an appropriate symbol for construction) represented in familiar perspective view. Each cube appears to have two black exterior faces and one white one—the mind supplies the lacking edges because it prefers a neat, complete figure. However, the arrangement of the shapes permits several completions, which now begin to emerge, contradicting the first. The white "faces" may appear open; the cubes vanish. The black may become negative, and a white cube appears in the center. No matter how long we look, the fluctuation goes on: the eye and the mind will never resolve their differences.

"Reverse & Obverse," 1962, by Josef Albers (U.S., b. 1888). India ink on paper. 23 x 14⅝". Courtesy Sidney Janis Gallery, New York. Photo by Eric Pollitzer.

The theme of "Reverse & Obverse" is the cube, which appears opened up as a cardboard carton might be opened, with flaps protruding in every direction. Albers has fashioned these two figures with precise ink lines, as though making a perspective drawing of planes in space. The lines define each construct completely, and at first glance the planes seem related in a rational manner. But when we examine each assemblage in its entirety, we find that it is physically impossible. No matter how we interpret the relationship of the parts, they cannot be reconciled spatially. Balked by this conflict, our perceptions shift back and forth.

The figures are visual mazes of wonderful complexity. Now one plane seems to advance, now another; at times they seem on the verge of dissolving into mere lines on a flat surface. We are never able to resolve the figures as wholly linear, however. In addition to using a number of heavy lines, which strongly suggest edges (and, therefore, forms that extend in three dimensions), Albers has carefully composed the figures of diagonal lines only. As in the Saks trademark **(Perception 19)**, we perceive them as receding—or advancing—in space, like traditional perspective lines. This interpretation is accentuated by the horizontal "horizon" and "ground" lines at top and bottom of the composition. These puzzling images created by Albers, which like the Saks trademark are capable of several meanings, are called "equivocal figures." Although unstable, they exist in dynamic equilibrium, and in "Reverse & Obverse," this illusive and elusive relationship works on two levels—not only within each figure, but between the two.

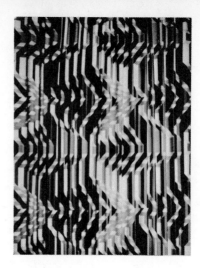

 Color

"Cross," 1968, by Anne Brody (U.S., b. 1932). Hooked wool.
7 x 7'. Tapestry commissioned by Gueron, Lepp and Associates,
Architects, for the Manhattan Rehabilitation Center, New York
State Narcotic Addiction Control Committee. Courtesy of the
artist. Photo by Malcolm Varon.

Designed as a wall hanging for an interdenominational chapel,
this tapestry is a striking and unusual example of optical art.
The pattern, based on geometric shapes arranged in strict
symmetry, produces an image with symbolic meaning, but our
immediate response to the work is purely perceptual—and this
is clearly the dominant concern of the artist. Like Komodore's
"Sun City" **(Perception 17)**, "Cross" virtually assaults the eye.

The pattern of the work is a progression that emanates from
the checkerboard at the crossing. The squares are altered
sequentially, becoming elongated either vertically or horizontally
as they move outward from the dynamic "target" area; each of
the rectangles along the major axes in turn generates a similar
progression. This orderly distortion has a kinetic effect. It
produces the illusion of movement into space (the smaller
shapes appear farther away) and across the surface (the shapes
between the arms of the cross seem to be drawn inward toward
the cross). But the artist's use of color is what really makes the
surface dazzling. While Komodore creates contrast by opposing
black and white, Anne Brody has chosen intense colors of equal
value. Not only are they opposites in terms of "warmth" and
"coolness," so that one tends to advance, the other recede;
they are also complementary colors. When complementaries are
placed side by side, each is heightened by contrast. Their
juxtaposition also affects the illusion of color afterimage, which
is the complementary of the color viewed. Thus, orange induces
a blue afterimage, blue an orange one. The result is the brilliant,
pulsating surface of this work.

 Color

"Extension," 1968, cotton print fabric, designed by Haydon
Williams. Courtesy Heal Fabrics, Ltd., London.

A painting need operate only in terms of a single, stable frame
of reference no matter where it is displayed. A fabric design, in
contrast, must be versatile enough to work in a variety of
situations that the designer is unable to foresee. Fabric design
is applied to a flat (or, in the case of textured materials,
relatively flat) surface, but seldom will it be seen this way. The
fabric may be cut into any number of shapes and sizes; curved,
so that the design is distorted; or draped, so that only certain
portions of it can be seen. For this reason, fabric designers
generally eschew patterns that suggest depth or create optical
illusions, since both depend on a carefully calculated arrangement of the elements. Disruption of the surface would simply
destroy the *trompe-l'oeil* effect of Harnett's painting, "Music
and Good Luck" **(Perception 14)** and the equivocal figures of
Albers' "Reverse & Obverse" **(Perception 20)**.

These examples notwithstanding, the fabric shown here is
successful both aesthetically and practically. Haydon Williams,
the designer of "Extension," has departed from tradition, going
out of his way to create a pattern that not only appears three-
dimensional but also is optically active. In doing so, he has
actually made the changing character of the fabric surface into
an advantage—a positive element of the design. When the fabric
is seen flat, the pattern consists of severely geometric shapes—
blocks of color and angled bands of color. The diagonals of the
design create the illusion of shallow space. As the fabric is
gathered into folds, the design elements are displaced and
compressed, and the bands appear to extend farther and farther
into space. Instead of destroying the pattern, the changing
depth factor evokes a lively sequence of three-dimensional
effects of color and form.

"80 Onward," 1968, by A. Richard DeNatale (U.S., b. 1925). Ruled lines and film. 8¾ x 8¾". Courtesy of the artist.

There are one hundred apertures in this composition; the eightieth, which should be an indentation on the right-hand side, is filled in. This almost unnoticeable variation in the pattern is a reference to the eightieth birthday of Josef Albers, the occasion for which DeNatale created the work. The number one hundred represents the designer's wishes for Albers' continued health and vitality.

The choice of design for "80 Onward" was an appropriate tribute to the artist who created "Reverse & Obverse" **(Perception 20)** and whose work is permeated by a concern with perception. The black field, with its regular pattern of white bars, is full of perceptual surprises. The relationship of figure and ground cannot be determined securely: the composition appears variously as a black figure in which openings have been cut or a black ground on which white figures have been superimposed. The treatment of the edges further complicates the interpretation, as the white bars merge into background and the black, in turn, becomes positive.

These observations are but preliminary impressions; further concentration reveals the workings of other perceptual phenomena, especially those effected by the strong contrast of black and white. The glowing afterimages of the white bars appear in the black area. The bars themselves seem to swell and enlarge, their light spilling over into the surrounding black— this illusion is called "irradiation." The black, too, becomes energized: at times we see, cutting horizontally between the white bars, a series of bands that seem darker than the remaining black background.

"Sky and Water," 1938, by Maurits Cornelis Escher (Dutch, b. 1898). Woodcut. 17¼ x 17¼". Courtesy Oldbourne Press, London.

"Sky and Water" is based on the simple illusion of equivocal figures, but Escher employs it in an extraordinary way. While Albers, in his "Reverse & Obverse" **(Perception 20)**, and Saks, in his trademark design **(Perception 19)**, use reversible abstract images, Escher uses reversible literal ones. He depicts a fantastic race in which, above the central horizon line, birds emerge from the negative shapes of fish as fish merge into the negative space of the white sky and gradually disappear; while below the horizon, the creatures of the air metamorphose and finally become one with the black water, the negative element in which the fish swim. On either side of the center the negative and positive of the two forms are equivalent, each determining and being determined by the other.

Accompanying the mysterious transformation of fish into birds and air into water is an evolution of the simple to the complex and the reverse, the uppermost bird and lowermost fish being most detailed. Similarly, an exchange of the balance between dark and light takes place in the lines that serve to frame the woodcut.

The concept behind Escher's composition is stunning—it is an analysis of the transaction between figure and ground, positive and negative, fish and fowl. The result carries us into an enchanted world where opposites correspond, exist independently, and are mutually dependent; it constitutes a conundrum that is visual, intellectual, and of the imagination.

Portfolio 8, Space

Space in Art

In the broadest sense, space is all around us, stretching to infinity. But although we tend to think of it as a void, negative and the opposite of mass, space is a positive visual element. It is not only an expanse that contains forms; it *has* form. Space and mass interact, and a change in one brings about a change in the other. Two-dimensional space is defined by length and width, or area; three-dimensional space by length, width, and depth, or volume. (Kinetic art, of course, also involves changes in space through time, the fourth dimension.)

When the sculptor shapes a block of wood or a lump of clay into an expressive form, he organizes and defines space—both the space surrounding the form and the space within it; the architect similarly deals with interior and exterior space. These artists are concerned with real space, space we can walk around or in or through. The painter and graphic artist, on the other hand, work on the flat surfaces of canvas or other materials—and they can create only the appearance of depth or volume. But this illusionary space is nonetheless visually real—and it can stretch to infinity, if the artist wishes. It is, in fact, virtually impossible to eliminate depth from two-dimensional art. Because we live in a three-dimensional world, we are accustomed to interpreting what we see in spatial terms, and we tend to attribute spatial qualities to images even when they are actually flat (consider how we interpret the space recorded by the photographer). Whether an artist works with real space or illusionary space is less important, therefore, than how he shapes it, for this is what expresses his purpose and moves us to respond to the work of art.

Space

Color

Salicin crystals, 1967, polarized light photomicrograph by Mortimer Abramowitz. Nikon EFM Microflex photomicrographic camera mounted on a Nikon S-Ke polarizing microscope. Kodachrome IIA film. Courtesy of the photographer.

Because we live in a three-dimensional world, we instinctively interpret what we see in terms of its relationship to the space in which it exists. We use such information as shape, direction, color, and relative size and position to determine if an object is near or far, standing still or in motion, deep or shallow (taking up a lot of space or a little). The same clues can create striking illusions of three-dimensionality even on a flat surface. The crystalline structure shown here, colored by polarized light and seen through a microscope, is only a few thousandths of an inch thick, yet the photomicrograph conveys a feeling of great depth: the rainbow-hued forms appear to extend into, move through, and be surrounded by limitless space.

The spatial quality of the photograph is produced by a variety of visual elements. For example, the juxtaposition of larger and smaller similar forms, many of which overlap, suggests that there are several planes or levels of space; in general, the larger forms appear to be in the foreground, the smaller ones farther away. In addition, diagonals dominate, implying that the forms are oriented obliquely—that is, they extend through more than one plane. The variation from brightly colored, sharp-edged shapes to ones that are muted in tone and soft-edged, as though in shadow, reinforces the impression of forms distributed in deep space. There are no points of spatial reference, such as base line or horizon, but only a featureless black background; this, and the apparent extension of shapes beyond the edges of the picture, suggest that the crystalline structure is set in infinite space.

Interior of Trans World Flight Center, John F. Kennedy Airport, New York, 1962, designed by Eero Saarinen (U.S., b. 1910, d. 1961). Courtesy Trans World Airlines, Inc. Photo by Ezra Stoller Associates.

Space is the medium of architecture: with wood, brick, concrete, and steel the architect defines and interprets space. While a beautiful building may strike us as sculpture on a large scale (since mass and space are also the materials of the sculptor), there is one essential difference. The primary consideration of the architect is *function*. Every building has a purpose—to provide shelter, work space, or be otherwise used—and unless that purpose is served, it is not successful architecture.

Saarinen's TWA airline terminal is a masterwork of architecture, a structure that is as functionally efficient as it is pleasing to look at and walk through. Mass and space are organized on a monumental scale: ten million pounds of concrete and one and a half million pounds of reinforcing steel were used in its construction, and the roof spans one and a quarter acres. These proportions were required to accommodate an unending stream of arriving and departing travelers. But instead of presenting the vast halls and familiar angular constructions of traditional architecture, the building's volume is articulated in sweeping, graceful curves. The lines of solid concrete structural elements—the arched shells of the roof, walls, supports, ramps, and stairways—flow uninterrupted, defining the interior in a series of continuous space lobes. Widening in the central hall (shown here), funneling into passageways, and curving gently to link different levels, the space provides travelers with a sense of direction. In addition, curving windows relate interior to exterior space; the building is pervaded with light and a feeling of spaciousness that is wholly appropriate to its space-age function.

 Color

"Spatial Metamorphosis," 1958, photograph by Herbert Matter (U.S., b. 1907). Courtesy of the artist.

The theme of this study in space is the Möbius band, a continuous surface that has only one side. (A simple Möbius band can be made by holding one end of a strip of paper, twisting the other end through 180°, and fastening it to the first end.) In his use of this phenomenon, the artist investigates the nature of space and our perception of dimension. The central device, itself a seeming contradiction in terms, actually is seen to define space. The one-sided plane has not only length and breadth but also depth; it resembles a three-dimensional G clef. Its three-dimensionality is emphasized by the stripes of color on its surface: as they increase and diminish in width, they indicate the advancing and receding of the form in space. Careful lighting, too, illuminates portions of its edge brightly and with sharp definition, while other portions are shadowy, appearing farther away.

Despite certain peculiarities apparently created by its convolutions in space, the form is convincingly three-dimensional. The background, in contrast, appears flat: in addition to the linear pattern drawn upon it, we can discern faint shadows cast by the construction. Unlike the black background in Abramowitz' photomicrograph of salicin crystals **(Space 1)**, here a flat surface limits depth. But the treatment of this surface adds an element of subtle ambiguity to what we see. In their striped, narrowing width and swirling shape, the linear figures echo the qualities of the three-dimensional construction with which they are visually interwoven.

 Color

CBS building, New York, 1965, designed by Eero Saarinen (U.S., b. 1910, d. 1961). Courtesy of Columbia Broadcasting System, Inc. Photo by Gene Cook.

In appearance, structure, and the interrelation of mass and space, this soaring tower could hardly be more different from the TWA airline terminal **(Space 2)** designed by the same architect. The terminal expresses and serves its purpose with open, free-form curves; the CBS building is severely rectilinear, possessing an elegance and dignity appropriate to one of the world's largest communications corporations.

Designed to house the main offices of CBS, this skyscraper packs 800,000 square feet of floor space into its 38 stories. The structure of the building is a direct and simple statement: a rectangular solid supported and defined by triangular granite piers that, in vertical lines uninterrupted by any cross-members, rise from the base in regular alternation with gray glass window panels. The result, however, belies the apparent simplicity. Ingeniously conceived, the shape and arrangement of the columns generate a visual effect that changes with the position of the viewer and the time of day. Thus, at one moment a passer-by will see granite alternating with glass, at another, the faces of the piers alive with light and shadow. At an oblique angle, this pattern of vertical textures compresses into a solid granite wall softened by the subtle shading of the stone: the permutations are innumerable. The full impact of this building can best be felt when it is experienced in relation to the surrounding space—the activity on the street, the textures of the buildings around it, and the narrow sheath of light and air through which it rises.

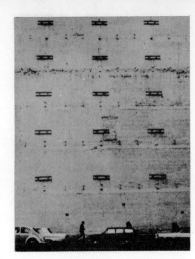

Space

⑤

"City Space," 1968, photograph by Sheldon Brody. The Reinhold Visuals Collection.

Space is constantly qualified by scale, which is a comparative measurement based on relationships of size. Scale has an important influence on our interpretation of and response to what we see, and "City Space" is an example of how the artist can use scale to create a particular effect. The photograph has been composed so that the human figures (and the automobiles, which are related in scale) are necessarily compared with a vast space defined by a seemingly endless wall. The immensity of this space reduces the human scale to insignificance. At the same time, the monotonous solidity of the wall, unrelieved by details (such as windows, doorways, or decoration) and extending beyond the edges of the visual field on three sides, engenders a sense of confinement—it constricts and presses down on the figures at the bottom of the picture.

Some of the ways in which the artist can manipulate scale to create widely different effects may be demonstrated by a simple experiment. If we cover the lower portion of the photograph so the figures cannot be seen, no basis for scale remains. Without the exaggerated discrepancy of size, the dimension of depth is lost, and the photograph becomes a study in surface and texture. If, on the other hand, we cover most of the wall, a completely new emphasis emerges. Now space is scaled to the human figures; an ordinary street scene, dominated by cars and passers-by, becomes the subject.

⑥ Color

"Love Generation," 1968, photograph by Burt L. Stern. Detail of painting by Robert Indiana. Photo courtesy of the photographer.

This unposed photograph provides a light-hearted illustration of some varied aspects of space. It is a straightforward record of actual space; although two-dimensional, the photograph represents the spatial situation clearly. The couple, standing in front of the painting, occupy a plane in the foreground. We seem to look over their shoulders into space, as we might see it through a window, and, in fact, their feet touch the bottom edge of the photograph as though it were the base line in a perspective rendering. The lines on the floor, also "in perspective," appear diagonal, indicating extension in space; they pass under and beyond the plane created by the partition on which the painting hangs and recede into the distance.

The painting itself occupies a plane just in front of the partition, as we infer from the shadow it casts. In addition, however, the painting presents us with another kind of space—pictorial space. Unlike traditional pictorial space, in which such devices as perspective create the illusion of three-dimensionality, the space in Indiana's painting is non-representational, ambiguous, and optical. At first glance it may seem flat, existing only on the one plane of the canvas surface, but we soon find that something is "going on" in the space of the painting. One letter tilts, others reverse into their mirror image, and the strong, contrasting colors vibrate, animating the relationship of figure and ground. The heroic-sized letters seem to push their presence into the museum space and interact with the viewers: the angular informality of the whole composition seems to echo the casual stance of the couple!

 Color

Ford Foundation building, New York, 1967, designed by Kevin Roche, John Dinkeloo and Associates, Architects. Courtesy The Ford Foundation. Photo by Ezra Stoller Associates.

The Ford Foundation building in New York City is the result of a singular spatial concept: instead of setting the architecture within the space of its immediate environment, the surrounding space has been incorporated within the architecture. One-third of the total space inside the structure is devoted to the immense courtyard garden shown here. Its size may better be comprehended when we know that it contains more than three dozen 30-foot-high trees, 999 kinds of shrubs, and a profusion of aquatic plants in a large pool (visible in the lower right-hand corner). The garden is completely enclosed. On two adjacent sides rise 12 stories of windowed offices; set backs carry the planting area above the multilevel main court. On the two remaining sides, glass walls separate the garden from the noise and weather of the city outside, and two more stories of offices roof the garden in.

The 12-story core of greenery and light is an environment completely controlled by air-conditioning and thermostatic heating, chemical fertilizers and automatic irrigation, which provide ideal conditions for both plant growth and human enjoyment. The building is remarkable, however, not for its use of twentieth-century technology to create a "perfect" environment, but for the humanistic concept underlying the exchange of so much premium urban space for space that cannot accommodate desks and filing cabinets. This design is functional because it brings the serenity of nature into the midst of business, the beauty of landscape to the routine of daily work, and the free space of the open air to the glass and steel of the city.

 Color

"Computer Numbers," 1962, photograph by Herbert Matter (U.S., b. 1907). Study for advertisement for Wyandotte Chemicals. Courtesy of the artist.

As in Robert Indiana's painting shown in **Space 6**, familiar symbols are the design elements in this composition. The numbers are arranged, like Indiana's letters, in a pattern that includes logical relationships (the numerical sequence of the small numbers) and arbitrary placement (the large numbers). But the overall pattern here does not have a specific meaning and literal value, as does the word "Love." The numbers serve, rather, as evocative images in an abstract dramatization of computer calculation, and the complex spatial nature of this mathematical process is reflected in the treatment of the numbers.

Matter's technique is more complex than Indiana's. Instead of placing the elements next to one another on a single surface, as the painter does, he has actually built up his pattern three-dimensionally, using layers of cut-out colored acetate. Although the final, printed design is flat, it presents a variety of spatial effects that are the result of the overlaying technique. Thus, the small numbers—lined up in rows suggesting the punched-out code system of computer cards—are formed by superimposing the cut-outs slightly off register. This creates an optical vibration that infuses the numbers with energy, translating the computer's electronic activity into visual form. The transparency of the acetate establishes different levels of depth as overlapping and color mixing occur. The interaction between these planes, involving shifts of size and shape as well as color and depth, is both subtle and intricate—reminding us of the computer process itself.

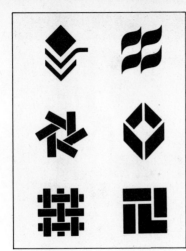

Space

Trademarks. Top, left: James S. Ward; right: Arnold Saks and James S. Ward. Center, left: Arnold Saks; right: Arnold Saks and James S. Ward. Bottom, left: Arnold Saks and James S. Ward; right: Arnold Saks. Courtesy Arnold Saks, Inc., New York.

A trademark must be unique and expressive of the owner's identity, yet it must also be simple enough to recognize at a glance. The design of a trademark might be compared to the writing of a haiku (a Japanese poem of three lines, with a set number of syllables per line)—both compress a great deal of meaning into a limited space, the haiku through word images, the trademark through visual images. Thus, in a trademark, every bit of space must be utilized, and the whole must be organized as economically as possible.

Each of the trademarks shown here is composed of a bare minimum of visual elements; in every symbol but one (top, left), the elements are identical, or derived from a single basic shape. But the results have variety and complexity, achieved through repetition, shifts of position, reversed and mirror images, or implied overlapping of the basic shapes. Equally important is another factor. We have taken the *black* areas to be the basic shapes—the figure, or positive space, in these designs; the white areas have been considered ground, or negative space. But if we look more carefully, we find that the white spaces are also active elements. In the symbol at center, left, a whirling form appears (this trademark was designed for a car-rental company); at bottom, right, the letters *TL* (Time-Life) emerge, and various different optical effects become evident in the other designs. Immediately legible, these trademarks are dynamic, provocative forms that also gain interest with prolonged viewing.

Color

"Ingenious Packaging," 1958, by Herbert Matter (U.S., b. 1907). Study for advertisement for Container Corporation of America. Courtesy of the artist.

Packaging is, in essence, the solving of spatial problems. Neatly and graphically expressing this theme, Matter's construction is indeed an "ingenious package." It presents a spatial problem in the form of a perceptual puzzle—the volume it defines is ambiguous, and it is virtually impossible to decide exactly how the elements are organized in space.

The geometric preciseness of this work is deceptive, rather than an aid to interpretation. The strongest elements of the design—the black bands—describe a two-dimensional, six-pointed star, but this figure also encloses space. Repeating the paradox, the white bands form a hexagon, but, as extensions of the black bands, further delimit space. Together, the black and white bands compose a three-dimensional frame that supports one sheet of transparent plexiglass and rests on (or encloses, at the base) another sheet. The floor, marked off in modular units that form a pattern of perspective cubes, adds ambiguity, serving both as ground and background to the construction. Finally, at the center of this puzzle is the most tantalizing element—the tricolor "contents" of the ingenious package. We perceive a cube, positioned in the center (or is it a corner?) of the space defined by the plexiglass and black and white frame. But this central element of the design is completely flat. It consists of flat colors, and the form that pushes its way into three-dimensionality is a pseudo-cube of the artist's contriving and our mistaken perception of space.

Color

"Diamond Light Floor," 1968, by Lila Katzen (U.S.). Construction of acrylic sheet and yellow and ultraviolet light. From a series of experimental environments presented by The Architectural League of New York. Photo by Robert A. Propper.

Lila Katzen's medium is environmental space—in this case an exhibition room, which is transformed not by altering its structure or dimensions, but by visually redefining its volume. On the floor of the room, over an array of yellow and ultraviolet fluorescent lights, the artist has placed a diamond-shaped, compartmented construction of clear acrylic sheets. From beneath its surface emanates the brilliant light that illuminates the environment both directly and by reflection from the mirrored walls and ceiling of the room.

The effect of combining these materials, transparent and reflective, with light is to dissolve the boundaries of the space enclosed by the room. The shallow acrylic construction on the floor assumes an illusionary depth, shimmering like the surface of a deep crystal pool; walls and ceiling disappear as the room, pervaded by light and color, is reflected to infinity. The familiar solidity of surfaces is replaced by an expanded, unlimited, continuous color-space that surrounds the viewer, delighting and confounding the senses with its ambiguity.

Color

"Personal Values," 1952, by René Magritte (Belgian, b. 1898, d. 1967). Oil on canvas. 31⅝ x 39½". Courtesy Jan-Albert Goris Collection, Brussels.

As we look into the space depicted in "Personal Values," we are confronted by paradox. No matter how intently we study this room and its contents, we will not be able to decide whether it is an ordinary-size room filled with some giant-size objects, or a miniature room in which objects of regular, everyday size appear gigantic. Is that an enormous comb on an ordinary bed, or an ordinary comb on a doll's house bed? Furthermore, is the room enclosed by four walls papered with highly imaginative wallpaper, or has it been transported, complete but without its walls, to the sky, which accommodatingly turns corners without the slightest effect on the clouds? Scale is purposely distorted; familiar relationships have gone haywire, and the inconsistencies cannot be reconciled.

Magritte establishes the spatial reality of the room and its furniture by a conventional use of perspective. Within this space, except for size, everything behaves in the expected way: forms are faithfully modeled by light and shade, the appropriate shadows are cast, glass is transparent, and mirrors reflect. It is the very regularity of the individual elements that baffles us, for just when we seem to have gotten things under control, illogic creeps in and frustrates our command. The essence of the painting is the creation of a convincing reality of space that is simultaneously denied. This is the world of fantasy and dreams, where reality is not subject to the laws of nature. We have been granted the ability to see what lies behind the surface appearance of things, to watch the enactment of an uncanny domestic drama—the small articles of someone's personal use expand and lead their own private lives while their owner is away.

Space

"Minu-Phone," 1967, by Martha Minujin (Argentinian, b. 1941). Electronically programmed construction. Ter Biorn, technician. Courtesy The Howard Wise Gallery, New York. Photo by Geoffrey Clements.

Step into this telephone booth, deposit a coin, and dial a number —the telephone really works. As you begin to speak, the colored lights that illuminate the booth begin to change, regulated by the timbre of your voice. Colored liquid contained in the glass "sandwiches" that form three sides of the booth slowly begins to rise, so that, from inside, the booth appears to be submerging. As you continue to talk, the opening minutes of your conversation are played back; meanwhile, currents of air blow, puffs of smoke appear, and, on a panel, a series of instructions light up. You are told to look down: your image appears on a television screen that forms the floor of the booth. When you hang up and step out of the booth, you will be presented with a photograph taken automatically—a souvenir of your fantastic phone call.

We enter, every day, a series of diverse spatial "packages" such as telephone booths, cars, houses. Each of these environments is organized to serve a function (communication, transportation, shelter), and we therefore *use* them rather than *respond* to them. Environmental art such as Lila Katzen's "Diamond Light Floor" **(Space 11)** makes us aware of the space around us by transforming it aesthetically, but it removes us from ordinary experience. Minujin, in contrast, invites us to participate in a startling, amusing, even baffling encounter with our environment. We enter a familiar spatial situation to find ourselves bombarded with unexpected and unique events that force us to respond, to re-examine our ideas about what everyday experience is and what it can be.

"Mirrored Room," 1967, by Lucas Samaras (U.S., b. 1936). Environmental construction. 8 x 10 x 8'. Courtesy Albright-Knox Art Gallery, Buffalo; gift of Seymour H. Knox. Photo by Malcolm Hart (Frank Cowan Studio). Courtesy The Pace Gallery, New York.

Infinite space is a concept beyond ordinary comprehension. We are accustomed to dealing with areas and volumes that can be measured or that we can relate to in familiar terms, such as scale. Without these points of reference, space becomes abstract—we cannot imagine what it looks like. Thus, we cannot depict infinity; we can only attempt to represent it by means of symbols or other artistic devices. The repeated mirror image is one of the most fascinating of them.

The room constructed by Samaras measures eight feet wide, ten feet long, and eight feet high. When this photograph was taken, the mirror-lined cubicle contained a girl, the photographer and his equipment and lights, and a mirror-topped table; through an open door, spectators were looking in. Yet the room is transformed by reflection into a magical, mysterious space filled with people and lights that seem to go on beyond what we can see or count or measure. There is an air of unreality about this space. We cannot determine which are the "real" figures, which reflections, and which reflections of reflections. (Try turning the picture upside down: the mystery only increases.) No matter where we look, the dazzling surround seems just out of reach. The ordinary clues by which we orient ourselves are jumbled, bombarding us from every conceivable point, and drawing us deeper and deeper into the paradoxical distance.

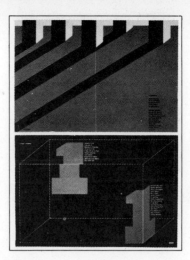

"Endless Variation #1," 1967-68, by Arman (French, b. 1928). Lacquered wood. 24 x 24 x 24" (main cube). Courtesy The Sidney Janis Gallery, New York. Photo by Frank J. Thomas.

The cube possesses particular fascination for artists concerned with the potentialities of three-dimensional space, perhaps because it is the most basic volumetric form (we even measure volume in "cubic" terms). To use the cube is, in a sense, to deal directly with three-dimensional space. "Endless Variation #1" is a lacquered wood cube with four sides composed of a series of diminishing squares. Each of the squares is hinged to the preceding one; thus, a total of 16 units can be opened and extended inward and outward from the largest squares that form the main framework.

When closed up, as in the top picture, Arman's cube appears solid, revealing nothing of its inner structure. But the moment we move a single element, we not only discover the cube's interior space—we simultaneously rearrange it by injecting a plane, and by linking it to the space outside. One change provokes another, and, until we close this "Chinese puzzle" up again, we are involved in creating new and increasingly complex spatial relationships. Without changing the length, width, or height of the component squares, we nevertheless change the dimensions of the space they define. We can organize and re-organize the space endlessly, telescoping it within and extending it beyond the original boundaries of the cube. Recession is suggested by the repetition of squares within squares and accentuated by the play of light and shadow on the angled planes, producing a sense of labyrinthine depth.

Color

Posters for The Visual Arts Gallery, New York, 1965 and 1968, designed by Milton Glaser (U.S., b. 1929). Courtesy of the artist.

Both of these posters are based on optical effects achieved by manipulating three-dimensional figures on a two-dimensional surface, but each one has a distinct identity expressive of the particular exhibition for which it was designed. In the top poster, for five sculptors, Glaser uses five pillar-like forms. Composed of angular, hard-edged planes, they nevertheless have a strong three-dimensional quality, reflecting the sculptor's concern with volume. The feeling of mass is created by the contrast of black and white shapes that define two "sides" of the pillars and the long black "shadows" cast diagonally across the poster. This abstract indication of solid forms seen in perspective is convincing—but Glaser injects a note of ambiguity. The diagonal lines of the shadows are parallel to each other instead of converging, as the rules of perspective demand, and the result is a spatial puzzle that makes the poster visually intriguing.

In the second poster, emphasis is placed on the space within a three-dimensional form rather than on its mass, and by defining it with lines instead of planes, Glaser allows us to see into and though it. This, however, makes it possible to interpret the form as a box seen from the top or the bottom; further ambiguity is created by the device of parallel diagonals. While the large numerals at first seem to clarify the volume—one by wrapping around a corner, the other by appearing to be half on the "near" side and half on the "far" side of the box—they actually create contradictions. To be spatially consistent, the type on the right should be angled, and the whole number on the far plane should be visible. In denying us resolution of the volume, the poster reminds us that the painter and printmaker deal in illusion, for they depict spatial form on a flat surface.

Space

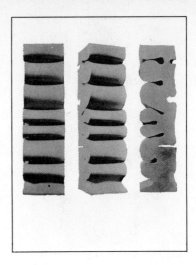

"Playground Space," 1968, photograph by Sheldon Brody. Detail of playground, New York City, designed by Charles Forberg. The Reinhold Visuals Collection.

A playground is often merely a certain space delimited by a fence or some other barrier and designated "playground"—nothing but the barrier, and perhaps a row of swings and a few benches, distinguish it from its surroundings. Such space cannot be said to have been designed at all, much less designed for the purpose of play. The playground designer must shape an environment, as the architect does, to serve a particular function. The space in a playground is usually linked more closely to the landscape than the space in a building, since it is not separated from the out-of-doors by walls and a roof, but it does have boundaries (of height as well as area), and it is arranged as purposefully.

This playground, of which we see only a portion, is composed of elements that both define and subdivide its space. These elements—concrete slabs, masonry, walls—form an environment that provides opportunity as well as encouragement for creative activity. The components are all simple in themselves, but there is sufficient variety to invite exploration and experimentation. There are places to hide behind, squeeze between, climb over, jump through, run along, ride around, and sit on. There are surfaces, shapes, and patterns to look at and touch. Everything is set within a gently inward-sloping circle, obviating the need for a barrier (there is more to do "inside"), and everything is proportioned to the child—the walls are low enough to see over; the concrete slabs are tall but not towering, and the top of the highest structure in the playground (from which this photograph was taken) provides a not-too-high vantage point for surveying the space as a whole.

"Soundless Symphony," 1968, by Minoru Niizuma (Japanese, b. 1930). Canvas over wood. 8' x 24" x 26". Courtesy The Howard Wise Gallery, New York. Photo courtesy of the artist.

Painting can be viewed only from one direction—the front—and its depth can be explored only visually. Free-standing sculpture, extending through three dimensions, almost demands that we move around it, not only to understand its volume but also to experience the full range of mass-space relationships that it presents.

From one point of view (left), "Soundless Symphony" shows us a solid, deep-rippling surface that flows with a varied but even rhythm. As the title of the work implies, this undulating mass moves through space as music moves through time. Another aspect of the sculpture is revealed in the second view—the confines of its curving mass. It gives the impression of pushing its way through space with an inner energy, as though its folds had been produced by the compression of a tall, pliant form that threatens to spring back to its full height. The third view is both a contrast to and completion of the others. Instead of the soft modulation of light and shadow on flowing curves, we see the even illumination of a plane. Its contours echo the curves, and its sharp-edged flatness suggests that their movement has been frozen; mass and space are balanced in dynamic tension.

Space

 19

Sketch for poster announcing concert of Dionne Warwick, 1966, by Milton Glaser (U.S., b. 1929). India ink on paper. Courtesy Push Pin Studios, Inc.

We see, in the work of many artists, how three-dimensional space may be represented convincingly on a flat surface by the use of such devices as overlapping, modulation of light and shadow, and perspective: Magritte, for example, depicts space quite realistically in his painting "Personal Values" **(Space 12).** In this design for a poster, in contrast, Milton Glaser eliminates completely or almost completely every familiar spatial clue and limits himself to the basic elements of line and plane, black and white. He defines the figure of the singer primarily by tracing its outline, reducing detail to a minimum. Form is suggested schematically, rather than molded, by the curvature of the lines and abstract black shapes that indicate its main contours. Echoing the figure, in flat silhouette, are the stark shadows that rise on either side; projected diagonally from its base and angled suddenly at the horizon line, they push the figure slightly forward. But for this, there is little in the pattern of black and white to indicate depth at all.

The result of this flat design, however, is a spectacular graphic image, which puts across the poster's meaning with dramatic directness. Instead of rendering the outward appearance of the singer's presence on stage, Glaser captures the feeling—the electrifying atmosphere—of the theater. Without the need for words, easily grasped from a distance, this poster unmistakably conveys the unreal quality of stage space in which background disappears and form is flattened by the harsh glare of spotlights, and all attention centers on the dazzling sound and personality of a great performer.

20 Color

"The Three Younger Sons of Shah Jahan Riding Together," Indian, Mughal school, ca. 1635. Watercolor on paper. 6¼ x 4½". Courtesy The Victoria & Albert Museum, London. Photo Crown copyright.

Depicting three-dimensional space in a realistic way was of little importance to the artist who painted this scene; his primary interest, as we can see at a glance, was to portray three royal personages, sons of Shah Jahan, the great ruler who built the Taj Mahal. But the painter nevertheless possessed an exact understanding of the means of representing space on the flat page, and he used them or eschewed them with skillful purpose. Thus, the distant landscape is rendered in perfect aerial perspective (through which far-away objects become hazy and soft in color). The expanse of the center ground is treated summarily, however, providing a neutral backdrop to the figures; the tree, while more detailed, is delicately pale and does not distract attention from the horsemen.

In the foreground, the color is intense, and close attention is given to the most minute details: every leaf and petal along the riders' path and, especially, the elaborate and decorative patterns of the horses' trappings and princely accoutrements. At the same time, however, the conventions of space are overturned. The spatial relationship of the figures and their mounts is described by emphatic overlapping, each pair occupying a different plane. But the ground does not recede at the same rate (it would take up too much room); as a result, the horses seem to prance incredibly in the air. More remarkable is the reversal of the expected decrease in size with increasing distance. The spatial relationship of the figures has been subordinated to their social relationship. The largest is the most important; the smallest, the least, and the artist has expressed this by direct pictorial means.

Space

"Japanese Wrestler," 1958, photograph by Sheldon Brody. The Reinhold Visuals Collection.

In contrast to the painter, who may work entirely from imagination, the photographer can record with his camera only things that actually exist. Within this limitation, however, his work is fully as expressive as the artist's, for like the artist he controls the elements of his composition and uses them to interpret ideas and feelings. Brody's treatment of his subject matter here is straightforward and literal rather than impressionistic, as it is in "Christmas Window" **(Space 23)**, but this is not a casual snapshot. It has been composed with care—not by posing the wrestler or arranging the objects around him, but by creating a spatial framework that gives all the elements meaning and coherence.

The mood of the scene is calm and tranquil: we seem to have caught the wrestler in a rare moment of unself-conscious relaxation. Although the figure is the most important element in the picture, it is not centered in the space, but set off to one side and partly covered by the strong shape of the parasol. On the other side, a wood post and bundles strewn on the platform claim attention, as does the rope ring on which the wrestler seems to rest his eyes. Everything is in equilibrium—the figure is balanced by the upright, the parasol by the ring. The foreground space is balanced by the background space—the edge of the platform forms a central plane (in which the wrestler is positioned), dividing the photograph horizontally. But while there are no intense contrasts, no drama, to disturb the tranquility of the scene, there is underlying energy. The camera, subtly angled, causes the central plane to slant gently, creating movement into depth.

"Black Zero," 1965, by Aldo Tambellini (U.S., b. 1930). Calo Scott, cellist, in multimedia theater production; graphics by Aaron Rose. Photo by George Ehrlich, courtesy of Aldo Tambellini.

Theatrical or stage space is a special kind of space, one that changes with every performance and production that takes place in it. From the passive emptiness of the deserted theater, it is transformed by light, sound, scenery, actors, and action into a kinetic environment that is, for the moment, any place and any time. Traditionally, theatrical space is designed to create an illusion—of a landscape, a street, a room. We are all familiar with the box set in which a fourth "wall" is missing, enabling us to see in. Many painters have used the same convention to depict space on a two-dimensional surface: Magritte's "Personal Values" **(Space 12)** is an example.

Tambellini uses the stage in a way that has nothing in common with the illusionary box set, although illusion is a major part of his mixed media production. The chief visual elements of "Black Zero" are light projections—abstract black and white shapes and patterns that offer us a new spatial experience. While an array of screens serves as a background, its function is not to enclose space: the lights that play over it and spill onto the walls and ceiling dissolve the solidity of these surfaces and produce changing illusions of depth. Space is expanded and indefinable; the location and substantiality of forms in it are ambiguous. The cellist, silhouetted, could be in front of, or behind, or projected on the screens. A balloon, inflating to enormous size and deflating with a hiss, becomes inseparable from projected polka dots. Spatially disoriented, bombarded by changing images and sounds, the audience does not look in at, but becomes a part of, the phantasmagorical drama.

Color

"Christmas Window," 1966, photograph by Sheldon Brody. The Reinhold Visuals Collection.

At the other end of the spectrum from Tambellini's black and white, sense-bombarding, abstract production, "Black Zero" **(Space 22)**, is this pastel impression of Christmas in the city, but "Christmas Window" is equally theatrical. Space here is illusionary, but with a very different purpose and effect. Instead of drawing us into mysterious depths created by light and shadow, Brody's picture merges near and far into one hazy, shimmering vision. Under the soft focus of the camera (created by placing a sheet of glass with a thin coat of vaseline in front of the lens), the well-defined space of a store window and the objects displayed in it appear broken down into their component light and color, like the trees in Monet's impressionist painting, "The Poplars" **(Color 3)**.

The space of the window, transformed into a fairyland scene of insubstantial images, presents all the familiar symbols of the season: the tree decked with tinsel and starry lights, glittering ornaments, angels, and other figurines. But while the picture has a Christmas-card quality, the photographer has not conceived of it merely as a reminiscence of childhood feelings. With a combination of sentiment and sophistication, he has caught in the window the reflection of towering buildings, and in the photograph he blends the cityscape into the decoration, the decoration into the cityscape, misting over both with the warmth and magic of the season.

Color

"Sky 1," 1967, by Joe Tilson (British, b. 1928). Screen print with vacuum-formed and vacuum-metallized objects. 49 x 27" Courtesy Marlborough Graphics Gallery, New York. Photo by Malcolm Varon.

"Sky 1" is composed of spatial incongruities. Against the background of a night sky in which stars stretch, seemingly, to infinity, looms an enormous envelope that is made minuscule, in turn, by a giant thumb. Whatever the size of the envelope, however, the space it denotes is insignificant compared to the sky. But dotted lines suggest a paper cut-out; moreover, it extends past the sky at the top. Envelope and sky, we must conclude, are equally flat. Another contradiction appears: the stars fade out, creating the illusion of recession into space, as though they formed a roof over the great metropolis below. With the New York skyline, however, the artist changes his frame of reference again—and yet again, in the view that is reproduced in photographic detail, upside down and postcard size, on the envelope. Finally, at the bottom of the composition, we find a handful of tiny metal trinkets. The only really three-dimensional objects used, they assume disproportionate reality and dwarf the city behind.

The actual spatial identities of all the images in "Sky 1" have been altered drastically by one or another means, so that our concepts of two- and three-dimensionality lose meaning. The most extraordinary spaces become inconsequential, and vice versa. The shrinking of the heavens by such objects as an airmail envelope and an airplane, among other hints, might well be interpreted as a comment on man's conquest of space. But whatever our interpretation of Tilson's paradoxical work—and many are possible—one clue seems clear. In writing "Envelope Here" and "Spanner," with pointers, on the sky, Tilson affairms that their placement is an artistic act, and he shows us that the artist's exploration of space is poetry, untrammeled by objective reality.

Portfolio 9, Light

Light

Without light there can be no form, no images, no visual reality. Whether a subject is fixed instantaneously on photographic film, or painstakingly modeled in paint, light is the element that establishes its physical and visual identity. This is true for any period, technique, or style. And, no matter what the medium, the artist's use of light largely determines whether his work is dramatic or subtle, straightforward or elusive.

In two-dimensional work, the portrayal of light and shadow gives the impression of mass, it suggests the quality and diversity of surfaces. In three-dimensional work, the nature of the material itself—how its surfaces reflect or absorb light, how the shadows are cast—gives definition, and establishes the essential character of the work.

Besides its physical importance, light has long been a means of evoking psychic and spiritual meanings. Light sets the mood; it is hard to imagine the portrayal of certain moods—the uncanny, the miraculous, the eerie, the contemplative—without special light treatments. And light is often used as a sign or symbol, to convey specific meanings to the viewer.

At times, artists have concentrated on using light in their work: the Impressionists, for example, were intent on the physical qualities of light; the Surrealists chose imaginative uses of light to establish the dreamlike quality of their themes. Today, in the electronic age, light has achieved new significance: in place of the painter's canvas there may be a television or movie screen, in place of the brushstroke, a light-charged neon tube.

Light

Color

"Domain of Lights," 1953–4, by René Magritte (Belgian, b. 1898, d. 1967). Oil on canvas. 76¾ x 51½". The Peggy Guggenheim Foundation, Venice, Italy.

The illogic of representing night and day simultaneously within the same painting is so effectively resolved by Magritte that we are at first unaware of the incongruity. It is only after the first look at "Domain of Lights" that we see the contradiction.

Magritte's artistic legerdemain works because he treats the elements of light in his composition in a perfectly straightforward manner. There is no conflict within each component: the daytime sky is as bland as a picture-postcard snapshot, and the glow of the windows and street lamp at night are just as matter-of-fact. The juxtaposition is arresting, however. The scene, with its various and contradictory sources of illumination—natural light and artificial light, interior light and exterior light, daylight and night light—becomes mysterious and provocative. The boulder in the foreground, the shuttered windows and blank walls, the dark woods suddenly all loom a little sinister.

As in his "The Castle of the Pyrenees" **(Mass 11)** and "The Pleasure Principle" **(Light 16),** Magritte leads us into fantasy through the presentation of the impossible as ordinary. Here light serves as the means by which the artist transports the imagination. Light—not logic—rules the painting; hence the title. Magritte painted eight other versions of this scene: in all of them, light is the central image and the departure point for fantasy.

Color

"Young Woman with a Water Jug," date not known, by Johanes Vermeer (Dutch, b. 1632, d. 1675). Oil on canvas. 18 x 16". The Metropolitan Museum of Art, Gift of Henry G. Marquand, 1889. Photo by Malcolm Varon.

Light, not the young woman with the water jug, is the real subject of this painting. Vermeer's light is natural light—the soft sunlight that comes in at the window. It infuses his canvas, animating colors and textures and giving form to objects.

In terms of light, Vermeer assigns equal importance to each object in the painting. He explores with the same level of interest how light and shadow define the delicate folds and creases of the woman's coif; the soft contours of her face and head; the rounded flesh of her forearms; the hard, shiny, reflecting surfaces of the jug and bowl; the heavy folds and rich patterning of the Oriental table-covering; the finial of the chair; the corner of the room, and even the blue cloth on the chair. How characteristic it is that Vermeer devotes such attention to the way light and shadow define the draping of this blue cloth, an object we cannot identify! Is it a cloak or a coverlet or what?

It is primarily through light and shadow that we perceive physical volume, and Vermeer uses this form-defining quality of light to create the illusion of space in his painting. It is with light that he establishes the identity of each object as volume, each with its own unique attributes: rough, smooth, transparent, opaque, hard, soft, solid, yielding.

Color

"Magic Glasses," date not known, by Edwin Romanzo Elmer (U.S., b. 1850, d. 1923). Oil on canvas. 14 x 10½". The Shelburne Museum, Shelburne, Vermont.

So important is light in visual perception that artists who are adept in the use of shadows and highlights can fool us into taking the representation of a thing for the real thing, as Harnett does in "Music and Good Luck" **(Perception 14).** There *trompe l'oeil* serves to heighten our perception of the painted objects. Here, in contrast, the artist is only secondarily interested in the objects he depicts. Elmer's main interest is in the reflections, which he paints in loving and meticulous detail. Many artists utilize this property of light—for example, the contemporary artists Pistoletto in "Standing Man" **(Perception 11)** and Estes in "Grossinger's" **(Light 4)**, as well as many fifteenth-century Dutch and Flemish painters who delighted in scenes reflected in drinking glasses, crystal gloves, mirrors, and other shiny surfaces. But Elmer's painting is unique in its concentration.

"Magic Glasses" offers a multiplicity of reflections. Most intriguing is the phenomenon of the landscape reconstituted on the lens of the magnifying glass, with its inverted image reflected from the other surface of the lens. This image transmission by means of light rays is indeed "magic."

Glass is a challenging subject for the artist, since it is transparent; were it not for reflected light we would not be able to see it at all! Yet Elmer has been able not only to create convincingly an image that exists entirely *outside* the painting, but to show us several different layers of a transparent substance: the magnifying glass rests in the mouth of a glass vase (note the details of its form), and the landscape is seen through window panes.

"Grossinger's," 1972, by Richard Estes (U.S., b. 1936). Oil on canvas. Approx. 50 x 30". Collection Mr. Robert P. Kogod. Courtesy The Allan Stone Gallery, New York. Photo by Eric Pollitzer.

Light, falling on sensitized film, produces the image in photography (the word *photography* literally means "light-writing"). It is not surprising that this oil painting bears a striking resemblance to a photograph because Estes, a "photo-realist," paints from photographs rather than from life or fantasy. The result, as this black-and-white reproduction shows, is an image depicted wholly in terms of the amount of light reflected from its component parts.

It is fascinating to compare this painting with Elmer's "Magic Glasses" **(Light 3).** Both painters are absorbed with the theme of reflections in glass—the re-creation of images by reflection, reflections within reflections, double reflections. Yet "Magic Glasses" possesses an element of fantasy that is not present here. Despite Elmer's *trompe l'oeil* technique, his painting emphatically remains a painting. It reveals the imagination of the painter although it seems to be based on scientific observation. Estes's work, on the other hand, can momentarily be taken for the carefully composed photograph on which it is based; it has a stark, cold, crisp remoteness. Only momentarily, however, can we take "Grossinger's" for a photograph, since a close look discloses that it is far from being just a good copy of a photograph. The painter has interpreted the scene in terms of powerful areas of light and dark held together by dynamic diagonals. Some forms have been reduced to essentials (the trays of baked goods, the sidewalk and masonry), while others are depicted with photographic precision (the reflected buildings). The overall result is a surprisingly abstract yet classically structured composition.

Light

Color

Two untitled pieces, 1972, by Larry Bell (U.S., b. 1939). Vacuum-plated glass. *Left:* three panels, each 96 x 72 x ⅜"; *right:* two panels, each 84 x 48 x ¼". Courtesy The Pace Gallery, New York. Photo by Albert L. Mozell.

These two light-capturing environments, shown in gallery installation, consist of sheets of glass arranged at right angles so as to create a complex space through and around which the viewer can walk. Each glass wall has been treated so that it changes imperceptibly from complete transparency to translucent, smoky cloudiness to mirror opacity. The placement of the panels, interacting with the light in and around the gallery, creates a complex of shimmering surfaces, glossy reflections, light distortions, and other optical effects. At one moment the environment may seem to be a large glass box, but if the viewer changes his position even slightly, he experiences a completely new set of sensations. He may see figures and objects either through a transparent wall, reflected and re-reflected, or distorted as in a fun-house mirror; the same subjects may disappear before his eyes as in a cinematic dissolve, or he may suddenly confront his own mirrored image.

With these pieces, it is impossible to maintain the physical neutrality permitted by traditional works of art—a painting hung on the wall, or even a sculpture on a pedestal. Here the viewer is a participant, constantly made aware of himself as part of the environment and in relation to the work. The artist has set up a laboratory in which light, activated by the viewer, is the agent of change and the source of experience.

"Second Hand," January, 1971, by Vito Acconci (U.S., b. 1940). Live performance, one hour. Photos by Shunk-Kender. Courtesy The Sonnabend Gallery, Inc., New York.

Acconci's work is so ephemeral that we know it mainly through the medium of photographic documentation. Like other "conceptual" artists, he is concerned not primarily with the production of an artifact but with an idea or an interpretation of life and its processes.

These four photographs record four moments in an hour-long performance. It consisted of Acconci walking slowly around a suspended 1,000-watt light bulb while he concentrated on the movement of the hands of the clock, so that in following it he "became" part of the clock itself.

Acconci's work is often referred to as Body Art because it is concerned with the relationship of his body to a given environment, or the reaction of his body to events and stimuli. In "Second Hand," he deliberately isolated and explored the interrelationship of three elements—the artist, the clock (time), and the light bulb (light). Thus, in a literal way, light played a leading role in the event. Light heightened, if it did not create, the dramatic impact of the performance. This is evident in the photographs, which record the movement of the artist's shadow on the walls of the stark alcove in which the performance took place, and it is notable in the artist's verbal expression of what is happening: ". . . my shadow is on the wall (I've entered the surroundings)—my circle moves me into my shadow (I'm going into myself) . . ."

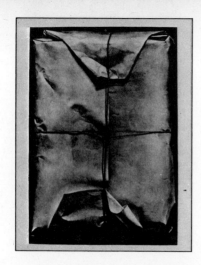

"Untitled," 1967, by Claudio Bravo (Chilean, b. 1936). Chalk, brush, pen and ink, pencil. 29½ x 43⅜". Collection, The Museum of Modern Art, New York. Inter-American Fund. © 1975, The Museum of Modern Art, New York.

Light is the primary visual indicator of volume in art as in the real world around us; that is, we generally perceive the mass of an object by interpreting the way light models its surface. Like Estes's painting "Grossinger's" **(Light 4)**, this drawing depends completely upon the artist's rendering of shadows, highlights, and the range of tones between them for the astonishing realism it achieves. In his minutely detailed observation of the way light acts on a particular subject, Bravo's eye resembles the lens of a camera.

Bravo employs the traditional illusionistic means of rendering a three-dimensional object on a flat surface, but his subject matter is unconventional: a banal paper parcel. The parcel fills the picture. It has no background, no context; it is not part of a "story." The associations we may bring to the image are our own affair; the artist has merely presented it, without comment or explanation. Yet he has rendered every fold and crumple of the paper, every twist of the fibrous twine, with meticulous care. He has expressed the texture and mass of the parcel. If we compare Bravo's parcel with the head-dress in Vermeer's "Young Woman with a Water Jug" **(Light 2)**, we find that the interest of the contemporary artist is not so different from that of the seventeenth-century painter. Both works are essays in light modulation; it is in point of view that they differ!

Color

"Repetition XIV," 1969–70, by Robert Bidner (U.S., b. 1930). Serigraph. 34 x 24". Courtesy The Barney Weinger Gallery, New York. Photo by Albert L. Mozell.

The shapes that make up the figure in this silk-screen print are not modeled by light and shadow—they consist, rather, of solid areas of flat color—yet the image evokes a remarkable sense of depth. We perceive the figure as a series of rectangular planes placed, with space between them, in four neat stacks in space. We seem to be looking down at them at a slight angle. It is very difficult, in fact, to see the figure two-dimensionally, as four parallelograms and a series of visually implied but not actually completed parallelograms.

Bidner creates the impression of depth by taking advantage of our tendency to interpret visual stimuli in a meaningful way. Overlapping, for instance, implies an arrangement in space. Similarly, the progression from light to dark implies extent in space. So strong is our tendency to interpret visual clues logically that even if the progression from light to dark proceeds in steps as it does here and is not continuous (as light modulation actually is), we still perceive the change as spatial. Thus, by making the top parallelograms bright yellow and each remaining shape in each stack darker than the one above, the artist leads us to conclude that the yellow ones are "closer" than the dark violet. If we turn the print upside down, we perceive quite a different spatial arrangement! The perceptual clues have been reversed, and so, therefore, is our perception.

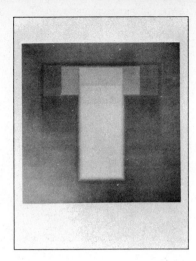

Light

Color

"Color Sound II, or Homage to the Square No. 3," 1972, by Karl Gerstner (Swiss, b. 1930). One of a series of eight serigraphs. 31½ x 31½". Published by Editions Denise René/Hans Meyer, Düsseldorf, Germany. Courtesy Galerie Denise René, New York. Photo by Geoffrey H. Clements.

Like many twentieth-century artists, Karl Gerstner dispenses with subject matter in the traditional sense in order to experiment directly with color and light. He uses these inseparably related elements for the optical sensations they can evoke, rather than symbolically or to explore form. In this he may be compared to Josef Albers, whose "White Line Squares" **(Color 16)** are also a study of light.

We must know something about the physics of light to analyze "Color Sound II" although not to experience its effect. The artist has composed planes of two colors that are at opposite ends of the visible spectrum: red-orange, with a long wavelength and low frequency, and violet, with a short wavelength and high frequency. The contrast of the hues and gradations of value (the amount of light in the hue) are minimal but carefully calculated, and the juxtaposition creates remarkable optical sensations. The print appears to glow with light; it is almost incandescent.

The overlapping planes of color create a feeling of depth, as in Bidner's "Repetition XIV" **(Light 8)**, but the T-shaped arrangement of these implied squares is visually ambiguous, and our perception of the space shifts if we look at the composition steadily. The color planes seem to vibrate, as a result of this shifting, and the combination of glowing colors and their vibration produces a "color sound" that is the visual counterpart of the buzz of neon or fluorescent light.

Color

"Glass Door Knob," 1971, by Bruce Everett (U.S., b. 1942). Oil on canvas. 74 x 57". Courtesy O.K. Harris Works of Art, New York. Photo by Eric Pollitzer.

The meeting of hardware-store crystal and light is, in this six-foot-high painting, no ordinary sight. Because of the painter's handling of light, which infuses each glass facet with pulse and energy, transparency becomes something tangible, so that a commonplace doorknob is transformed into an optically charged object. All the slopes and planes of its interior are illuminated.

If Everett's purpose, however, were merely to describe meanders and sparkles of light, he would have eliminated all else, as in the photograph of cut glass **(Surface 8)**. Instead, he shows us the drab solidity of the door's hardware, a bland background, even a shadow—all deliberate reminders of the banality of the subject. Deliberate, too, is the painter's treatment: Everett analyzes the paths of light and, although he is selective in what he reveals, he never tampers with the physical appearance of the fixture itself. Everett's doorknob is not luminescent, it does not glow. By remaining a careful observer and by a subtle and evocative use of light, Everett is able to present an altogether humdrum object and, at the same time, a visual experience worthy of a much grander subject.

Color

"Rouen Cathedral," 1894, by Claude Monet (French, b. 1840, d. 1926). Oil on canvas. 39¼ x 25⅞". The Metropolitan Museum of Art. The Theodore M. Davis Collection. Bequest of Theodore M. Davis, 1915.

While "Domain of Lights" **(Light 1)** is a synthesis of different times of day, this study of the cathedral at Rouen is about one time of day, one set of atmospheric conditions, one specific and transitory kind of light, and the visual sensation of this light upon the stone. Light is not used here to define form, as in Vermeer's painting **(Light 2)** or even in Bravo's painted parcel **(Light 7)**. Structural form is subservient to surface impressions, and Gothic architecture bows to the artist's analysis of the effects of sunlight on an intensely complex and variegated surface.

Monet made a methodical and systematic study of the cathedral under varying light conditions. He worked on this series of some forty paintings over a period of years, both in a room at Rouen and then back in his Paris studio. Yet each painting conveys a sense of visual immediacy, as if the artist rushed to finish his canvas before light, shadow, and color glints changed. By using broken color, Monet achieved this remarkable luminosity, perhaps enhanced here because the subject has almost no context—a portion of the cathedral fills nearly the entire picture plane—and a limited range of tones provides for all the color richness.

Variations of color within the sunlit areas of stone are extremely subtle. There, the pasty application of paint has a texture of its own, a heaviness appropriate to the subject. The areas in shadow are another story; the paint strokes are short and free, and the bold violets, corals, and blues against the creams and the bright yellow door are testimony to Monet's genius in analyzing sensations of light and color.

Entrance Passageway, 127 John Street, New York City, 1971. Owner-builder: William Kaufman Organization; architect: Emery Roth & Sons; lighting: Howard Brandston, Lighting Design, Inc.; graphics and ground floor design: Corchia, de Harak Inc. Courtesy William Kaufman Organization, New York. Photo by Albert L. Mozell.

The entrance to 127 John Street in New York City's bustling financial district is unusual because it is more than just the "empty" transitional space between out-of-doors and indoors that forms the lobby of most office buildings. In place of the vast expanses of marble or glass we have come to expect, here are three short connecting corridors in the shape of a T. Through the simple use of neon tubing and corrugated steel, they have been made into light-ringed tunnels that seem spacious as a result of the perspective effect of the receding rings of light and metal ribs. The pattern of line and light formed by these two elements is the sole decoration as well as the delineator of the space. The two elevator banks that service the building are located off the ends of the cross-bar of the T; a dazzling light-bulb sculpture at each end proclaims the floors served by that group of elevators (1-16 and 17-32; only the number 32 is visible in the view shown here).

The designers of this lobby have organized the space in such a way that it clearly directs people to the elevators—thus fulfilling the functional requirements of the space—but they have, at the same time, created a stimulating environment meant to be enjoyed by the people who use the building. The designers' imaginative manipulation of light transforms the workaday action of entering the building into a sensory experience: the architecture has become a huge walk-through sculpture.

Light

"Window or Wall Sign," 1967, by Bruce Nauman (U.S., b. 1941). Blue and peach-colored neon tubing. 59 x 55'. Photo by Rudolph Burckhardt. Courtesy The Leo Castelli Gallery, New York.

"The true artist helps the world by revealing mystic truths." Bruce Nauman presents his message in much the same manner as a brewery might advertise its beer: in glowing neon. Like Antonakos in "Marie's First Neon" **(Line 18)** and Chryssa in "Fragment for the Gates to Times Square II" **(Color 12)**, Nauman has made use of the resources of modern technology to enrich the vocabulary of the artist. For paint, ink, and the other media of drawing, he has substituted the brilliant line of neon light. But unlike Antonakos and Chryssa, who manipulated neon as pure line and color, Nauman has fully utilized the connotations of the medium—that is, he has created a kind of commercial message for art.

Although reduced to the bare essentials of imagery—words enveloped in a simple spiraling line—Nauman's sign is an expression of the artist's feeling and an attempt to communicate with the viewer. It is a revelation rather than an exhortation, and in this sense is comparable to Blake's illustration for the Book of Job **(Light 14)**. Nauman has used light in a literal way to convey his thought. He has constructed a visual-verbal pun: viewers who grasp the message may be said to "have seen the light"!

"The Spirit passed before my Face," plate from the Book of Job, 1825, by William Blake (British, b. 1757, d. 1827). Engraving. Plate size: 8½ x 6⅝". The Metropolitan Museum of Art. Gift of Edward Bement, 1917.

Bruce Nauman's description of the true artist (see **Light 13**) can appropriately be applied to William Blake, for all of Blake's work—his poems, paintings, and engravings—were aimed at revealing mystic truths to the world. Blake was a visionary, who believed that he saw God, and he wished to convey his experience to others. His problem was that of all artists who undertake to represent the unrepresentable nature of spiritual experience. The element of light has a special value for such artists, because it has a rich double meaning. It not only serves to make form visible by illuminating it; it can also refer, in a symbolic sense, to understanding.

Thus, Blake employs a blinding burst of light as the dominant compositional force in this engraving: the strong contrast of light and dark creates the visual tension of the illustration. At the same time, the light that radiates from the heavens and haloes the vision of God is the artist's graphic metaphor for the Divine Spirit. The rays of light that thrust diagonally through the picture space identify the source of illumination and highlight the fear and wonder of man in the presence of God.

Color

"The Adoration of the Shepherds," 1594–1612, by El Greco (Domingo Theotocopouli) (Spanish, b. in Crete 1548, d. 1614). Oil on canvas. 9'10" x 5'11". Courtesy The Prado Museum, Madrid.

El Greco's work represents a high point of religious art. "The Adoration of the Shepherds," executed to hang over the artist's tomb as his own memorial, is one of the most intense and passionate paintings ever done; it is the product of a fiercely pious man who lived in a fiercely pious era, only a little more than half a century after the Spanish Inquisition was established.

"The Adoration" is not meant to show the scene of the shepherds and the Christ Child realistically. The figures are elongated and distorted; their bodies are twisted into unnatural positions, and their limbs are strangely gnarled. The shepherds seem not to be planted on firm ground, but rather to float in air like the angels that hover above. There is no discernible setting—behind the Virgin is the suggestion of an archway, but we cannot distinguish whether the scene is interior or exterior. Clouds and darkness hang above; in the foreground bull and rocky ground merge into shadow. Yet through the darkness shines the unearthly light that emanates from the Christ Child. It illuminates the group that clusters around the Child so that they appear to be composed not of flesh but of flame. The drapery is rendered in the bright colors of fire—red, orange, yellow, green. The forms are built up in shapes of light and color.

The painting is not formalized, like the "Crucifixion" from the workshop of Duccio di Buoninsegna **(Organization 11),** nor is it a religious narrative, as is Botticelli's "The Three Miracles of St. Zenobius" **(Organization 15).** It is, rather, a rendering of the artist's inspired inner vision, sacred and mysterious and awesome, expressing the intensity of religious ecstasy through a dramatic use of light.

Color

"The Pleasure Principle," 1937, by René Magritte (Belgian, b. 1898, d. 1967). Oil on canvas. 28¾ x 21¼". Courtesy The Edward James Foundation, Chichester, Sussex, England.

Look long enough at the "head" of this ghostly portrait and you will begin to see a face: this is entirely the creation of your own imagination, and every viewer will imagine something different. The "sitter" is presented matter-of-factly in frontal view; there is nothing remarkable in the rendering of the everyday business suit and drab necktie, or the table with wood grain painstakingly delineated to appear solid and real. In contrast, the astonishing burst of light in place of the figure's head shocks us: we do not know what to make of it. We look again, and find that there is no clue to the identity of the figure—it is anonymous. What is the meaning of the pitted rock on the table? Again, there is no clue.

The title of this painting refers to an eighteenth-century philosophy called Utilitarianism, but this information does not lead us to any further understanding of the work. "The titles of my paintings," Magritte once said, "accompany them in the way that names correspond to objects, without either illustrating them or explaining them."

As in his other paintings—see, for instance, "Domain of Lights" **(Light 1),** "The Castle of the Pyrenees" **(Mass 11),** "Personal Values" **(Space 12)** Magritte uses visual anomaly to open the door to personal fantasy. Here the mystery resides in the viewer's interpretation of the meaning of the light.

Light

Color

Bust of Sassanian king, Shapur II (?), fourth century. Silver-gilt. 15⅜ x 9 1/16 x 7⅞". The Metropolitan Museum of Art. Fletcher Fund, 1965.

In painting, the artist manipulates light to suggest space and form or optical movement on a two-dimensional surface. But sculpture invites real light to play over its surfaces, emphasizing the particular nature of its material—the earthbound quality of wood, as in the Kongo ritual figure **(Fantasy 21)**; the muted ceramic surface of the Chinese court lady **(Mass 22)**; the monumental sheen of a bronze Benin head **(Surface 6).** Here the designer chose hammered silver, its opulent polish a perfect match for his desire to ennoble his subject and create an elegant aristocratic portrait.

Much is made of finely incised pattern—the thin repetitive lines of the beard, the snakelike curve of the moustache, the hair neatly flaring out to a symmetrical mass of curls, balanced by the graceful ballooning crown with its fluting and its careful border of raised circles. All this rich decorative detail serves, as it does in the Benin sculpture, to give a sense of volume to the head and to heighten the impact and nobility of the face itself, which has smooth, lustrous, uninterrupted planes. The forehead is unfurrowed, the gaze of the eyes direct, and the lips have a distinctive curve. A proud and worthy monarch is conveyed by these features, and the flicker of light over the metal—the shimmer of silver highlights and the soft modeling of silver shadows—adds to a mood of ancient splendor.

"Positive-Negative," 1970, by Keith Sonnier (U.S., b. 1941). 16mm black-and-white film, silent, 12½ minutes. Photo by Richard Landry. Courtesy The Leo Castelli Gallery, New York. Film distributed by Visual Resources, Inc., New York.

These four images of a girl's profile are distinct portrayals of the same subject because of variations in light values. In the manner of the Impressionists, the artist invites us to examine a subject under changing light conditions, but this is a work of art composed only of light; there is no canvas, no paint, no wood, no stone—only electronic signals captured on light-sensitive film. What we are seeing are two frames from a black-and-white silent film shot from a videotape. When the production is viewed as a whole, the continuous split-screen negative-positive image shows the head rotating full circle from profile to full view. But the artist intends us to view the work as we do here—not as a continuum with a beginning and end, but with contemplation, on more than one occasion, as we enjoy a picture in a gallery.

If we compare these frames to Kendall Shaw's painted images of football players **(Movement 7),** we can appreciate how Shaw uses positive and negative for dynamic tension and movement, while Sonnier is working only with the subtlest gradations of light as they transform his rather bland and traditional portrait subject. Here, positive becomes negative, and high-contrast flatness becomes tone and modeling. As he controls his light treatment, the artist capitalizes on the inherent physical qualities of his medium: The ever-present but ever-changing pattern of horizontal lines composing each image contributes the unique striated view of the subject (characteristic of video transmission), adding both an intriguing graphic element and a reminder of the fact that each image is an electronic mosaic of light signals.

Illustration for Zeiss-Ikon Voigtlander advertisement, designed by Albert E. Markarian, Kalmar Ad/Marketing, Englewood Cliffs, New Jersey. Courtesy of the artist and Zeiss-Ikon Voigtlander.

Many modern artists use evidence of technical processes as a dominant element of their image. The photograph of an egg **(Mass 9)** and the unusual screen-print portraits **(Perception 6** and **7)** make exaggerated use of the dot pattern typical of the photoengraving screen most often used to reproduce photographs on the printed page. Here, Markarian has chosen not a dot screen but a horizontal line screen that dispenses with tonal gradations and instead distributes distinct darks and lights across the picture plane. Our eyes reassemble the original photo information much as they would "read" an Impressionist painting, automatically reconstituting the tonal qualities of normal visual experience. This same ability to interpret images broken into arbitrary patterns is what allows us to merge the horizontally distributed electronic pattern of the black-and-white television screen into a fully tonal picture. In fact, we are so accustomed to making this visual adjustment that we almost take the pattern of lines in Keith Sonnier's film **(Light 18)** for granted.

As the eye sorts out the relationships of the optical striations in this illustration, we become conscious of how light patterns not only define shape and form, but also indicate even the most subtle of depth-space relationships. The eye is challenged by these light patterns, and an ordinary newspaper sports photograph becomes a compelling kinetic rendering of the subject. With this light composition, Markarian has made us conscious of the optical process of perception, a theme perfectly suited to an advertisement for a major lens manufacturer.

Color

Detail from "Invitation to the Side-Show (La Parade)," 1887–88, by Georges Seurat (French, b. 1859, d. 1891). Oil on canvas. 39½ x 59¼". The Metropolitan Museum of Art. Bequest of Stephen C. Clark, 1960.

The Impressionists felt they could best describe an object under light by juxtaposing colors rather than blending them. The viewer would do the mixing himself and have a heightened sense of the way a scene truly presents itself to our eyes. Seurat's method, called Pointillism—painting an endless number of tiny dots, each calculated for maximum vibrancy in relation to the others—was an effort to shape the Impressionists' notions about color into a formal methodology with a firm scientific base.

The tiny dots of color used for each area of the painting, for example the green façade at the right, represent the color components of that object. They are interspersed with flecks of yellow-green to tinge the area with the overall glow and radiance of the gaslight illuminating the scene. (The overhead gas jets are not actually seen in this detail, but we see the interior lamps in the background.) The resulting vibration forces the viewer to be active; his optical involvement prompts him to perceive the surfaces as lit by real light—dancing, sparkling, and alive.

Although light is a revealer of color in this painting, we also have a strong sense of shape and form. In Monet's painting **(Light 11),** towers, portals, and carvings are felt, not seen. Seurat, on the other hand, has his own way of delineating figures and structures into their most basic form so that all elements—the quivering dots, the simplified and expressive shapes, the almost whimsical repetition of heads and hats—give us a sense of the artist's unique interpretation of visual experience.

Light

"Time Study," 1971, by Ned Harris (U.S., b. 1925). Black-and-white photograph. Courtesy of the photographer.

This photograph is almost pure pattern—no tone, no modeling, no reflections, no depth. Just rows of lines and dots in pure white on sharp black, and a curious figure that has at once the flattened toneless quality of graphic design, and the unprepossessing look of a "real" image.

Photography is dependent on light in its every aspect; the creative photographer realizes that he must contend with this above all other elements in shaping his mode of expression. He may choose a style of startling realism, as does this same photographer in his photograph of a demolition site **(Fantasy 16).** But he may, as in this picture of a man changing light bulbs on the face of a Times Square electric billboard, work with light to create a provocative abstraction in which real-life subjects become elements in a black-and-white formal field.

Harris limited the composition of his original photograph to a tight range of subject matter and then further reduced it in the darkroom. His high-contrast darkroom treatment produces stark blacks and whites that flatten depth and intensify the design significance of each detail in the photograph. The photographer had a keen sense of how well the flattening would work for his image. His eye was especially keen in noting how the unusual shadow effect erases the horizontal lines between the rows of bulbs and breaks up the overall pattern, making the shadow, in fact, as important as the man himself.

Top: "Highway U.S. 1, Number 5," 1962, by Allan D'Arcangelo (U.S., b. 1930). Synthetic polymer paint on canvas. 70 x 81½". Collection, The Museum of Modern Art, New York. Gift of Mr. and Mrs. Herbert Fischbach. © 1975, The Museum of Modern Art, New York. *Bottom:* "Standard Station," 1966, by Edward Ruscha (U.S., b. 1937). Serigraph. 25⅝ x 40". Collection, The Museum of Modern Art, New York. John B. Turner Fund. © 1975, The Museum of Modern Art, New York.

Both of these paintings use the haunting imagery of the superhighway, not by day, but in the chilling loneliness of the night. In D'Arcangelo's painting (top), the unrelieved perspective is broken only by two remote signs and the luminous center-lane marker that seems to rush irrevocably into the distance. The foliage would soften the scene by daylight; here it appears as a dark, almost forbidding, mass. Most of us have known the interminable monotony of night driving at high speeds, blinded by oncoming headlights, fatigued by long stretches of blackness punctuated only by the brilliant neon constellation of a roadside burger joint or a service station. Ruscha's "Standard Station" is just such a break in the darkness— brightly lit, full of accurate detail, but nevertheless coldly impersonal, a structure out of a mold, its slick polished surface bearing no reassuring reminder of a specific locale or a specific proprietor. Not a single person, not even a car, appears in the painting.

Through a distinctly intellectualized use of light, both artists characterize the subculture of the superhighway, a world experienced at seventy miles per hour. Both make use of a harsh, flat quality of light to epitomize the impersonality of a machine environment. As Pop artists, they seem to report the contemporary scene in obvious terms, working with the most direct and simple compositional elements. In fact, they show us another aspect of our lives that we take for granted, expressing, and perhaps evoking in us, a sense of uneasiness and disenchantment.

Color

"New York Skyline," by Jack Zehrt. Color photograph. From the files of Freelance Photographers Guild, Inc., New York.

Now York City views—the skyline, the bustling harbor, the familiar landmarks—have been a recurring subject for some of the finest photographers. It is not the subject, however, but what the photographer does with it that makes for a great picture. Control of light decides whether a photographer's vision will be banal or dynamic. Jack Zehrt had the daring to forego the subdued and graphic grays of traditional photographic cityscapes and to choose instead the burning hues of sunset. But he has controlled his camera—his light machine—so as to honestly depict a sunset panorama in clear-cut and unsentimental terms.

Skyscrapers silhouetted against a heavily clouded sky provide a low-keyed background for a mosaic of bright light caught on the reflecting surfaces of windows, waterfront machinery, piled cargo, and rooftops. Shafts of light from the setting sun dart through breaks in the clouds to illuminate some parts of the cityscape while leaving others in shadow. It is this partial illumination and partial shadow that makes for the diagonals of dark and light that, as in "Grossingers" **(Light 4)**, unify the composition. Those portions of the scene that are revealed have both a literal value, invoking the "hardware" of the city, and an important functional value, as a series of basic shapes that echo each other and carry the eye back and forth across the picture plane. For all its stormy violets, burning oranges, and white-hot golds, this photograph is actually a dispassionate and carefully structured statement of its subject.

Color

Top: "Sunrise, with a Boat Between Headlands," ca. 1835–45, by J.M.W. Turner (British, b. 1775, d. 1851). Oil on canvas. 36 x 48". *Bottom:* "View of the Thames," 1959, by Oskar Kokoschka (British, b. 1886 in Pöchlarn of Czech-Austrian parentage). Oil on canvas. 36 x 48½". The Tate Gallery, London.

These two paintings are both descriptions of the same environment, the river Thames. But in the one above, painted by Turner, we can hardly make out water, the two riverbanks, or a boat. The artist had obviously reached a point where the quality of heavy mist, the atmosphere drowning in the light of the sunrise, was of more importance than literal forms and outlines. Paint is used almost metaphorically; it is up to us to explore the images latent in the ever-so-subtle nuances of vaporous whites, pale yellows, blues, and denser golds.

In contrast, Kokoschka's interpretation of the subject in "View of the Thames" is frank and crisp. He uses light to express something bold and energetic, to dramatize the dynamism of modern London. Vigorous brushstrokes and hasty washes, even in the bright midday sky, are meant to convey the hectic traffic and river activity of the Thames and its London environs. Every detail, the bright colors, the smudges of paint, the repetition of strokes, even the way the flag whips about its pole, is meant to express lively motion. Where Turner's light treatment made for a diffuse and suggestive image, Kokoschka uses light to be explicit, and to communicate, instantaneously, a psychological mood.

Portfolio 10, Fantasy and Illusion

Fantasy and Illusion in Art

All artists ask us to believe in their visual statement, whether it be a traditional studio painting of a landscape or a portrait or the exhilarated slashes and streaks of paint across a canvas. Some artists, however, challenge us in this very act of believing—the fantasist intriguing our imagination, the illusionist challenging our intellect.

In fantasy, the artist creates an unusual visual situation: If we accept his frame of reference, each subject element, no matter how literally illogical, takes on a believable and convincing quality. Fantasy presents us with a unique and extraordinary reality—it may be exotic or commonplace, threatening or benign, a nightmare or a vision of delight; it may be a journey in search of mystery, a source of escape, or a way of sounding the meaning of existence.

In illusion, the artist rearranges elements of reality to create a visually arbitrary and paradoxical situation in which the sum of the parts adds up to conflicting totals. He takes advantage of the fact that we form our ideas of reality on the basis of selected visual cues rather than by assessing the totality of the visual field; by providing multiple, often contradictory sets of cues, he can present us with more than one optical entity within the same work of art.

In fantasy and illusion we experience both good-natured jokes and puzzles and arresting speculation. Whatever the artist's intent, however, the bizarre and unconventional manner in which he either boggles the imagination, or toys with optical reflexes, heightens our perception of both concept and reality.

Fantasy and Illusion

" 'Undecidable' Monument," 1970, by Roger Hayward (U.S.). Ink drawing. From "Mathematical Games" by Martin Gardner. Copyright © 1970, Scientific American, Inc. All rights reserved. Courtesy W. H. Freeman and Company, San Francisco.

There is pleasure to be savored in the surprise ending of a short story. We look back in amusement at our gullibility in accepting what the author led us to accept. The visual surprise, the paradoxical image, is similarly based on our tendency to be visually gullible; let the draftsman or the artist suggest the mere bare beginnings of an object and we tend to fill in the rest. The jolt, of course, comes when the artist leaves us midstream and introduces a totally contradictory set of images. The basic figure—originally called a "blivet"—that Roger Hayward has whimsically embellished in this drawing contains just such a pair of visually contradictory images.

We are, at first, so baffled and disoriented by the monument that our eyes flit from top to bottom and back, in an effort to reconcile the two messages. That the passageway of the arch is not a space but a solid seems impossible. That the two rectangular uprights could become three rounded columns seems incredible. In fact, the addition of the low hills and the sailboats proves to be incidental; the monument is confusing with or without accessory details.

The best way to tackle this puzzle is to ignore the literal value of the image. The viewer is then free to savor the paradox and enjoy whichever perceptual version presents itself. As with the short story, he can thus look back and appreciate how much he was ready to construct on the basis of a few suggestive lines.

"A Fish Story," episode from "The Upside-Downs of Little Lady Lovekins and Old Man Muffaroo," 1903–05, by Gustave Verbeek (U.S., b. Nagasaki, Japan 1867, d. 1937). Ink drawing.

It takes a highly imaginative artistic talent to trade on the double meanings of images. Gustave Verbeek's "upside-downs" made their debut at the beginning of the comic-strip era, but historians of the medium consider them among the most ingenious. Each installment in the ongoing narrative of Lady Lovekins and Old Man Muffaroo consisted of six panels, providing twelve episodes. Followed right side up, the panels contrived a predicament for the heroine; the reader would find the continuation of the story, as well as the solution, by turning the panels upside down and reading the second set of captions.

Unlike the specimens of type shown in negative (**Fantasy 4**) where the viewer works hard to find the letter amidst the complexities of figure and ground, here the effect is due primarily to the ingenuity of the artist. He does rely, however, on certain habits of visual perception that contrive to his benefit. The illusion works here, as in "Undecidable Monument" (**Fantasy 1**) because the viewer so readily constructs images from a few visual cues. In this case, the viewer brings added memories and associations so that the rather crude forms that serve as claws and that even more crudely serve as trees are immediately understood, as is the beak that becomes a canoe. Still more fascinating are the visual hieroglyphics that serve as the frightened face of the girl and the moustached, bulbous-nosed face of the man. But the viewer is selective; he conveniently discards the lines that confuse or are extraneous to the image, and this tendency is cleverly used by the artist.

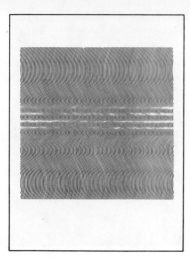

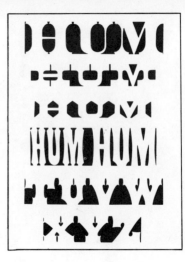

"Current," 1964, by Bridget Riley (British, b. 1931). Synthetic polymer paint on composition board. 58 ⅜ × 58 ⅞". Collection, The Museum of Modern Art, New York; Philip Johnson Fund. © 1973 The Museum of Modern Art, New York.

The illusions produced by optical art, such as this energy-charged painting by Bridget Riley, are purely perceptual. The viewer is expected to leave all associations, memories, and expectations behind and simply enjoy the tricks his own eyes play upon him. In the case of "Current," the assault is so potent that the eyes experience a disturbing loss of focus that is both unsettling and enthralling. The illusion is thus one of pulsating motion produced by a painted reality that is in fact static.

At first, the focal point of the unstable plane is the intense horizontal of swirls that forms a band across the painting. It cuts not only a dizzying center pathway, but eddies and furls in and out of another dimension. Slowly then, a second motion—this time vertical—billows across the broader curves above and below the frenzied band in the middle. Images and afterimages reinforce the motion that carries us many times in and out of the third dimension, making the title, with its implication of tides and irresistable pulls, entirely appropriate.

This complexity of physical sensation is actually achieved by the relatively simple device of positioning undulating lines—stark black on glaring white—painted with machine-like precision, at exactly regular intervals. There are only slight variations in width. It is through this concentrated repetition of a single linear element, not unlike the insistent repetitions of electronic music, that Riley casts an illusionary spell which enchants but enervates us.

Specimens of original 19th-century American wood type. From *American Wood Type* by Rob Roy Kelly. Copyright 1969 by Litton Educational Publishing Inc. Courtesy of Rob Roy Kelly and Van Nostrand Reinhold Company, New York.

Typography is a set of visual symbols that we usually take for granted. We absorb the messages of books and the impact of posters and advertisements without noticing the subtle marriage of message and typeface. But because these examples of nineteenth-century wooden type (used for billboards and poster displays) are printed in negative, the ambiguous reversal of black and white, we must play the intriguing game of finding the letters. In the process of unraveling the visual puzzle, we discover the counterpoint of negative and positive and the significance of the spaces surrounding alphabetic forms.

Rob Roy Kelly's presentation has the on-off character of a typographical illusion; we see the letters and then we don't, seeing instead only white areas floating amidst black abstract forms. This permits us to explore the vegetable-like forms growing progressively simpler in the top three lines, and the medieval ornateness of the fleur-de-lis patterns in the lines at the bottom. The interplay of figure and ground is so strong and evocative that an exciting graphic composition emerges, as it does in "Sky and Water" (**Perception 24**). But while Escher's composition plays on the negative and positive shapes of fish and fowl, the type specimens transcend their utilitarian values and an abstract rhythmic progression of subtle black and white shapes leaps forward, not unlike Ray Metzker's photomontage (**Perception 9**), where we find ourselves delighting in the sheer enjoyment of sensitively related forms.

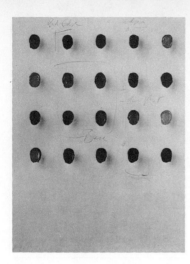

Fantasy
and Illusion

COLOR

"Untitled," 1972, by George Stever (German, b. 1940). Acrylic and pencil on paper. 30 × 24″. Courtesy O. K. Harris Works of Art, New York. Photo by Eric Pollitzer.

This is certainly a rarefied painting; it does not actively stimulate our thoughts or our senses. Yet we can trace it to certain artistic traditions. Like Harnett's trompe l'oeil painting (**Perception 14**) which treats objects on a cupboard door with every shadow of the real image, George Stever arranges objects of a very different sort—twenty daubs of putty-colored paint and some casual notations—and treats them, shadows and all, as if they were really there. But, we may ask, as if they were really where? Artists have been known to create paintings about their painting, as in Jasper John's "Field Painting" (**Surface 24**). But the Johns painting is "painted"—surfaces are streaked, dripped, awash with color—and shadows are produced by such objects as real cans, a knife, and a light switch. In its extreme simplicity, Stever's untitled painting might be a more terse statement about the artist's craft, the daubs of paint might be resting on a sheet of glass (some artists prefer glass palettes to compare subtle values) in preparation for some monochromatic work. The cast shadows around the color and in some of the penciled lines would support this possibility. But, a few of the lines and all of the writing are without shadows to contradict this impression. We sense that this painting is more about the concepts of the mind than about the process of painting itself and that there is a tension set up between reality and the painted illusion, but we can only speculate about the artist's true intention.

COLOR

"Crucifixion (Corpus Hypercubus)," 1954, by Salvador Dali (Spanish, b. 1904). Oil on canvas. 76½ × 48¾″. The Metropolitan Museum of Art, Gift of The Chester Dale Collection, 1955.

Artists often make their innermost fantasies known in coolly realistic fashion, shattering only here and there the veneer of credibility. In Magritte's painting of a rock floating in the air (**Mass 11**), there is such a shattered realism but we are strangely at ease with its illogic. Dali, too, has disrupted the laws of nature in this Crucifixion, but he has created a universe of illusion that so overwhelms our perceptions that rationality is for a moment suspended and we accept what we know can never be.

Taken one by one, the elements are only unusual because of the brilliance of Dali's execution. It is, however, their placement in space that gives the painting its special significance. The figure of Christ retains its time-hallowed stance, painted with the full classical force of anatomical realism. The rich velvety sky with its baroque theatricality is reflected in the equally baroque drapery costuming the lone witness. And yet the Christ hovers in space in front of the Cross, as if the forces of nature had been miraculously reinterpreted for the event. The body reveals none of the traditional wounds; the nails themselves are symbolized by four free-floating cubes. They echo the larger, almost architectural, cubes that form a Cross that is fixed in time and space, independent of the laws of gravity. The rich monochromatic tones and the dramatic spotlighting suggest the luster of another world; the size and placement of the witness figure seem out of key; the face of Christ is never seen. Rational and irrational thus hang in suspended balance in this singular interpretation of the Crucifixion.

"Self-Portrait as a Drowned Man," ca. 1972, by Doug Prince (U.S., b. 1943). Black-and-white photograph. Courtesy the artist and Light Gallery, New York.

To create this composite photograph, Doug Prince sandwiched and blended together four different negatives taken over a period of six months. The photographer is not duty bound to record reality as it is; he can use photographic processes and equipment to manipulate and recompose visual data with all the freedom of the painter or the graphic artist. Extracting the visual situations that he needed from each negative, Prince has created a new reality, a unique blend of sheer fantasy and the authenticity of the photographic image.

All the force of the evocative composition is centered in the face of the drowned man. Our attention is first drawn to the serene features by the intensity of the light that surrounds them. The same almost phosphorescent light illumines the water and the rocks immediately above the head and reappears in the band of light sweeping across the distant landscape, picking up the iridescent glow of the sky, strengthening the composition, and endowing it with an ephemeral, magic quality.

The importance of the moon, which seems to exist more as a poetic element than as a source of light, is accentuated by its symmetrical placement and by the repetitions of its shape in the lens flares below the horizon. The flares also highlight the chasm that so powerfully evokes all the mystery of the depths of the earth. The photographer might have eliminated these lens flares but didn't; they not only lead our eyes back to the face but their presence also reminds us that Prince's fantasy is after all a photographic one.

"Artist in Chair," 1971, by Duane Hanson (U.S., b. 1925). Polyester and fiberglass, polychromed. Collection The Morgan Gallery, Kansas. Courtesy O. K. Harris Works of Art, New York. Photo by Eric Pollitzer.

Just as the viewer is wondering what distinguishes this particular photograph, he learns that the subject is not a man but a life-size polyester and fiberglass sculpture. This kind of deception is, of course, the ultimate in artistic illusion. Duane Hanson achieves such acute realism (often known as verist or new realist sculpture), by making molds of the limbs, head, and torso of his subject, casting them in polyester and fiberglass, and combining them to duplicate the original pose. He uses paint to reproduce flesh tones; he includes details such as hair, and here has added eyeglasses and a hat—the kind of accessory that so particularizes a person. For clothes, he often uses the belongings of the sitter himself. The casually held catalogs identify both the sitter, Mike Bakaty, and Hanson.

A painting showing a candid-camera pose of a figure in paint-stained denims, treated as a naturalistic study of an artist, would not be this unusual. But a sculptured figure is less tied to such momentary details as stance and dress; it does not normally pinpoint a moment in time. By expressing himself in such precise and meticulous detail, by making this an almost living, breathing person, Hanson has created an eerie replica of artist Mike Bakaty—far closer to the real than a wax museum figure. Thus, this work is an example of how extreme illusions can grow out of realism.

Fantasy
and Illusion

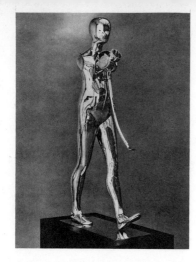

Study from Falling Man series: "Walking Man," 1964, cast 1965, by Ernest Trova (U.S., b. 1927). Chromium-plated bronze. 59 ⅝ × 11 ⅜ × 26 ½". Collection, The Museum of Modern Art, New York; Gift of Miss Biki Laura List. © 1973 The Museum of Modern Art, New York.

If, in a gallery, we could see Trova's gleaming figure alongside the Hanson sculpture (**Fantasy 8**), the juxtaposition would provide a volley of contrasts. The deft illusion of a real figure in one would heighten the anatomical fantasy of the other. The textures—cloth, hair, paper, wool, and fleshlike body—would underscore the high polish of the chrome finish, sleek and impenetrable, reflecting the viewer and the surrounding room in a shimmer of patterns. The abundance of specific detail—fingernails, shoelaces, the crease of the face—in Hanson's sculpture would bring home the lack of such human elements as arms, ears, facial features, and the intrusion of the puzzling fixture on the chest, the nail-like addition on the shoulder, in Trova's study. Trova's figure is like a robot, fashioned by a machine that could duplicate it a thousand times, a science-fiction figure controlled, we might imagine, by external commands.

We might decide that the sculpture is a comment about man's dilemma—trying to feel human in a world of chrome, glass, gadgets, and machines, a world of nine-to-five jobs and worship of the dollar. But this analysis would overlook pure sculptural beauty—the grace of the forms, the gentle curve of the torso, the harmony of each part perfectly tooled and matched to the next. "Walking Man" has all the distance and austerity of an ancient Egyptian figure and the supra-human form of a traditional deity. The fantasy of the image thus permits us to ponder the reality of being human and the aesthetic beauty suggests man's transcendence of his destiny.

"Man who Tore Himself in Two," 1969, by David Hockney (British, b. 1937). Illustration for *Grimm's Fairy Tales* (Petersburg Press). Etching and aquatint on copper. 18 × 13". Courtesy André Emmerich Gallery, New York. Photo by Eric Pollitzer.

The tales and play of children abound in fantasy, as does the oral history and traditional wisdom of primitive peoples. Fantasy is a way of dealing with the world, making sense of situations where we only have partial knowledge. And psychologists tell us that a child's often morbid flights of imagination help him in the healthy socialization process, projecting onto terrifying creatures the angry behavior he learns is not acceptable.

This illustration, dramatizing a scene in the famous Grimm's tale, Rumpelstiltskin, describes the dwarf's exasperation when the Princess guesses the answer to his riddle. "He rends himself asunder," said the early versions of the tale, and David Hockney has given us this phrase in almost comic-strip fashion in a four-paneled version. Many phrases in our daily language, such as "she cried her eyes out," or, "he laughed until his sides split," are pure fantasy disguised as metaphor; if interpreted visually they would be as bizarre as Hockney's illustration. But Hockney has saved the translation from word to image from morbidity by portraying the most grisly aspects of the situation openly, but with a whimsy that makes the near gro-tesque become good fun. Hockney's dwarf is a very droll figure with his hairy arms and fuzzy suit, faced with the ridiculous task of pulling off a leg, then flinging it with both arms in the air. It is only in the bustling third scene that we might flinch; in the end all is calm, innocent parts floating decoratively in the air. Fantasy is thus one way for the artist, much as in the oral tradition, to deal with events that defy the limita-tions of rational, naturalistic situations.

COLOR

"Seated Women II," 1939, by Joan Miró (Spanish, b. 1893). Oil on canvas. 63 × 50 ¾". Courtesy The Peggy Guggenheim Foundation, Venice, Italy.

The spontaneous and often discordant depths of the psyche was the wellspring of surrealist inspiration. Some surrealist painters challenge us with familiar and well-rendered elements articulated into a nonsensical or paradoxical whole. Others, like Miro or Tanguy (**Fantasy 17**), use a visual language all their own while they work in seemingly realistic themes.

If we think of "Seated Woman II" as following in the tradition of stately portraiture we are all the more curious to penetrate the mystery of its bizarre elements, sensing that physical identities have been disintegrated and then reconstituted into a strange, new reincarnation. This most original interpretation of portraiture retains no semblance of the sitter's appearance, yet the artist has kept to the rich painterly techniques of the past, contrasting flatness and decorative clarity with the nervous brushwork and overpainted layers of the background.

The dulled red and weighty black alert us to a somber mood. Forms with a life of their own flit about the composition—tiny combinations of insects, snails, antennae, fishes, waving cilia, a monstrous head, an impossibly elongated neck, impressions of a dress, a piece of jewelry, an eye. But then these very forms slip back into the composition, serving as foils in a subjectively decorative counterpoint, making us at ease with the most astonishing detail. In the compelling authenticity of Miró's fantasy, the unreal becomes real, the incredible becomes credible.

COLOR

"The Surrealist," 1947, by Victor Brauner (French, b. Romania 1903, d. 1966). Oil on canvas. 23 ⅝ × 17 ¾". Courtesy The Peggy Guggenheim Foundation, Venice, Italy.

Just as the poet fashions words into new realities, shocking the torpor of everyday language, the surrealist artist dips into his own dreams, the memories and pieces of his childhood, and his unbridled imaginings, to create a new and transformed reality, one that defies the physical laws of nature and the mundane laws of common sense. Victor Brauner tells us of these magical feats through his own provocative and metaphorical vision. He transports us to the landscape of another time and insistently plants before us a dreamy-eyed magician with an impossible coiffure, crowding the picture frame like an oversized dwarf. The magician's table is aglow with wondrous qualities of transformation. First we discern a fish on legs that could surely walk, then a larger insect with delicate wings, jewel-like eyes, and pert ears, feeding from a pink storybook flower while a ball of mysterious flames flickers in the water.

At the sight of provocative symbols (taken from the Tarot cards)—the Hebrew letter, the twisting figure eight, the sword, the money, the goblet, the glowing insect eyes—the viewer feels tempted by a mystery to be unraveled, a story to be told. But the artist's use of imagery is not meant to lead us to reason. His fantasy, so alive with glowing color and exquisitely invented forms, is linked only to the world of magic, where time is a continuum and logic and causality are unheard of.

Fantasy and Illusion

COLOR

"Cut Out and Send," 1968, by Joe Tilson (British, b. 1928). Screen print. 40 ¼ × 27 ⅛". Courtesy The Barney Weinger Gallery, New York. Photo by Eric Pollitzer.

Pop art takes a long look at the images of our daily lives and collage is an excellent way to display its wares without comment; for juxtapositions have a telling story of their own. In this screen print by Joe Tilson, unrelated bits from the mass media are presented as vertical slices of printed imagery arbitrarily stripped together, somewhat like the artist's baggage of painted surfaces in Jim Dine's "The Studio (Landscape Painting)" **(Surface 18).** But while the Dine painting suggest the "reality" of the artist's creation, "Cut Out and Send" avoids the implication of either a pictorial, an intellectual, or even an artistic reality.

The artist dispassionately gives equal value to each subject element—the Apollo blast-off; the blown-up image of a woman's eyes, possibly from a fashion photo; the photographer's color and gray scales; and scenes from Laurel and Hardy and King Kong in the sequence of movie stills. Taken as a whole, Tilson's collage is in turn artificially removed from the total frame of the picture with the decorative border of a photo motif, and treated whimsically as a coupon with the familiar words, "cut out and send." Then, as if our imagination were too weak to visualize the act of snipping, the screen-printed image of a scissors, replete with shadow and highlight, is added in typical "how-to" fashion. (As if to disown this last addition, the artist signs his name below the coupon.) With all its irony, this aggressive juxtaposition of media information thus attempts no cohesive or believable setting. Free of all preconceptions and visual entanglements, we are left to ponder our own fantastic reactions.

COLOR

"Siva and Parvati with their Children on Mount Kailasa," ca. 1745, Guler (Punjab Hills), India. Watercolor. 10 ¾ × 7 ¼". Courtesy The Victoria and Albert Museum, London. P. C. Manuk and Miss G. W. Coles Bequest through the National Art Collections Fund, 1949. Crown Copyright, The Victoria and Albert Museum. Photo by Sally Chappell.

As we pondered the meaning of "The Surrealist" **(Fantasy 12),** we realized that Brauner's private fantasy must remain a mystery. Quite the contrary for this Indian miniature: if only we knew the subtle symbolism of color and imagery characteristic of eighteenth-century Hindu painting, we would recognize the meaning of each detail and know the exact identity of the deity figures. Here is Siva as an ascetic, meditating in the Himalayas, accompanied in domestic tranquility by Parvati, the Divine Mother. Throughout the painting are threatening allusions to another, less benign, manifestation of these deities. The garland of human heads is being prepared for Siva, who wears them when he rides about on terrifying missions of destruction. Thus, what seems like extraordinary fantasy is actually full realism in terms of Hindu iconography.

The modern Western viewer needs no interpreter, however, to feel perfectly at home with this miniature's stylistic qualities. The languid, flowing line describes the animals and figures with a delightful stylization and economy, but manages to express a remarkable vocabulary of textures: the smoothness of Nandi the bull, the softness of the lion's fur, Siva's hair, Parvati's wiry tendrils. Disarmed by the pictorial freshness of another century and another culture, we allow ourselves to slip away from a familiar and perceptually comfortable environment to explore the strange and mysterious imagery.

Fantasy
and Illusion

COLOR

"Untitled," 1972, by Mel Pekarsky (U.S., b. 1934). Outdoor advertising. Oil over acrylic. 80' high. Courtesy of the artist. Photo by Eric Pollitzer.

Nothing better illustrates the precept that the symbol is more evocative than the real than this outdoor celebration of color in lower Manhattan. How else could the artist enrich the bleak urban environment and bring a bit of nature—its freshness, its poetry, its freedom and limitlessness—to one of the city's gloomier quarters?

If we pause below the mural, the lazy lines and gentle rainbow colors create for us a fantasy oasis, a slab of quiet carved out of the discordant noise and jarring visual jumble surrounding it. Horizon and hill lines, one piled above the other, with no suggestion of perspective or modeling, seem to call from memory a succession of stunning landscape vignettes. The yellow and lavender bands are like a vibrant dawn and a soothing twilight; within each the rolling contours of the dark hill shapes are outlined with a luminous sliver of color. The wide and narrow bands of complementary colors make us stop for a while before our eyes rise to the ethereal blues and the graceful repetition of lines above. There, a narrow band of browns breaks up and thus reinforces a feeling of great spatial distance.

Pekarsky's seven-story painting is a compelling apparition. Competing with city distractions, the mural beckons to the passerby, inviting him to participate in a fantasy where he can escape the pressing drabness of bricks and mortar to find the long-gone vistas of nature.

"Apocalypse," 1969, photograph by Ned Harris (U.S., b. 1925). Courtesy of the artist.

In "Self-Portrait as a Drowned Man" **(Fantasy 7),** Doug Prince created a fantasy in the darkroom. Here, the photographer found and captured a fantasy in the street. This odd sight of a billboard advertisement out of context, swept up in the urban fever to destroy and rebuild, might have amused others passing by; the photographer found and framed a composition that would bring out the full visual impact and tell an "apocalyptic" story. By eliminating distracting and useless details from his print, Harris gives us a greater sense of the outrageous scale of the bottle, the ice, and the glass, while the tilt of his camera creates a downward avalanche of wrenched wires and the crumbling innards of an old building.

Realizing the potential interplay between the garish, oversized realism of billboard painting and the wreckage of a demolition site, the photographer lets us explore the meanings of his title, "Apocalypse." There is wry humor in the contrast between the convivial cocktail and raw destruction; we think of decadent revelry in the midst of tragic ruin. There is also humor in the way the flow of gin seems to be the cause of it all. We might also think of more serious implications—destruction in the life of the slave to alcohol; destruction in a society that is slave to the advertiser who knows no limits in creating desires for that which is not needed.

145

Fantasy and Illusion

 COLOR

"Mirage le Temps," 1954, by Yves Tanguy (U.S., b. France 1900, d. 1955). Oil on canvas. 39 × 32″. Collection The Metropolitan Museum of Art, George A. Hearn Fund, 1955.

Shapes and spaces can be wondrous and palpable even though we have no clear notion of their identity. Yves Tanguy draws and modulates his surfaces with such precision that we seem to understand the stuff of his dream universe. The cool range of blues and grays, the occasional reds, oranges, and browns, the interlocking sculptured forms, the soft and wispy suggestions of atmospheric perspective—all tempt us to linger and examine the clutter of implausible yet monumental debris and to explore the limitless expanse.

No sound, no movement intrudes upon the solitude. The imagination is free to find in the icy mood of this landscape a lonely moon desert, or a forgotten and abandoned beach, even the far depths of the ocean bottom. There might be memories of the past, of children playing; some of the intriguing shapes could have been smoothed and rounded by endless pounding of the sea. Although Tanguy's subject matter is not of our world, his techniques as a painter are very familiar—cast shadows, highlights, careful modeling of surfaces, haziness to suggest distance—all working to reassure us about the physical properties of his environment, without giving us any tangible clues about the true subject. Tanguy's art is the most sophisticated kind of fantasy, an abstract visual poetry that defies all rational interpretation.

 COLOR

"Drawing for The Valley Curtain Project," 1971–72, by Christo (Christo Javachef) (U.S., b. Yugoslavia 1935). Drawing, collage, photograph. 28 × 22″. Courtesy the Allan Frumkin Gallery, New York.

Occasionally, the artist's imagination takes him far from the studio and the usual tools of the craft. This working drawing is one of the plans for an actual event, a monumental "happening" in which Rifle Gap, Colorado, was transformed by a huge orange curtain. The project took years of planning, $750,000 worth of engineering and installation costs, and extensive cooperation between the artist, engineering firms, state authorities, and the construction workers, itinerant laborers, and students who were there to secure the 200,000 square foot "Valley Curtain" to its moorings. On August 10, 1972, at 11:00 a.m., the project was completed; the artist, Christo, was dunked in Rifle Creek, skydivers floated down on multicolored parachutes, motorists and horseback riders vied to be first through the twenty-four-foot arched opening.

This strange expression of beauty and fantasy was not meant to serve any practical purpose. There it would be, just after a bend on Highway 325, its surface billowing like the sails of a ship, its bright nylon folds lit by the glare of the strong summer sun. But it did not last. Twenty-eight hours later, powerful gale winds, over sixty miles an hour, forced the dismantling of the curtain. For the artist, there was no great disappointment for his object all along was to "erect the curtain—not to perpetuate it." The unusual act of nature that caused it to destroy itself, so to speak, only added to the magic of this incredible mingling of art, technology, and the environment.

COLOR

"Split Yellow," 1971, by Stephen Posen (U.S., b. 1939). Oil and
acrylic on canvas. 90 × 76″. Courtesy O. K. Harris Works of Art, New
York. Photo by Eric Pollitzer.

Both Christo **(Fantasy 18)** and Stephen Posen work in extremes,
one of fantasy and the other of illusion. "Split Yellow" is a meticulous
painted likeness of yard upon yard of yellow cloth, draped, stretched,
folded, and massed upon a backing of cardboard boxes. The way the
color deepens as the fabric disappears into a crease; the way the
stripes are interrupted and distorted in their paths; the way the light
hits the tight and the soft folds, the crumpled parts, and the places
that still bear the original neat creases—all this ultra-specific information is carefully reported to the viewer.

Posen takes months to complete his exacting reportage. He begins
by tacking an arrangement of boxes to his studio wall and draping
cheap cotton cloth until he is satisfied with the effect. Then he works
on a forklift to maintain an eye-level perspective, painting in exact
scale a completely frontal view of his assemblage. The result is a
strange accomplishment, since Posen acknowledges having no interest in cloth and boxes. Nor could he expect us to. This very detachment gives full force to the illusion.

Yet it is hard not to read overtones of meaning into this large painting, every square inch of it rendered with the exquisite precision of a
miniature. "Split Yellow" pulsates with a mysterious energy; hidden
behind its tucks and folds there seems to lie more than mere illusion.

COLOR

"Barbarian Sacrifice," 1932, by Paul Klee (Swiss, b. 1879, d. 1940).
Watercolor. 24 ¾ × 18 ⅞″. Collection The Solomon R. Guggenheim
Museum, New York.

In the work of Paul Klee, the image takes on a life of its own. Often, it
has the inexplicable immediacy and poetry of music. "Barbarian
Sacrifice" is both ambiguous and clear, sophisticated and naive,
whimsical and profound, spontaneous and careful in its expression.
The artist reveals the intensity of his introspection and intuition, but
only through a curious range of personal symbols and allusions to
exotic cultures and customs—always with a light touch and an amazing economy of means.

The methodical repetition of tiny squares lends a ritualistic mood to
the painting. It has the look of an old piece of tribal cloth and a
primitive flatness out of which shapes emerge either by a muddying
of tone or a washing away of the mosaic. Some of the shapes are
described by plainly drawn outlines of red and black. Overtones of
Moorish architecture can be sensed in the three main arches and
even in the teardrop shape of the two quizzical faces, while the
overall mosaic pattern, particularly in the luminous upper area, keeps
this distinctive Mediterranean flavor.

Despite the cartoon quality of the faces and the childlike quality of
drawing, lightness and humor is swallowed up in the sophisticated
elusiveness of the work as a whole. Nor does the title help in de-
ciphering meaning; it suggests instead a kind of tribal ritual, where
the viewer is initiated into mysteries that he cannot fully understand.

Fantasy
and Illusion

COLOR

African nail figure, Kongo tribe, Republic of Congo, late 19th—early 20th century. Wood, nails, and glass. Courtesy of The Brooklyn Museum.

When we put images from distant cultures in our museums we usually lose sight of their true original function. What seem like bizarre echoes of frenzied tribal ritual were actually the normal accoutrements of a most reassuring and useful healing figure for members of the Kongo tribe. Driving these sharp nails and spikes into various parts of the figure was a way of bringing relief to the sick; for the suffering and affliction was thought to be transferred to the figure itself. Just as seemingly fantastic details in the Hindu miniature **(Fantasy 14)** were part of a deeply accepted system of myths and beliefs, so the symbols in this figure—even the strange mirrored opening on the abdomen—all take their place in a rich fabric of custom and ritual.

That an object so valued for practical and religious use could at the same time have such intrinsic aesthetic dignity helps us to understand how, for "primitive" peoples, an object's artistic value is inseparable from its tribal or communal significance. For modern man, who lives most of his days with a great bareness of spirituality and whose art stares down at him from a museum or a decorator's walls, this potent union is difficult to grasp. We can, however, take vast pleasure in the figure in purely sculptural terms. With great simplicity the shapes define the torso, the neck, and the joints at the knees, elbows, and pelvis. There is in the whole pose—the tilt of the head, the solid planting of the feet, and especially the trusting, receptive features—a gesture of acceptance and confidence that must have given a sense of great comfort to the sufferer of ills.

COLOR

"Family Supper," 1971–72, by Ralph Fasanella (U.S., b. 1914). Oil on canvas. 70 × 50". Courtesy of Jay K. Hoffman Presentations, New York.

Wishes, memories, and a great need to tell, in an immensity of detail, about the city, the poor, and another era, are the driving forces behind Ralph Fasanella's primitive painting. Now he runs a gas station and paints as much as he can, but there were many years spent as an activist in the early labor movement, when Fasanella was thrown from one factory job to the next because of his outspoken political involvement. He remembers his father's bitterness and endless hours of work as an iceman, and his own unhappy experiences of running away from home.

Intent on giving the viewer intimate and vivid details of 1920s immigrant family life, the artist resorts to a schematic version, showing an apartment in cross section, like a child's dollhouse, much in the tradition of medieval religious painting. In this same tradition, he freely adjusts his use of scale so that important figures are enlarged. And, like other primitive or self-trained artists, he reports composite memories by cramming his canvas with physical detail—the endless windows and neighbors, not an object forgotten in the room. But he also adds the dimension of a deeply felt social consciousness and expands reality for emotionally charged material. His mother is shown atop the dresser, clasping children to her waist, her feet in a bucket and clotheslines snaking through her arms, as a reminder of the drudgery of her existence; his father, the iceman, is pinned to the Cross in a religious painting on the wall. Yet, "Family Supper," in a merging of fantasy and wish-fulfillment, also gives an idealized sense of family, the glow of comfort and sharing in a hostile world—a memory that probably never was for Fasanella.

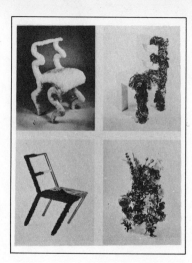

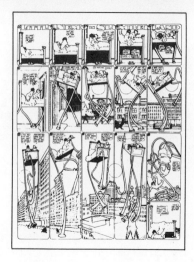

 COLOR

Chair transformations by Lucas Samaras (U.S., b. Greece 1936).
Top left: "Chair Transformation #17," 1969–70. Cotton on wood.
36 × 19 × 16″. *Top right:* "Chair Transformation #10," 1969–70.
White formica and colored yarns. 38 × 20 × 20″. Collection The
Whitney Museum of American Art. *Bottom left:* "Untitled," 1965.
Pins, wool, and paint on wood. 36 × 19 × 16″. Collection Robert
Mayer. *Bottom right:* "Chair Transformation #25," 1969–70. Plastic
flowers on wire. 42 × 20 × 22″. Collection The Whitney Museum of
American Art. Courtesy The Pace Gallery, New York.

Where verbal metaphor ends, visual metaphor begins. Words could
not be used to dislocate familiar and commonplace objects in quite
the same way as this theme and variations on a chair, in which basic
form is released into exciting extensions and reinterpretations of
itself. In "Pastry Case" **(Surface 12),** we are forced to stretch our
imagination when confronted by the shining banality of a banana split
thrust into the realm of sculptured mass. So Samaras's outrageous
inventions sharpen our perception of the intrinsic qualities of a chair,
and indeed of all the materials and surfaces unearthed by the artist's
fertile imagination. As the structure dissolves into a tangle of mul-
ticolored yarn, as it crouches into a bent and woolly shape, as it
proclaims itself as a spray of plastic flowers, as it is tilted to an absurd
and functionally impossible angle—each time some new aspect of
the chair is altered. Never, however, do we lose recognition of the
chair as the subject of these ridiculous and disorienting transmuta-
tions. What is destroyed is the chair's practical identity; instead of an
object for sitting the artist gives us a visual pun. And, since it is not
only the chair that is out of context, but the formica, the yarn, the
cotton, and the flowers as well, Samaras isolates the commonplace
materials that make up our physical environment and allows them to
have fresh and unusual potential.

Episode from "Little Nemo in Slumberland," from the Sunday New
York Herald, July 26, 1908, by Winsor McCay (U.S., b. 1889, d.
1934). Ink drawing.

The artist has an incredible range of means and materials at his
disposal to display his fantasy. But he may choose to resort to the
most basic of all—the rich and fluid use of line. Line and pictorial
organization make of these Little Nemo stories—tales of a boy, his
wild dreams, and how he awakens to find himself safe, but usually
tumbling out of bed—wondrous excursions into the unreal that are
above all vastly satisfying visual pieces. Their creator, Winsor
McCay, considered the inventor of the comic-strip format, was able
to keep an audience of children and adults engrossed (the stories
appeared in the Sunday edition of the New York Herald from 1905 to
1911 and briefly during the 1920s), because of the richness and
inventiveness of his imagery.

The high point of this episode is the manner in which McCay transforms a bed into a fluidly changing variation of itself, just as Samaras
(Fantasy 23) with the same talent for varying a basically simple
theme, transforms his chairs. The bed takes on a convincing life of its
own in part because of the artist's marvelous sense of pacing, his
sense of scale, his mastery in achieving remarkable shifts in perspective, his brilliant use of pictorial space. McCay not only commands the space of each panel, he alters the shape of the panels to
suit his needs, making them taller to fit a growing bed. Notice how
panels 13 and 14 are actually a single scene, in which the characters
are shown twice. This expertise of technique makes of fantasy a
delight; it captivated the audience of McCay's time and is winning
over a new audience today.

Index of Artists

Subject Index

Abstract expressionism 2:14; 5:4
Advertising 5:8,23; 7:19; 8:8,9,10; 10:13,15,16
African art 1:21; 3:16; 4:6; 10:21
Air art 6:4,15
American Indian art—see Native American art
Animals 1:1,16; 3:13,16,24; 5:21,24; 6:16; 7:24; 8:20; 9:19; 10:2,14
Architecture 1:4,7,8; 2:13; 3:5,15; 6:3,4; 7:1; 8:2,4,5,7; 9:11,12,23; 10:1,15
Armor 2:5,24
Asian-Oriental art 1:14,16; 2:1,8,22; 3:7,24; 4:13,16; 5:21; 8:18,20; 9:17; 10:14
Assemblage 3:17; 4:3,4,11,12,24; 10:19
Automobiles 2:18,19,20; 4:1; 6:10; 7:3; 9:22; 10:15

Body art 8:13; 9:6

Cartoons—see Comic strips
Children 2:12; 3:10,20; 5:22; 6:15
City environments 1:8,17,23; 2:15; 3:18,20; 6:4; 7:1,2,3; 8:5,7,17; 9:4; 10:15,16,22
Collage 6:1; 8:24; 10:13,19
Comic strips 2:19; 5:7; 7:15; 10:2,10,24
Computers 1:3; 4:9; 6:20; 8:8
Conceptual art 8:13; 9:13; 10:18,19
Construction 1:2; 2:2,17; 3:17; 4:4; 6:12,24; 8:3,15,18; 9:5; 10:23
Costume 1:10; 2:22,24; 5:21,22; 9:2; 10:8

Drawing, Line 1:13; 7:20; 8:19; 10:1,2,24
Drawing, Mixed media 9:7
Drawings, Watercolor 1:15,16; 7:8; 10:14,20

Environmental art 7:11; 8:2,7,11,13,14,17,22; 9:12; 10:15,18

Figure-ground relationships 2:5,6; 3:7; 7:9, 19, 20, 23, 24; 8:9,10,19; 9:18; 10:4
Food 2:9,23; 3:9,13,14; 4:12,24; 5:2,15; 9:2,4; 10:22
Furniture 1:5; 10:23,24

Games—see Sports and athletics
Glass 1:19; 4:8; 5:7; 9:3,5
Grafitti 1:17; 3:8,18

Hard-edge painting 1:11; 2:17,19; 6:7
Heads 1:21,22; 4:6; 5:22,23; 7:5,8; 9:16,17,18; 10:13,20
Human figures 1:1,10,13,14,15; 2:1,3,5,6,7,22,23,24; 3:10,11,16,20,21,22; 6:6,7,17,19,20; 8:6,19; 9:14,15,16,20; 10:6,7,8,9,10,11,12,14,21

Illusions—see Optical illusions
Impressionism 5:3; 9:11,24

Kinetic art—see Op art

Landscapes 3:13; 5:3; 8:20; 9:1,22,23,24; 10:1,6,7,14,15,17,18
Lettering 1:3,16,17; 3:3,4,8; 4:19,24; 5:13,15; 8:6,8,16; 9:13,14,21,22; 10:4
Light environments 5:10; 8:11,14,22; 9:5

Machine art 1:3; 4:20; 5:12,19; 6:5; 8:13; 10:9
Masks 1:21; 2:24; 3:2; 4:16
Medieval-Renaissance art 3:5,11,15; 5:6,14; 6:18; 9:2
Minimal art 1:11,12; 2:4,17
Mirrors 3:2; 7:11,12; 8:14; 10:21
Motion 1:15; 2:5,6; 6:4,5,6,8,17,21,22,24; 7:5,16; 9:19; 10:10
Motion pictures 6:21
Multimedia presentations 5:17; 6:13; 7:16; 8:22
Murals—see Wall paintings
Musical instruments 2:3,7; 7:5,14; 9:20

Naive art 3:13; 10:22
Native American art 3:2
Nature 2:9; 3:6; 4:14,15,17; 5:5
Neon 1:18; 5:12; 6:11; 9:12,13
New Realism 2:23; 4:12; 9:13; 10:8,19

Op art 1:2,3,11,12,20; 3:4,7,12; 4:4,5,20; 5:7,11,16,17,18,19; 6:2,3,14; 7:17,18,20,21,22,23,24; 8:9; 9:8,9,19; 10:3
Optical illusions 7:17,18,19,20,24; 8:9; 10:1,2,3,4,5

Performance art 8:13; 9:6
Photography, Abstract 5:8; 6:12,22; 7:6,7,9,13; 8:3; 9:19
Photography, Action 2:5,12; 4:10; 6:5,6,8,10,13,15,16,17,22; 7:5,10; 8:22; 9:19,21
Photography, Candid 1:10; 2:3; 3:9; 4:10; 7:3,5,10; 8:6
Photography, Close-up 3:6; 4:14,19,23

Chronology of the Visuals

Pre-Twentieth Century Art

1766-1122 B.C.	Shang Dynasty, Chinese bronze ritual vessel 2:8
1122-255	Chou Dynasty, Chinese bronze ritual vessel 4:13
1st century A.D.	Pre-Inca Peruvian textile 1:1
4th century	Statue of Sassanian king 9:17
300-900	Mayan clay whistle statue 2:7
618-907	T'ang Dynasty, Chinese ceramic tomb figure 2:22
ca.1249-ca.1287	Middle Kamakura Period, Japanese Heiji scroll paintings 1:16; 3:24
13th century	Painting by Duccio 3:11
ca.14th century	Nepalese statue 2:1
15th century	Venetian painting, early 15th century 5:14
	Painting by Hieronymus Bosch, ca. 1495 5:6
16th century	French armor, 1555 2:24
	Painting by Pieter Bruegel the Elder, 1565 6:18
	Painting by El Greco, 1594-1612 9:15
17th century	Mughal school, Indian painting, ca. 1635 8:20
	Painting by Johanes Vermeer 9:2
18th century	Kulu School (Punjab Hills), Indian painting, ca. 1720 5:21
	Guler School (Punjab Hills), Indian painting, ca. 1745 10:14
	Japanese print by Sharaku, late 18th century 1:14
19th century	Engraving by William Blake, 1825 9:14
	Painting by J.M.W. Turner, ca. 1835-45 9:24
	Drawing by Honoré Daumier 1:15
	Painting by Vincent van Gogh, 1887 4:15
	Painting by Seurat, 1887-88 9:20
	Painting by William Michael Harnett, 1888 7:14
	Painting by Claude Monet, 1891 5:3
	Painting by Claude Monet, 1894 9:11
	Favrile glass vase by Louis C. Tiffany, late 19th century 1:19
	Painting by Henri Rousseau, late 19th century 3:13
	African statue, Kongo tribe, late 19th-early 20th century 10:21

Twentieth-Century Art

Abstract Expressionism
- 1950   Painting by Mark Rothko 2:14
- 1960   Painting by Willem de Kooning 5:4

Machine Art
- 1959   Motorized construction by Nicolas Schöffer 4:20
- 1962-64   Polarized construction by Karl Gerstner 5:19
- ca. 1965   IBM computer print-out 1:3
- 1965-67   Motorized statue by Preston McClanahan 6:5
- 1966   Neon construction by Chryssa 5:12
- 1967   Electronically programmed construction by Martha Minujin 8:13

Minimal Art and Hard-edge Painting
- 1964   Painting by Kenneth Noland 1:11
- ca. 1965   Painting by Ellsworth Kelly 1:12
- 1965   Construction by John McCracken 2:17
- 1966   Sculpture by Tom Doyle 2:4

New Realism
- 1962   Assemblage by Claes Oldenburg 4:12
- 1964   Mixed media sculpture by George Segal 2:23
- 1971   Sculpture by Duane Hanson 10:8
- 1971   Painting by Stephen Posen 10:19

Op Art
- 1938   Woodcut by Maurits Escher 7:24
- 1962   Drawing by Josef Albers 7:20
- 1963   Construction by Günther Uecker 4:4
- 1964   Paintings by Bridget Riley 6:2; 10:3
- 1964   Painting by Richard Anuszkiewicz 1:20
- 1965   Painting by Bill Komodore 7:17
- 1965   Painting by Richard Anuszkiewicz 5:11
- 1966   Paintings by Victor Vasarely, 2:16; 3:12
- 1972   Serigraph by Karl Gerstner 9:9

Photo Realism
- 1967   Drawing by Claudio Bravo 9:7
- 1971   Painting by Bruce Everett 9:10
- 1972   Painting by Richard Estes 9:4

Pop Art
Surrealism